THE GARDENS OF THE SUN

THE GARDENS
OF THE SUN

A NATURALIST'S JOURNAL
OF BORNEO AND
THE SULU ARCHIPELAGO

BY
F. W. BURBIDGE

With an Introduction by
FRANCIS S. P. NG

SINGAPORE
OXFORD UNIVERSITY PRESS
OXFORD   NEW YORK
1991

Oxford University Press

Oxford New York Toronto
Delhi Bombay Calcutta Madras Karachi
Petaling Jaya Singapore Hong Kong Tokyo
Nairobi Dar es Salaam Cape Town
Melbourne Auckland
and associated companies in
Berlin Ibadan

Oxford is a trade mark of Oxford University Press

Introduction © Oxford University Press Pte. Ltd. 1989

First published in 1880 by John Murray, London
Reprinted in Oxford in Asia Hardback Reprints *in 1989*
Reissued as an Oxford University Press paperback 1991

ISBN 0 19 588993 2

Printed in Malaysia by Peter Chong Printers Sdn. Bhd.
Published by Oxford University Press Pte. Ltd.,
Unit 221, Ubi Avenue 4, Singapore 1440

INTRODUCTION

FREDERICK WILLIAM BURBIDGE was born in March 1847 in Wymes-wold, Leicestershire, England. His father was a farmer and fruit-grower, and young Frederick started work as an apprentice gardener when he was still a boy. After his apprenticeship, he entered the Royal Horticultural Society Gardens at Chiswick as a student, and in 1868, at the age of twenty-one, joined the staff of the Royal Botanic Gardens, Kew. He stayed only a few years with Kew, but maintained a life-long association, visiting Kew for a few days almost annually to study its plant collections.

In 1870 or 1873 (biographers differ over the date), he joined the editorial staff of *The Garden*, a horticultural publication, in which he expressed his considerable skills in writing and botan-ical drawing. During this time, he published two books which were to become standard references for many years—*The Narcissus: Its History and Culture* (1877) and *Propagation and Improvement of Cultivated Plants* (1877)—as well as a handbook on the *Art of Botanical Drawing* (1873), and various horticultural papers. All these were remarkable achievements for someone with relatively little formal education.

In 1877–8, Burbidge was commissioned by the British horti-cultural firm of James Veitch and Sons to collect new and beautiful plants, especially pitcher plants, from Borneo, for intro-duction to cultivation, and thus began his first, and apparently only, adventure in the Eastern Archipelago.

His collecting efforts were concentrated mainly in what is now the Malaysian state of Sabah, although on the way he made brief stops at Penang and Singapore. From Singapore, already a busy

F. W. Burbidge, after being awarded an honorary Master of Arts degree by
Dublin University in 1889.

city fifty-eight years after its founding by Stamford Raffles in 1819, Burbidge made a short trip to the summit of Gunung Pulai in Johor, in August 1877.

In September 1877, Burbidge arrived at Labuan Island, which the British had occupied as a Crown Colony in 1846, and from whence British influence had spread to the mainland of North Borneo. Indeed, just before Burbidge's arrival, a private syndicate, later to become the British North Borneo Co., had obtained grants on the mainland from the Sultan of Sulu and the Sultan of Brunei, and hence Burbidge's arrival coincided with the transfer of control of North Borneo to a British company.

Burbidge first landed on the Borneo mainland at Lawas, at the northern tip of Sarawak, which was easily reached by an eight-paddle rowing boat from Labuan. He returned to Lawas several times in the next two years to collect specimens, especially of *Phalaenopsis*, and other orchids.

In order to obtain the famous pitcher plants of Mt. Kinabalu, Burbidge made two ascents of the mountain. The first was accomplished on foot, starting from Gantissan on 30 November 1877, and continuing through Tamparuli, Bawang, Kelawat, Kaung, and Kiau.

For the second ascent, Burbidge started from the mouth of the Tumpasuk River on 5 August 1878, journeying through what is now Kota Belud, and up to Kaung and Kiau. This time, Burbidge rode on a water buffalo, which he greatly admired for its intelligence, strength, and dependability, and which probably saved his life on one of the many dangerous river crossings he made.

Burbidge did not spare himself on his great adventure in the eastern tropics, and he returned to England in a weak condition as a result of the malaria he contracted. However, this did not stop him from completing and publishing an account of his travels within the relatively short period of two years.

From a horticultural and botanical point of view, Burbidge's trip was a great success, especially in terms of the *quality* of the specimens he collected. Among his living introductions were the beautiful giant pitcher plant of Mt. Kinabalu, *Nepenthes rajah*, which Hugh Low and Thomas Lobb had earlier tried to obtain without success, and *Nepenthes bicalcarata*. In all, Burbidge's living and dried collections amounted to some 1,000 species. Several plants were named after him, for example, *Aerides burbidgei*, *Alsophila burbidgei*, *Burbidgea nitida*, *Dendrobium burbidgei*, *Globba burbidgei*, *Polypodium burbidgei*, and *Wormia burbidgei*; and *Nepenthes burbidgei* was named by Burbidge for his wife.

The Gardens in the Sun: or a naturalist's journal on the mountains and in the forests and swamps of Borneo and the Sulu Archipelago, published in 1880, is Burbidge's account of his travels. It is very much more than a naturalist's dry journal. Rather, it is a delightful record of travel and discovery through what Burbidge terms 'the enormous conservatories of beautiful vegetation—great Zoological Gardens inhabited by rare birds and curious animals'. Burbidge had a keen eye and was interested in and described many things—peoples, customs, industry, agriculture, plants, and animals. In addition, he visited and described the royal courts of Sulu and Brunei, both of which were in a state of political decline, Sulu being under pressure from the Spanish government at Manila, and Brunei being much reduced after having granted the territory of Sarawak to James Brooke in 1841.

In the manner of many travellers of his time, Burbidge had strong views about the customs and behaviour of the peoples he met, and he readily stereotyped people. Although some of his opinions are now painful to read, we must keep in mind that this book was written in the tradition of the nineteenth-century traveller to the East.

For those interested in the agricultural economy of Sabah before British rule, the book also contains a great deal of information. Burbidge was specially enthusiastic about fruit trees and took great pleasure in evaluating and describing the many native fruits of Sabah. We learn, for example, that the cultivation of citrus fruits—oranges, mandarins, and pomelos—was already very advanced in the Sabah of 1878, well before the introduction of modern agricultural technology. Overall, little seems to have escaped Burbidge's eye during his journeys through Sarawak, Labuan, and the north of Borneo to Sulu, and he is equally at

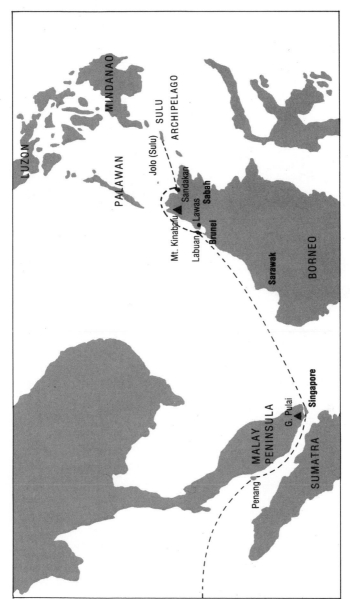

The Route followed by Burbidge, 1877–8

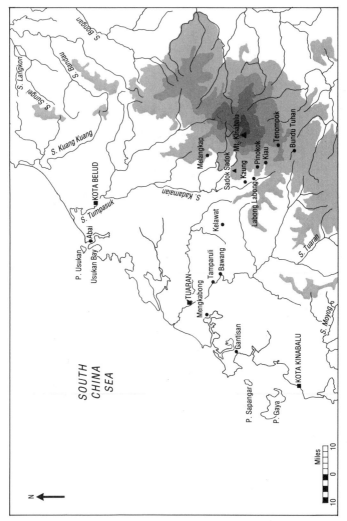

Mt. Kinabalu and Its Vicinity (after Jenkins, 1978)

home describing his encounters with the people he met on the way and their way of life as he is in writing about the world of Nature.

On his return to England, Burbidge briefly rejoined the editorial staff of *The Garden* but shortly after, in 1879, he was offered the curatorship of the Botanic Garden of Trinity College in Dublin. He held this post until his death in Dublin on 24 December 1905 at the age of fifty-eight, a few months after the death of his wife Mary.

Burbidge's career in Dublin was professionally distinguished. In addition to curating the Botanic Garden of Trinity College, he was Keeper of the College Park from 1894. He was also a member of the Royal Irish Academy, the Linnean Society, and the Royal Horticultural Society. As a lecturer and writer about plants and gardening, he was reputed to have few equals. In 1889, he was awarded an honorary Master of Arts degree by Dublin University, and in 1897, the Victorian Medal of Honour by the Royal Horticultural Society. After *The Gardens of the Sun*, he published *Chrysanthemum* (1884), *Wild Flowers in Art and Nature* (with J. G. L. Sparkes, 1894), and *Book of Scented Garden* (1905).

Burbidge was a popular and genial figure in British and Irish botanical and horticultural circles, and on his death no fewer than six obituaries were published in various journals. The only indiscretion that he is known to have committed was his endeavour to add variety to the flora of Ireland by scattering seeds of exotic plants around Dublin, which earned him the disapproval of local botanists.

Burbidge's collections of botanical specimens were deposited in the herbaria of Kew, the British Museum, Oxford University, Leningrad, Berlin, Vienna, and Singapore, and visitors to the British Museum can still see 40 plates and 115 original sketches of Borneo prepared by Burbidge, which he presented to the Museum in 1886.

Forest Research Institute Malaysia   Francis S. P. Ng
January 1989

References

Obituaries in *Gardeners' Chronicle* 38 (1905) 460, *Kew Bulletin* (1906) 392–3, *Hortus Veitchii* (1906) 75–8, *Journal of Botany* 44 (1906) 80, *Gardeners' Chronicle* 39 (1906) 10, and *Journal of the Kew Guild* (1906) 326–7.

Jenkins, D. V. (1978), 'The first hundred years: a short account of the expeditions to Mt. Kinabalu 1851–1950', *Kinabalu, Summit of Borneo*, The Sabah Society, Kota Kinabalu, Sabah, Malaysia.

Kurata, S. (1976), *Nepenthes of Mount Kinabalu*, Sabah National Parks Trustees, Kota Kinabalu, Sabah, Malaysia.

Wyse Jackson, P. S. (1987), 'The Botanic Garden of Trinity College Dublin 1687–1987', *Botanical Journal of the Linnean Society* 95: 301–11.

MALAY DANCING GIRL.

THE

GARDENS OF THE SUN:

OR

A NATURALIST'S JOURNAL

ON THE MOUNTAINS AND IN THE FORESTS AND SWAMPS OF

BORNEO

AND THE

SULU ARCHIPELAGO.

By F. W. BURBIDGE,

TRINITY COLLEGE BOTANICAL GARDENS, DUBLIN, AND FORMERLY OF
THE ROYAL GARDENS, KEW.

WITH ILLUSTRATIONS.

LONDON:

JOHN MURRAY, ALBEMARLE STREET.

1880.

I Dedicate this Work

TO

MY WIFE,

BECAUSE WHILE I WORKED ABROAD SHE WAITED AT HOME.

MOST OF US KNOW HOW EASY IT IS TO LABOUR—

ALL OF US KNOW HOW HARD IT IS TO WAIT.

PREFACE.

THIS record of a time spent among the less well-known portions of Malaysia may be interesting to those whom the goddess of travel has wooed in vain, as perchance to some of those "birds of passage" to whom the islands and continents of the world are as well known as the church-spires and mile-stones of their own land. In the islands of the Malay archipelago—the Gardens of the Sun—Nature is ever beautiful, and man, although often strikingly primitive, is hospitable to the stranger, and not often vile.

A voyage of a few weeks brings us to these beauty-spots of the Eastern Seas—to an "always-afternoon" kind of climate—since they are blessed with the heat and glory of eternal summer—to a place where winter is unknown—monsoon-swept islands oasis-like basking in a warm and shallow desert of sea. Warmed by perpetual sunshine, deluged by copious rains, and thrilled by electricity, they are really enormous conservatories of beautiful vegetation—great Zoological Gardens inhabited by rare birds and curious animals. In these sunny garden scenes man is the Adam of a modern Eden, primitive in habits and numerically insignificant; he has scarcely begun his battle with things inanimate, or his struggle for existence as it is known to us. At home we have man as in some sort the master of Nature, but in the Bornean forests Nature still reigns supreme. Here with us man wrests his sustenance from her—there she is lavish in the bestowal of gifts unsought.

The immediate future of an island larger in area than Great Britain cannot fail to be of interest to political thinkers, especially to those who belong to the "scientific frontier" school. Malay Government is weaker now than it was even at the time Sir James Brooke received Sarawak, and the aid of our own Government is now being sought in favour of the cession of the whole of Northern Borneo—from Gaya Bay to Sabuco—to a public company! Unaided by England, Borneo seems likely to suffer in two ways—either to be annexed by the Government of Manilla, or else to fall into the hands of the promoters of public companies. The Sulu Archipelago has already thus lost its independence; and the question which now suggests itself is, What will England do with her foster-colony, Borneo the Beautiful?

Borneo offers to the student of nature an ever-interesting field for research and study. The local government is very peculiar and interesting. Every village of any pretensions has its "Orang Kaya," or head man, and his house is at the service of the passing stranger. In any matter of dispute he may be referred to, and my own experience of these petty rulers was on the whole very satisfactory. I found them honest and just in their advice, although at times a little grasping in their bargains.

The ease with which food is obtained in such a tropical land is of course inimical to any great exertion or progress on the part of the natives. That most generous of all food-giving plants, the Banana, is everywhere naturalised in Borneo up to an altitude of 3000 feet. It fruits all the year, its produce being to that of wheat as 133:1, and to that of the potato as 44:1. With rice and a few esculent roots, all easily grown, it gives a profusion of food at a slight expenditure of labour—labour for the most part performed by the women. The Malays of Borneo are morally far inferior to the inland tribes ; and, wherever it is possible to them, live in voluptuous ease.

Borneo is the home of the " Orang-utan," or " wild man of the woods," an animal which, with its African relative, the " Gorilla," has occupied the attention of so many of the first thinkers of our time. Here, in its native forests, this large man-like ape lives in the great natural orchards, swinging itself from bough to bough with its peculiarly long arms, building its platform or nest of leafy branches, and eating its meal of fruit in peace. " Let any naturalist," says a modern observer, " who is prejudiced against the Darwinian views go to the forests of Borneo. Let him there watch from day to day this strangely human form in all its various phases of existence. Let him see it climb, walk, build its nest, eat, and drink, and fight. Let him see the female suckle her young and carry it astride her hip precisely as do the Coolie women of Hindostan. Let him witness the human-like emotions of affection, satisfaction, pain, and childish rage. Let him see all this, and then he may feel how much more potent has been this lesson than all he has read in pages of abstract ratiocination." After all, the Orang-utan is a poor creature, with but an outer resemblance to the human species. In intelligence he is not only far below the lowest savage, but even inferior to the horse or the dog. No amount of teaching will make the Orang-utan or any other ape practically useful to man. Do all we can for them in a state of confinement, they are simply big helpless monkeys to the last!

The avifauna of the island is very rich. Its pheasants rival those of China in beauty. The great hornbills abound in the fruit groves, and are giants in comparison with their representatives the toucans of South America. Here the humming-birds of the new world are amply represented by the sun-birds. Mound-building megapodia are common, their earth-works rivalling those of the termites; and the edible nest-making swallow works in its dark cave dwellings to satisfy the epicurean tastes of those Eastern aldermen, the mandarins of the Celestial Empire. One peculiar species of kingfisher always makes its nest in company with that of a colony of wild bees. Its young may be fed on the young larvæ, or perchance the company of the bees may be courted for the sake of their protection in the event of the nest being attacked.

Amongst my own introductions to European gardens is a singular species of pitcher plant or nepenthes, the urns of which are armed with two sharp and strong spines (see p. 341). Its pitchers always contain insects of various kinds, and I am convinced that the spines are present to prevent birds and insect-hunting animals such as the tarsier from removing these insects from the urns. The stalk of this nepenthes is swollen quite near to the pitcher in a singular manner, and is there punctured by a peculiar species of ant, but I could never satisfactorily account for their presence, unless it be in search of water.

Beccari, during his travels in Borneo, discovered a singular plant—Myrmecodia—parasitic on low jungle trees. Its economy is most interesting. The young seedlings, when about an inch in height, are punctured or bitten by an ant, an operation which causes the stem to become gouty and eventually hollow; in fact, a natural living hive in which the ants then shelter themselves. This is their own gain, and they in turn rush out to resent any attack which may be made on their living nest. A case analogous to this of mutual protection is recorded of an African species of acacia. The most singular thing in connection with this co-operative affair is that unless the young seedling plants are bitten in due course they are said by Beccari to die. I saw this plant daily for a long period, and often amused myself by attacking it in order to see how invariably the ants rushed out in force to repel the intruder. I also noted many young seedlings both living and dead, but of my own knowledge could scarcely venture so far as to say that the dead ones had succumbed owing to the ants having neglected to bite them !

An account of some of the more remarkable of my discoveries and introductions may be found in the Appendix to this volume, p. 339.

In conclusion, I may be allowed to say that the far interior of Borneo still remains to be explored. It is emphatically a wild land without roads or bridges, and a march right across the island from the north-east to the north-west coast, although a formidable undertaking, would if accomplished reveal much that is at present unknown.

F. W. B.

CONTENTS.

CHAPTER I.

EASTWARD, HO !

CHAPTER II.

SINGAPORE.

CHAPTER III.

VISIT TO JAHORE—GUNONG PULOI.

CHAPTER IV.

RIVER AND FOREST TRAVEL.

CHAPTER V.

CHAPTER VI.

CHAPTER VII.

CHAPTER VIII.

A CITY OF LAKE DWELLINGS.

CHAPTER IX.

A VOYAGE TO SULU.

CHAPTER X.

A ROYAL PIG HUNT.

CHAPTER XIV.

CHAPTER XV.

TROPICAL FRUITS.

CHAPTER XVI.

NOTES ON TROPICAL TRAVEL.

APPENDIX.

LIST OF ILLUSTRATIONS.

THE GARDENS OF THE SUN.

CHAPTER I.

EASTWARD, HO!

Gibraltar—Port Said—Suez Canal—Kantara—Aden—Life Afloat—
Floating Homes.

WHEN our ship had nearly reached the mouth of the
Mersey, on her outward voyage, the boatswain and his
men were busily engaged in lashing everything moveable
in its place on deck. "We shall get it to-night," said
that man of the sea; but on the vessel went as smoothly
as ever, and everybody was merry at dinner-time, hours
after the "Bosun's" prophecy. We watched the setting
sun, and a gorgeous after-glow of purple, grey, and gold.
Then came the twilight, and a sense of chilliness. The
land on the port-side was lost in a soft grey mist; then
it became colder and darker, and we went below. The
saloon looked bright and cheerful, with its sparkle of
glasses in the swinging racks, and the mellow light of
the lamps.

I read for an hour or more, and then "turned in,"
heartily glad to think we were having such a smooth and
pleasant time, and that the "Bosun's" prediction had
not been verified. I was soon asleep. How long I slept
I do not quite remember, but I dreamed that I was

falling down a well, and the crash made when I reached the bottom awoke me. I forgot for the moment where I was, but my first impressions were that, Zazel-like, I had been shot out of a cannon, and that I was whirling round chain-shot fashion. Instinctively stretching out my hands, I found myself in my berth, but the ship was plunging and rolling very much, and everything moveable was knocking about in all directions. Another crash, similar to the one which awoke me, told of loose crockery going to destruction in the steward's pantry.

I spent some time in trying to decide whether the ship was playing at leapfrog, or trying to turn a somersault. A " sea change " put an end to my deliberations. Sleep was impossible, and I was glad when morning came, and I held on to the berth with one hand, and dressed with the other. That man of the sea was right. We had " got " it, and no mistake; and we continued to " get it " until off Cape St. Vincent, when we regained smooth water.

Cape St. Vincent is a rocky bluff, crested with a ruined convent and a lighthouse, the white walls of which gleam out brightly in the sunshine, although we are fully ten miles away. After we have passed it, and look back, it forms a much more picturesque object than when seen directly opposite; and in front of the nearly perpendicular cliffs is a curious cone-shaped rock, and through the narrow passage between this and the mainland, tradition says an American skipper ran his vessel for a wager, and got through safely. The whole coast here is bold and rocky, but not dangerous. Large craft may ride close in under the cliffs.

A few miles further along is Cape Sartenius, a rocky headland, which rises perpendicularly from the sea, and is crowned with a fort and lighthouse; and from this point the rugged coast-line falls away towards Trafalgar Bay and Gibraltar, a distance of nearly two hundred miles. We were fortunate in seeing the red honey-combed rock at Gibraltar in the morning's sunshine, the pretty little town of St. Roque lying behind across the neutral ground. To the left the cork woods and Alge-siraz. Exactly opposite " Gib," on the African side, is Ceuta, with its lighthouse and fort on the hill, and square flat-topped Moorish houses below ; while Apes' Hill stands up clear and dark against the masses of fleecy white clouds. The straits here are about six miles wide, and it was near this point that the Moors used to cross, Pict and Scot fashion, into Spain in the olden time. Of course, like Mark Twain, we saw the " Queen of Spain's chair " on the hill behind Gibraltar, and a naturalist friend reminds me that the rock here is the only place in Europe where monkeys and scorpions are naturalised. The wag meant " Rock Scorpions " I sup-pose, but the monkeys are there all right enough. By the aid of a good glass, we saw patches of cultivated crops on the low coast hills, and whitewashed farm-houses were freely dotted amongst them. Now we were fairly into the blue waters of the Mediterranean, and the coast lines began to recede on either side. Here and there, however, over the coast hills we obtained glimpses of the snow-peaked Sierra Nevada mountains standing out clear and cool against the blue sky.

It was about the middle of June, and very hot during the day time, but chilly at night. The sea is of the most emphatic blue when you look down into it, but has a purplish glow towards the horizon. The sunsets are occasionally very beautiful, with their tints of crimson, salmon, grey, vermilion, and gold. It is pleasant at sun-rise, after a bracing salt-water bath under the hose-pipe, to watch the silvery dolphin as they follow each other in line and play around the bows of the ship, at times leaping clear out of the water. The velocity of these creatures is wonderful; they gambol around a ship, and keep up alongside without any apparent effort. A few black and white sea-gulls are the only aërial visitors, except that now and then flying fish are seen skimming the surface of the blue water with their glistening wings. In some places they may be seen by the hundred, rising in flocks from the water, to escape their enemies below. They fly for a distance of two or three hundred yards, rising and falling in a sinuous manner; and occasionally they dip into the crest of a wave for a moment, to moisten their wings, which enables them to prolong their flight. Many were washed or flew on board during the night, and were very delicate in flavour. The sailors say they fly at the lights, and thus fall on deck, which may be the fact, as it was only after dark that any were caught in this manner. Some specimens were sixteen inches in length, but about half that size appeared to be the average.

We caught a passing glimpse of Galita and Malta on our way. Both were once little more than barren rocks; indeed, Galita is so still; but Malta has been improved by cultivation, and now yields much of the early vegetable produce brought to the Paris and London markets. Tradition hath it that formerly vessels trading to Malta were obliged to bring a certain quantity of earth with them, so anxious were the Maltese to improve their tiny farms.

Port Said was our first stopping place; and, after a fortnight afloat, we were glad to see the lighthouse, like a yellow speck on the horizon. We went ashore, and saw the town, which stands close to the sea-beach, and

by the entrance to the canal, with which it is con-
temporaneous. Behind, as far as one can see, stretches
the arid desert itself. The old Arab town of square, flat-

EGYPTIAN WATER-COOLER.

topped houses, is nearly a mile away to the right. The
new town consists mainly of shops and hotels, with the
exception of the consular residences, the hospital, and
post-office.

I visited the hospital, with the young Irish ship's doctor

as a companion, and among the inmates saw an American suffering from fever and chronic rheumatism. In one of the cells, guarded by a couple of Arab sentries, we found a young, fair-haired, blue-eyed Greek sailor, who had murdered an Arab girl through jealousy the night before. I was struck by the gentle, inoffensive expression on his face; but I suppose he did not deserve the pity I felt for him. A public square, planted with trees, shrubs, and flowers, forms an oasis in the midst of the desert of dusty streets, and white-washed or stucco houses. Most of the houses are two-storied, and furnished with cool, shady verandahs; and in some cases they are covered with the green drapery of a large convolvulus, which adds much to the picturesque effect of walls and fences throughout the place. In the gardens, bananas, date-palms, bamboo, and other vegetation common to hothouses at home, here grow in the open air, with no other protection than that afforded by a belt of tall reeds. Nothing is produced here, even the necessary fruits and culinary vegetables being brought from Malta, or the Mediterranean ports. Soil and fresh water for the little gardens has to be procured from Ismalia, fifty miles away.

In the markets we found plenty of ripe grapes, fine pomegranates, water-melons, and great pithy-skinned oranges. Vegetables consisted of lettuce, onions, beet, the Egyptian turnip-rooted kind, peas, okre, and gourds. Most of the stands were attended by lazy Arab women, of various ages, who sat cross-legged among their goods, and kept off the flies with switches of horse-hair. A tight-fitting cap, ornamented with little gold coins, covered their heads, and their figures were enshrouded in great black cloaks, reaching to their heels.

We saw some old Arabs watering the hot and dusty streets with sea-water, which they carried in large skin

" bottles," slung behind them, so that the march of
modern progress has not yet obliterated all the old
customs and utensils of these singularly primitive people.
We took about a hundred tons of coal on board here.
This was brought to the side of the vessel in lighters,

SHE OF THE MARKET.

and carried up sloping planks by some fifty or sixty
swarthy fellows, who kept up a droning chant the whole
time.   They each carried up about a hundred weight
at once in a basket ; and the whole gang reminded one
of a colony of black ants, as they swarmed up one plank
in quick succession, and trotted down another, after
disposing of their dirty load.   Perhaps the Pyramids,
and other gigantic architectural erections, were reared by
myriads of ant-like workers, similar to these we now saw.
   Two mail steamers entered the Canal before us, and it

is a very odd sight to see the masts of the first one gliding away to the left, nothing else being visible but the flat
sea of sand as far as the eye can reach.   Pilots are necessary for the Canal, and notwithstanding their special
knowledge and skill, vessels frequently get aground.
Coaling over, we get under way and enter the strip of salt
water which connects the Mediterranean with the Gulf
of Suez, passing through the flat desert, a distance of
about eighty-seven miles.   The completion of this undertaking, apart from facilitating European and Eastern
commerce, has also, if local report speaks truly, benefited
the climate of the district as well ; a current of cool air is
now attracted along its route, and the precious burden of
the rain-clouds has also been brought to this tract of arid
sands, which previously were almost entirely destitute of
showers.   Another benefit to the dwellers on its shores is
the fish which travel along this strip of water-way and so
are caught close to the doors of those who live or who
are employed along its banks.   At five mile intervals
along the banks are stations for signalling purposes, and
as the strip of seaway is not broad enough for two vessels
to pass each other, the Canal is widened at each " gare,"
so that one vessel can make fast while the other passes.
The whole thing is regulated by a simple telegraphic and
signalling system.   Nearly all these stations have little
gardens, but the prettiest of them all in this way is that
at the old Arab town and ferry station of Kantara,
through which many caravans pass on their way to and
from Cairo.   Here is a tiny hotel, and several little
whitewashed houses with shady verandahs laden with
climbing plants of various kinds.   One of the houses is
sheltered by a row of poplars, and the colour and fragrance of the oleanders were delightful.   The Arabs call
this flower the " Rose of the Desert," and certainly at

this little oasis it might fairly be said that the desert had been made "to blossom as the rose."

We reached here at sunset, and the air was deliciously cool and fresh, and a sight of the dark green poplar trees was most cheering and home-like. Crickets chirped in the sand, and the splashing of the fish in the Canal was heard very frequently after we had made fast for the night. The tints on the vegetation and sand-hills by the banks just before sunset are most lovely, and the sunsets themselves very gorgeous as seen through the clear dry air. Two of the firemen had to be placed in irons soon after leaving Port Said, to prevent them from leaping overboard or injuring themselves. They were literally maddened by some villanous spirituous drink which had been smuggled on board during the hurry and bustle of coaling in the morning. Here and there we passed the bodies of dead camels, on which wolfish-looking dogs or vultures regale themselves. Flocks of flamingoes were seen in the distance. As the air becomes clearer after sunrise the distant sand-hills resemble islands in a broad lake or sea, an effect due to mirage; indeed, the semblance of a flat expanse of water lying in the full sunshine near the horizon is so perfect as to deceive all but the experienced. The hills of loose sand close to the banks of the Canal are swept quite smooth by the winds in some places, while here and there the surface is rippled like a snow-ruck, and the foot-prints on these "sands of time" made by the passing Arab are singularly like those made in frozen snow.

At one of the stations an old Arab offered a basket of very fine fish for sale which he had caught in the Canal the night before. We got a view of the Khedive's Palace and M. F. de Lessep's residence at Ismalia just before running through the "Bitter Lakes," and reached Suez before

sundown. The passage through the Canal takes about
two days, as the rate of progress is necessarily slow
to avoid washing down the banks, and there are frequent
stoppages.

Suez is a larger town and much older than Port Said,
but its inhabitants depend almost entirely on the few
residents connected with the Canal and Railway to
Alexandria, and the pilgrims who land here on their way
to Mecca and Medina, the birthplace and tomb of their
Prophet. After leaving Suez the climate becomes hotter

ARAB DHOW.

every day. The coast-line is backed by barren looking
copper-coloured mountains, and the air smells hot and
dry, like that of the greenhouse devoted to the cactus
family at Kew. Two or three steamers with pilgrims on
board for Suez were seen.

Among the visitors from the coast were great brown
locusts, a humming-bird hawk moth, and one or two
small birds. A quail flew on board, and flitted about
the deck for two or three days. Another little bird, as
elegantly shaped as a lark, stayed on board for several
days; it was brown in colour, with almost black wing-

tips ; it had a band of white just above the tail, and this gave the bird a characteristic appearance, especially during its jerky red-cap like flight.

We went into Aden, and I never felt the heat so much anywhere before or since. It is a huge Dutch oven of sunburnt rocks without a sign of vegetation as seen from the harbour. It is astonishing how soon one begins to take a personal interest in a ship on which a long voyage has to be made. The second mate was the skipper of a China trader, and tells me of the palmy days before the Canal was opened, and when freights were £12 a ton. One of the quartermasters was an ex-royal yachtsman, a civil and obliging old fellow, with a sharp eye for grog. One of the stewards has been a photographer, and another is a hairdresser—rather a luxury to have aboard ship. The old Welsh stewardess was a character, with nightly tendencies towards hot rum and water and old superstitious stories of the sea. The captain is a fat, red-whiskered old sea-dog, who knows all about everything, but evidently never enjoyed an introduction to Mr. Lindley Murray in his youth. His politics are peculiar, and his motto appears to be that of the ultra radicals, " Down with everything what's up."

Penang was our next stopping-place, and we got ashore for two days, and enjoyed a walk around the town and a ride to the " Falls " and the " Hill." Two days afterwards we stepped on to the Pile wharf at Tanjong Paggar or the " fenced cape " at Singapore, and our experiences of the tropics really began. The voyage for two days down the Straits of Malacca had been very pleasant, and we thoroughly enjoyed the smooth blue sea and clear sky, flecked now and then by tiny fleets of junks with their mat sails of a soft golden hue, reminding one of cornstacks at home. Bukit-Jugra, Cape Rachardo, and Mount Ophir towering up above the horizon behind the town of Malacca itself, were distinctly seen ere we reached the numerous islets near the entrance to the harbour and roads at Singapore.

A long sea voyage has its pleasures as well as its drawbacks; and in travelling eastward, more especially, it is quite possible, after crossing "the Bay," to get a smooth voyage all the way. There are times when the Mediterranean, the Indian Ocean, and the China Sea lie sleeping in the sunshine, and a steamer runs as smoothly as a canal boat. Of course a yachtsman of the old sea-dog school is disgusted with this sort of fine weather sailing; but it is most pleasant to passengers on board steamships who can lie and read under the cool side of the awning, drinking in the fresh ozonised sea air, untroubled for the nonce by the cares of business or the whirl and bustle of the town.

A curious feeling comes over one on viewing the boundless ocean for the first time on a calm, cloudless day. It makes one feel extremely small to gaze on what appears to be the eternity of sea around, with not a speck or a sail to break the view on all sides. Then when a breeze springs up a sense of freedom animates the breast as the vessel rushes through the water and shakes the milk-white foam from her bows, as though also glad to be free. The pleasure is akin to that of the saddle. The exhilarating motion of the ship stirs one's blood and sends it coursing through one's veins, as she "walks the waters like a thing of life," and the strong pure breeze fans our cheeks and the cool spray comes in our faces like a shower of dew. Well might Ruskin give our English pastime of yachting the first place amongst recreations. Nothing can be more refreshing than to stand on board a tight little vessel when there is, according to the poetry of youthful memory,

" A wet sheet and a flowing sea, and a wind that follows fast."

In the joy of the moment you do not wonder at the sea-fights, the brave sailors, and the corsairs of old ; the men who love the sea and can struggle with it through all its moods and phases, will be brave anywhere.   If the sea does not nerve a man to brave actions, nothing else ever will.   Life on the sea is most refreshing to the average landsman, and on board ship time flies more pleasantly perhaps than anywhere else, if it be true that " sweet do nothing " is the acme of enjoyment.   What an appetite the sea-breezes give one for breakfast, which is perhaps of all meals that least enjoyed by inland residents on shore.   Our floating cities are the triumphs of modern civilised ingenuity ; and during propitious weather in a warm climate, life afloat possesses for the time a freshness and novelty unobtainable elsewhere.

CHAPTER II.

Hotels—Singapore—An Eastern Port—A Tropical Island—Chinese Settlers—Chinese Play—Tropical Night—Climate.

THIS port, which is also the seat of the government of the Straits Settlements, has not inaptly been called the "Liverpool of the East," and the applicability of that title soon becomes evident to the stranger from "home," who finds himself on the landing-stage at Tanjong Paggar for the first time. Here is a range of warehouses or "godowns" for the storage of goods, and coaling sheds for the supply of the mail and other steamers moored alongside. One is soon glad to get away from the heat, the noise of the steam winch, and the coal-dust; and a gharry or cab having been procured, the dusky Jehu springs to his seat on the shaft, from which "coign of vantage" he uses both whip and voice in urging on at a gallop a plucky little pony, scarcely larger than a donkey, and most probably bred either in Sumatra or Pegu. You meet other little ponies in other little gharries coming full tilt down the road to the wharf, a string of buffalo-carts, or occasionally a neat little private carriage, and you soon become aware of the fact that Singapura, as it is still called, of the Malays is both hot and dusty. On you go, and the stuffy little gharry, even if it has no windows, soon becomes as hot as an oven, and the perspiration streams from every pore. By the time you reach the hotels the chances are that your shirt and collar are in the state best described as " pulpy ; " and if you are of a sanguine temperament, your face may be said to resemble " the rising sun." Of course you have kept your eyes open as you came along past the rough hedges on the right clothed with red lantanas, the neat police-station on the bank to the left, with those beautiful crimson and buff-flowered hibiscus bushes before the door. Then the rows of Chinese houses and shops, an elaborate Hindoo temple or two of white stone, and then street after street of whitewashed red tile roofed shops, until you reach the square, where you meet your agent, or to the hotels, nearly all of which are clustered around the tall spire of the cathedral, which you will have seen as the ship steamed slowly into harbour. The chances are you will have been recommended to one or other of the hotels by some knowing friend.

The Hotel de l'Europe is the principal one ; but at the time I arrived in Singapore the *chef-de-cuisine* had such a bad name that I was recommended elsewhere. One is sure to be comfortable at any of the first-class houses at prices varying from two to five dollars daily, or less by monthly arrangement. For this sum one may secure a more or less comfortable bedroom or suite simply white-washed, the floor covered with yellow rattan matting, which is both cool and clean. The walls, as a rule, do not boast of anything great in the way of pictorial embel-lishment ; at night, however, lively little insect-eating lizards disport themselves thereon ; and then, too, the hum of the hungry mosquito is heard. In the morning you rise soon after gun-fire (5 A.M.). It is daylight about 6 A.M. ; and after partaking of a cup of tea or coffee, and the inevitable two bits of toast, you have a walk. Every-body nearly seems astir. While dressing, the chances

are you will hear a gentle tap at the door, or hearing it
opened very cautiously, you turn suddenly, and are
startled by a dusky apparition in an enormous white
turban. It is an itinerant Kling, or Hindoo Figaro, who
seeing you are one of the new arrivals by yesterday's
mail, would like to shave you, or cut your hair, at a
charge of half a dollar.

Strolling outside into the main thoroughfares you see
a strange motley crowd. The markets are full to overflowing with edibles of all kinds ; meat, fish, vegetables,
and fruit lie about in glorious profusion. Here a heap of
fresh fish of the most vivid colours, there a pile of yellow
pine-apples or bright scarlet chilies, oranges, pomoloes,
mangosteen and rambutan, Chinese long beans, fresh
green lettuces and young onions, tomatoes, and the
hundred and one elements of native cookery, which are
perfectly unintelligible to any but native eyes. Chinese
coolies coming in from the interior of the island laden
with fruit and vegetables, or other commodities. Sleek
fat-faced celestials in black jackets, loose white trousers,
and white European felt hats, taking their morning's
stroll, and in every doorway gaunt-featured Chinese
artizans of the tailor and shoemaker type sit or stand
enjoying the cool fresh air and their morning's whiff of
tobacco at the same time. The Chinese predominate,
but you will find dusky spider-limbed Klings and the
more compact little brown Malays fairly represented.
You will notice gharries coming into town laden with
Chinese traders, and other vehicles bring in the European
storekeepers, agents, clerks, &c. You return about eight
o'clock, and have a bath, and then dress for breakfast.

As you sit in the verandah or open basement awaiting
the gong for breakfast being struck, various itinerant
traders, generally Klings or Chinese, try to tempt you

with their wares, for which they ask about five times as much as they are worth, or could be bought for in London. Japanese and Chinese fans, slippers, cabinets, lacquer ware, and carved ivory goods, all of second or third rate value, form their stock in trade in general, while some offer gold brocade worked for slippers or smoking-caps, crape handkerchiefs and shawls, or Indian embroidery, and even socks and white handkerchiefs of cheap European make.

Of course, to a new arrival, everything is strange, and not the least perplexing is the Babel of language on all hands. English, Dutch, German, Chinese, Javanese, Hindustani, Spanish, Portuguese, and Malay, the latter by far the most general—the lingua franca which all use in common. At last, bang! bang!! bang!!! goes the gong, and breakfast is ready exactly at 9 A.M. There is no ceremony. A little regiment,—an awkward squad rather,—of Chinese " boys " hand the dishes in turn. As a rule, everything is well cooked, and there is variety enough for everybody. Beef-steaks and mutton-chops, one or two well-made curries and rice, eggs and bacon, cold ham, boiled eggs, salads, vegetables, and plenty of fresh fruit. Coffee or tea is not so much in favour here in the East as at home, bottled Bass, claret, or Norwegian beer, being preferred instead. After a long morning's walk, however, scarcely any beverage is so grateful as an accompaniment to the post-prandial cigar as is a cup of freshly-roasted coffee. Breakfast over, the real business of the day commences. All the large stores and godowns are opened at 8.30 or 9.0 A.M., and from 10 until 12.30 everyone is alert and busy. Gharries are whisking about in all directions. The fattest and sleekest and richest of Chinese merchants arrive in their more or less imposing carriages, boats and sampans are going to or returning from the shipping in the roads, buffalo carts ply between the godowns in town and those at the wharf, the sun pours down its heat and light from the zenith, and everybody seems intent on making their hay while it shines.

All the principal stores and shops are either in "the Square" or its vicinity, and here you can procure home comforts of nearly every description, together with the latest books and home papers. You will procure the latest news at Little's Store, and will see many things there to interest you. Sale & Co.'s, and Katz's Stores, are also well worth a visit, and few of the Chinese shops will compare well with that of the late Hon. C. Whampoa, C.M.G., who was a most influential trader in the place. The "Square" is an oblong plot of turf planted with various tropical trees, and one of these, although fast going to decay, is well worthy of notice, being completely enshrouded with rare orchids of various kinds. This stands immediately opposite the Singapore Dispensary, and owes its interesting appearance to Mr. Jamie, who first planted it with orchids some years ago. Amongst other plants *Aerides suavissimum* is especially luxuriant, completely wreathing some of the principal branches with its glossy green leaves, and many seedlings of this species have germinated and are now promising little plants. *Vandas, Phalænopsis grandiflora*, and *P. amabilis* also grow and flower well here in close proximity to the dusty streets. In Singaporean gardens the rarest of moth orchids are planted in cocoanut-shells and hung from the verandahs, or placed on the mango or orange trees on the lawn, where they soon establish themselves. How many English orchid amateurs would wish for such a genial clime.

A morning in the "Square" gives one a tolerably clear

insight into the enterprise and trade of Singapore. You hear a good deal about the price of sago or gutta and rice, or about the chartering of steamers or sailing craft, or the freight on home or export goods. You are sure to meet two or three captains of trading steamers. Captain Linguard, perhaps, after one of his trips to the Coti river away on the south-east of Borneo, and then you will hear something of the rubber-market, or of the pirates, of whom, perhaps, few men know more than this energetic "Rajah Laut," or "Sea King," as he is called by the natives.

Another maritime celebrity is Captain Ross, a genial sailor, who owns the mail steamer "Cleator," which runs between Singapore, Labuan, and Brunei, on the north-west Bornean coast. Captain Ross is well acquainted with the principal places in the whole Malayan Archipelago; and few residents have an equal colloquial knowledge of their languages. He has been attacked by pirates more than once in the old days, and is quite a nautical authority in every way. That tall, dark young fellow yonder, with the heavy moustache, is Captain Cowie, who ran the gauntlet of the Spanish gun-boats so successfully during the Sulu war, carrying rice, powder, and arms for the Sultan's people; and here one also meets "old sea dogs" of nearly every nationality, but more especially English and Dutch.

One must of course look in at Emmerson's for tiffin, and a glance at the home papers and telegrams. Tiffin is much like breakfast, only nearly all the dishes are cold. The curries here are excellent; and a well-made salad of fresh green vegetables is a treat, when the temperature is 92° in the shade. The Raffles Institution is well worthy of a visit—an interesting museum of native curiosities and natural history specimens having recently

been formed; and there is here an excellent library of
books, on nearly all subjects. A collection of economic
products is in course of formation, and if well carried
out, will add much to the interest of the place. The
Botanical Gardens are situated at Tanglin, a distance of
about three miles from the town of Singapore; and as
the roads are smooth and level, it is a very pleasant
journey, either in the morning or evening. One night
each week the military band performs in the garden;
and then a good many of the residents ride or drive
out to " eat the air," and hear the music before dinner.
Good collections of orchids, palms, and economic plants,
are here kept up, and the place forms an agreeable
promenade morning and evening. In addition to the
plants, a small collection of animals and birds, for the
most part natives of the Archipelago, may be seen here.
The island itself is tolerably flat, the elevated portions
being in the form of low hills, or " bukits," the highest,
Bukit Timah, being about 400 feet above sea level.
Many of the rare plants, formerly found here, have died
out since the destruction of the old forest for cultivation.
Wild pigs are plentiful; but the tigers do not often
repeat the predatory visits of twenty or thirty years ago,
when two or three hundred Chinamen were devoured
every year. They now very rarely cross the "Old
Straits," a channel about half a mile wide, which separates
the island from the mainland of Jahore.

In the Singapore *Times*, however, for Feb. 1, 1879,
the following paragraph appeared, which shows that
the brutes have not quite lost their old-established
man-eating desires :—

" Tigers, it would appear, are approaching Singapore
town unpleasantly close. On the 29th January a Chinaman was taken away by one on a plantation only about

four miles from town; and unpleasant rumours are afloat that some have lately been seen in Sirangoon and Changhie."

Much fruit is grown; and there are cocoa-nut, gambir, pepper, indigo and gamboge plantations on a small scale. Vegetable crops here, as in San Francisco, are a monopoly of the thrifty Chinese gardeners. The trade in economic products of the soil of the neighbouring islands is an important one, and, ere long, when cultivation extends more fully into Jahore and Perak, this will be much increased. Some of the planters from Ceylon have already commenced extensive clearing operations in Jahore; and if these succeed, the rest is but a question of time. A few rare and interesting plants yet linger in the jungle, notably, the curious pitcher plant (*Nepenthes Rafflesiana*), which, singularly enough, is one of the first plants to spring up after a jungle fire. *Gleichenia dichotoma* clothes some of the hill-sides here as freely as the common brake-fern at home.

One of the most singular of native plants, however, is that known as *Amorphophallus campanulatus*, a relative of the " Lords and Ladies " of our English woods; but this tropical species is of Titanic dimensions, producing a lurid spathe, nearly two feet in circumference, and exhaling the most fetid and repulsive of odours.

In rambling about the island one comes across fertile little gardens and groves of mangoes, mangosteen, and other fruit trees, the tenants being generally Chinamen. The bye-streets of the town present some novel sights to a stranger, being tenanted for the most part by Chinese artizans and shopkeepers, the workshops being generally quite open to the street. Blacksmiths, tin-workers, tailors and shoemakers, carpenters, coopers, and basket-makers here ply their callings, and turn out excellent work, although some of the tools used are exceedingly clumsy in appearance from our own point of view.

Passing down some of the streets beneath the shade of the piazzas, one meets with general stores of every description, each with its little stall right outside the door close to the path. Here you can purchase almost everything; tools, nails and screws, needles, pencils, cotton, cutlery, ammunition, old Tower muskets—indeed nearly everything in the way of hardware goods, whether Chinese or European. The European goods are such as are especially made for this market, and the prices are surprisingly low.

It is curious to observe how some industrial products are universally used here to the exclusion of others. For example, " Bryant & May's " matches, so common at home, are here supplanted by a neatly made " Tänd-stickor," ten little boxes of which are made up into a packet, which sells for as low as six cents, although ten cents is always asked of strangers. In many Chinese and Kling shops European tinned provisions and patent medicines may be obtained at a very slight advance on home prices, as these petty traders watch the sales of old ships' stores very closely, and are thus enabled to purchase very cheaply.

The Chinese compete with all comers in cheap labour; and their innate capacity for imitation enables them to do so very often with advantage in the case of manufactures. If you can only give a Chinese workman a pattern or sample of the goods you require—whether boots, clothing, cabinet work, or jewellery, he may be trusted to imitate the same even to a fault. They are most industrious, having apparently no regular hours of labour, but often toiling from early morning until far into the night for a scanty pittance ; but no matter how small their earnings, they generally contrive to save something. Indeed it is difficult to say whether 'tis their industry or their thrift which most deserves commendation. Of course they have their faults as a people, and most serious some of them are ; and wherever they are admitted as emigrants, a strong hand is needed to keep them in order.

For opening up new trading enterprises or colonies in the East their aid is invaluable, as they are most frugal, and possess a peculiar habit of making the best of circumstances. In Sarawak, and also in the British colony of Labuan, the money derived from the opium and spirit farms form a main feature in the revenue, so that eastern colonies, in favouring Chinese emigration, add to their revenue by their expenditure as well as by their labour. Many, by thrift and frugality, rise to positions of affluence, and then it is curious to see how thoroughly they fall into the ways of the class to which they reach. This makes a Chinese colony so prosperous as a rule ; for if a man has money he is sure to spend it either in trade, or in a fine house, garden, servants, horses and carriages, and other luxuries. As a rule they deal with their own class, but they take to European luxuries very kindly. I was asked out to dine several times at the houses of wealthy Chinese whilst in the East, and was at first rather disappointed at the thorough European character of the repast. Clean cloth, knives and forks of course ; and every course might have been prepared in Pall Mall, if we except the curries; and it is but natural that the curries of the East are inimitable elsewhere. You get most delicately prepared pastry, and ten to one, roast beef and plum pudding, which are all the world over understood to be our national dishes.

A gentleman told me that once when in Paris, just

after the war, he was conversing with a friend near the Tuileries, when a wicked-eyed young *gamin* overhearing his bad French with an English accent, observed, " Ah, M'sieu rost-bif, God-dam," as he rapidly vanished round the corner. Many of the rich merchants speak English well ; if not, then Malay is the medium of conversation. And the wherewithal to wash down your food is not forgotten : indeed, many of the rich " babas " give excellent champagne breakfasts, and " Bass " and good Bordeaux are as common as at European meals. However addicted to " samshu " and " shandu,"—the baleful narcotic immortalised by De Quincey,—a Chinaman may be privately, you will find him courteous, and eagerly apprehensive as to the comfort and enjoyment of his guests on all occasions when he entertains Europeans.

Sometimes you meet with a surprise at a Chinese dinner—a surprise especially prepared for your benefit. I was present at one where we had small dishes of rice and condiments set before us, with " chop sticks " in lieu of knife and fork. Now a native to the manner born will use his two chop sticks as cleverly as Mr. G. W. Moore handles his bones ; and as he leans over his dish you see a constant stream of food running up to his mouth, while with your chop sticks awkwardly held you simply demonstrate what " eating porridge with a knitting pin " really means. Well, dish followed dish, and we began to think the whole thing " awfully slow," when the host arose and requested us to accompany him to the " dining-room."

Sure enough we found ourselves in a large and well lit interior. There was a dinner-table laid in European style, the silver and glass irreproachable, and floral decorations rather tastefully arranged graced the board. Of course there was a good deal of laughter as the neat

Chinese " boys " handed round the sherry and bitters as
we stood in groups ; and a few minutes afterwards the
gong was beaten for dinner in quite a homely fashion.
A jolly old Spanish priest was present, and our long-
tailed host did not omit to ask him to say grace, which
he solemnly did, first in English, standing the while, and
then we were all surprised as the rubicund-cheeked friar
rolled out a Chinese prayer interlarded with choice
maxims from Confucius, and all in the Hokien dialect of
Chinese. The whole thing was much enjoyed. We had
soup oxtail and " birds' nest," the latter extremely good,
but perhaps rather too sweet for European liking; fish
of several kinds, beef and mutton cooked in various
ways, also pork cutlets excellently cooked, as indeed only
Chinese cooks can prepare them ; pastry, cheese, and
such fruits for dessert as no money could procure from
Covent Garden. Fat juicy mangoes, delicate mangosteen, rambutan, bananas, and other kinds, never eaten in
perfection anywhere but in the tropics—the gardens of
the sun.

A " wyong " or Chinese play had been organised by
our host, one portion of his house being fitted up as a
private theatre, and to this we adjourned after dinner.
The performers were a celebrated troupe just arrived
from China, and very clever they were, especially in
pantomime. Of course we understood not a word of
what was spoken ; and yet so expressive were the actions
that the plot and motive of the play was perfectly com-
prehended even in detail. The music of shrieking two-
stringed violins, and the rattle of gongs and tom-toms
which accompanied them, however, might fairly be added
to Mr. Sothern's list of things which "no fellah can
understand." The plot was of an undutiful daughter of
poor parents who was beloved of a youth of her own age

and station. A rich mandarin, however, loves and marries her. Her young lover is the most dutiful of sons, and a good spirit helps him on ; while at the same time a bad one causes the mandarin heavy losses by sea and land. The undutiful daughter has her parents driven from her husband's gates, where they had come to beg, while her former lover succours them, and they ultimately die, blessing him. Eventually the mandarin is degraded, and the dutiful youth is elevated to his place for some service he has rendered to one of the emperor's favourite ministers. He then makes a speech, telling how good and clever he has been, and ultimately marries the tiny-footed daughter of the minister who has befriended him. Nor does the play finish until his "poor, but honest parents" and the audience are convinced by ocular proof that a son and heir has been born of the union, a piece of good fortune for which the rich but wicked mandarin before him had hoped in vain. The character of the youth was excellently played throughout by a young Chinese lady from Hong Kong, and I do not remember to have seen a male part acted much better by a female actress anywhere. So that the Lottie Venns and Kate Vaughans of our own stage must look to their laurels, as ere long they may possibly have to compete with the " cheap Chinese labour " of the Eastern mimes.

It was late that night as we drove back to our hotel, and such a night as one can see only in the tropics, where the moonlight is bright enough to read by, and streams down like a gloriously brilliant bridal veil over sweet-scented blossoms wet with dew, and the most elegant of palm-trees, over the gorgeous floral treasures of eastern gardens, and over the homes of thousands of dusky brides. The sounds heard during the otherwise still hours of evening or night are peculiar, the clucking sound of a lizard in the tree overhead is quite bird-like, you hear some frog-like croaking in the wet ditch beside the road, the subdued humming of distant tomtoms reaches you from the hut of a Hindoo Syce, and the

" KAYU KUTOH."

almost mournful cadences of a Javanese prayer chanted by a party of labourers in a garden-house or field-hut reach you on the cool breeze. Then comes the boom of the " Kayu Kutoh,"* or wooden gong on which the Malay " mata mata," literally " man with eyes," or watchman, beats the hour at one of the outlying police-

* This last instrument closely resembles the "teponaztli," an instrument still in use by the Indians in the Cordilleras of Mexico, the deep thudding sound of which may be heard a distance of several miles.

stations. Fires are not at all uncommon, and then you are roused out of a sound sleep by a couple of shots from the signal battery, which shake the whole place. As you lean from your window enjoying just the last sweet whiff ere turning in for the night you may, perchance, hear the silence broken by snatches of song familiar to your ears— the songsters being a party of rowdy sailors returning to the ship after a " wet night " on shore. I am sadly afraid that the low grog-shops monopolise much of "Jack's" time and money when ashore, notwithstanding that there is here an excellent " Sailor's Home," furnished with many conveniences, and supplying the comforts of an hotel at a cheap rate. Towards morning the chattering of sparrows and the shouting of rival roosters are among the most familiar of sounds which remind one of home.

The society of Singapore will compare favourably with that of any British Colony, and for genial hospitality its residents cannot well be surpassed. As in India, new comers are expected to call upon the residents first. In my own case I brought letters of introduction to some of the older inhabitants, and I must here acknowledge how handsomely those cheques were honoured by them. One scarcely knows how valuable genial hospitality really is at home, but far away it is pleasant to find how thoroughly English—British, one ought to say—is the welcome extended to strangers. Government House is the Court, of course, and it is needless to say, that all courtesies essential are there extended to both residents and others. Of course, in a community formed of many nationalities, and of people whose trade and other interests are liable to clash with those of their neighbours, there are sure to be little murmurings and bickerings, together with petty jealousies of various kinds. This is so, more or less, everywhere, but in the Colonies there are few, if any, old titled families to balance the commercial interest.   One may see some bonny English faces in the carriages which are here driven around the Esplanade just as along the " Lady's Mile " at home ; or one evening a week are gathered around the band-stand at the gardens.   The climate, however, is not well suited to the development of the rosy cheeks we see at home ; the peach-like bloom too soon gives place to the soft purity of the lily, and it often becomes necessary for the wife and children to return to a cooler climate, in order to regain somewhat of the health and strength of which a lovely but debilitating climate has robbed them for a time.   Here, as in India, this is a serious drawback to many residents.   Here, too, there are no hill stations sufficiently near, or, as yet, adapted to serve as Sanatoriums.   Now that Jahore is being opened up, however, it is to be hoped that a few bungalows may be erected on Gunong Puloi, on the summit of which the air is comparatively cool and bracing, much more so than on Penang Hill, and it may be readily reached from Singapore in two days.   The cost of living here, even in proportion to the large salaries received, is far in excess of that at home, and the mode of life itself is different.   Here, one must have a large house, and if there is a family, five or six servants at least are needed.   The wages paid to these appear small when compared with the cost of English servants, but at least three times as many are required. The master must have his " boy," the mistress her "ayah, then the cook, water-carrier, grooms, gardener, must be provided, to say nothing of nursery attendance. Native provisions are tolerably cheap, but many things essential must be imported from home at an advanced rate.   Furniture is dear, and pianos, and many other necessities, to say nothing of luxuries, must also be brought from the old country, and freight, if not commission, has to be added to the cost. The very nature of the currency used adds to other expenses. Many things purchasable at home for a shilling, here cost a dollar, at the least a rupee or two shillings, and the result of all this is that with an annual income of five hundred pounds in England, one must think twice ere a jump is made at what appears a tempting bait, namely, "a thousand a year" in the East.

The progress and importance of Singapore, commercially and politically, have never ceased to increase since 1819, when the British flag was first raised on the island by Sir Stamford Raffles.

CHAPTER III.

THIS mountain lies about twenty-five miles north·west
of the native town of Jahore, and is a trifle over 2,000
feet in height. To reach it from Singapore, one must
take post-horses or the coach which runs daily to Krangi,
a police-station on the margin of the "Old Strait," and
thence little steam ferry-boats carry one on to Jahore,
from which place the mountain is reached partly in boats
viâ the Scudai river, and partly on foot through the forest.

I had agreed to visit the Puloi mountain in company
with the government botanist, and leaving Singapore
early, we reached Jahore about 3 P.M., after several little
stoppages on the way. The ride from Singapore to
Krangi was a very pleasant one to me, fresh as I was
from the "old country." The roads are remarkably
smooth, and of a bright red colour, their margins fringed
with orchards of tropical fruits or rows of betel-nut palms.
Here and there are patches of sugar-cane, tapioca, or
indigo, little plots of great-leaved bananas, while at intervals one catches passing glimpses of neat white bungalows nestling amid tall cocoa-nut groves. Arriving at
Krangi, hot and dusty, we rested some time in a clean

bungalow or rest-house, built for the convenience of travellers by the Government. The native police were very attentive, and we took our luncheon here and strolled around the station, and saw abundant evidence of the wild pigs, which are said to be very plentiful. While we waited, the Maharajah drove up in a neat little carriage drawn by a pair of ponies. This was just before his visit to England, and we obtained a good view of him. He is a fine manly fellow, with a bushy moustache, and was dressed in white trousers and jacket, with a white sun-hat, and wore a coloured "sarong" around his waist. We informed him of our intended visit to the mountain, and he promised us that Mr. Hole, his secretary, should furnish us with guides and boatmen.

We had arranged with a Chinese sampan man to ferry ourselves and baggage over, but just as we were about starting one of the little steam ferry-boats came over, and leaving "Johnnie" to bring on our things and a Chinese "boy" in charge, we crossed in the steamboat. We took up our quarters with Mr. Boultbee, with whom we were to stay the night. Jahore itself we found to be a straggling place built along the margin of the strait, and consisting of the Istana and a mosque, together with a few whitewashed houses roofed with red tiles, and native palm-thatched cottages. The best of the tiled houses are occupied by Chinese shopkeepers, the principal wares being rice, fruit, fish, coopery, boxes, baskets, and miscellaneous stores. The principal industry of the place is the timber trade. Extensive steam saw-mills, fitted with good machinery, are here worked by the Maharajah, a good many natives being employed in the trade, while the timber finds a market in Singapore, where a depot exists for business purposes. A railway was projected to the forest near Gunong Puloi some years ago, and several miles of wooden tramways were actually laid down, but the work is now suspended. Were such a roadway completed, it would do much to open up a fertile country especially rich in fine timber, rattans, and other jungle produce. The culture of gambier (*Uncaria Gambir*, Roxb.), pepper and other products now cultivated by the Chinese settlers would also be facilitated. As it is, the timber is cut as near to the streams as is possible, and is then dragged by buffaloes through the jungle and floated down to the town, several logs being lashed together so as to form rafts, on which a man stands to steer it clear of snags and other obstacles.

Gambling is one of the curses of this place, and is publicly carried on in some large buildings near the saw-mills. As the Maharajah derives a percentage from the tables, gambling is not likely to be suppressed here, as it has been at Singapore. Mr. Boultbee's house, where we stayed, is a large and comfortable one of wood, and it stands on an eminence at the north-east end of the town. From the verandah a beautiful view of the old strait is obtained, reminding one of Windermere, only that the vegetation is more luxuriant, brightened as it is by a tropic sun. We walked in the garden and forest behind at sunrise, when every flower and leaf was bathed in dew, and were much pleased with the vegetation. The elk's-horn fern (*Platycerium biforme*) grew on the stems of several of the trees, and we saw it high up in the branches of the forest trees behind the house. *Nepenthes ampullaria*, and the noblest of all ferns, *Dipteris Horsfieldii*, were also abundant in the jungle quite close to the sea-beach, and tall gleichenias clambered up the bushes to a height of at least twenty feet.

Birds and butterflies were alike plentiful in the jungle, and some of the latter were very gorgeous in colour.

D

After our morning walk we looked over the saw-mills, and then returned with the manager to breakfast. We afterwards visited Mr. Hole at the Istana, and found that he had already obtained guides and boatmen, so that we at once had our baggage transferred to the boats, and prepared to start on our journey. Some delay arose, however, owing to the man having to purchase stores, and so it was after four o'clock before we bade Mr. Hole adieu on the steps of the Istana jetty and got fairly off. All our heavy baggage was stowed in a native boat, manned by four Malays, while we ourselves and our stores occupied a Chinese sampan. Our craft was pulled, or rather pushed, by its owner, a stalwart celestial; and as he had never been up the Scudai river before, we had an old Malay sitting on the prow to act as pilot, the stream being very narrow in places, with numerous snags and shoals. Notwithstanding this precaution, however, we were aground twice, and the boat heeled over in the current rather uncomfortably. " Johnnie " had to plunge out into the mud of this alligator's paradise to push our craft into deep water again. These were trifling discomforts, however, not worth a thought amid much that was novel and interesting. We ate our dinners in the boat just at dusk, and enjoyed the cool breeze which swept over the water as we glided up stream.

The silence of the night was unbroken, save by the regular dip of the oars; and as darkness increased, the tiny lamps of the fire-flies became visible here and there among the vegetation on the banks. As we glided onwards their numbers increased, until we came upon them in thousands, evidently attracted by some particular kind of low tree, around which they flashed simultaneously, their scintillating brilliancy being far beyond what I could have imagined to be possible. During my whole sojourn in the East I never saw them again in anything like such numbers. The moon arose about eight o'clock, revealing more distinctly the gradual narrowing of the river, the vegetation of which appeared to be very luxuriant, towering far above our heads. We could recognise the tufted leaves and tall stems of a slender-growing pandan, standing out clear and dark against the sky, and here and there the tall dead trunk of a giant tree added to the weird beauty of a scene, in which the lack of accurate knowledge left much to the imagination.

Our solitary Chinese boatman dipped his oars with the same easy swing as at starting; and about nine o'clock he finished a stiff pull of nine or ten miles by running our boat into the little creek at Kanka Kaladi, he having kept ahead of the Malays, who paddled the other boat, all the way. On our arrival, all the Chinese who live here were abed; so we hauled our craft up to a boat-house at the head of the creek, and got all our things into the loft overhead, and having spread our rugs, and lighted our lamp, we turned in for the night. Before we fell asleep some of the people, who had been disturbed by our arrival, came to have a look at us, and did their best to keep us awake by talking most of the night.

We awoke the next morning just before sunrise, and soon prepared our breakfast of soup and biscuit. We had a stroll around the village, which was entirely occupied by Chinese settlers. The houses were of wood, thatched with palm-leaves, and most of them were surrounded with fruit-trees and cocoa-nut palms. We tried to hire coolies, to carry some of our luggage on to the next village, Kanka Ah Tong, where we were to rest for the night, starting for the summit to-morrow. Unfortunately, the head man was away at Jahore; and some coolies, who expressed their willingness to accompany us, demanded a sum equivalent to five shillings per day for their services, so we decided to do without them; indeed, the Malays we had with us protested against this extortion on the part of the Chinese settlers, and said they would endeavour to carry all themselves.

We pulled out of the creek, and proceeded further up the river, finally landing at a place where there is an excellent road, leading through the forest to Kanka Ah Tong. Here we landed all our things; and our men were fortunate to secure a couple of Javanese woodcutters, who were fishing, and who were willing to carry part of our gear for a fair payment. We rested a little in a hut beside the road, in which were two men suffering from fever, and another, who had dysentery. We gave them medicine, and pushed onwards. Monkeys were very plentiful on the tall trees beside our path; and we saw several grey squirrels, and a few birds, including a curious shrike, and a barbet, which I had never seen before. The trees around us were very tall, and in many cases festooned with rattans, and other climbing-plants. Flowers were not plentiful; and although we made several *détours* in the forest, nothing of interest was seen.

It was very hot in the middle of the day. Our thermometer stood at 93° in the shade; and nearly all the way our path lay in the open, the sun being very hot overhead. After the first few miles we came to several open plots of land, under cultivation, gambier and pepper being the principal crops. We stayed at one place, where the raw gambier, or "terre japonica," was being prepared in a low shed. There were several low brick fire-places, over which shallow iron pans were placed;

and in these the leaves and young stems are boiled. The product, when finished, looks like wet red clay, and is packed in coarse bags, and sent to Singapore, where it realises about five dollars per picul of 133 lbs. Gambier is a very exhausting crop, literally ruining the land on which it is grown.

The Chinese whom we found here were very much interested and surprised at our visit, and gave us a supply of cocoa-nuts, oranges, and papaw fruit from their garden. The latter fruit are as large as a small Cadiz melon, with delicate red flesh, when perfectly ripe. They are not much esteemed; but I thought these very nice, having a flavour resembling that of apricots. The colourless milk of the young cocoa-nuts, fortified by just a *soupçon* of brandy, tasted really delicious, after our tramp under a hot sun. These thrifty Chinese had a fine flourishing plantation of bananas, but no ripe fruit; and clumps of yellow sugar-cane here and there attracted the attention of our followers, who helped themselves to the natural " sugar-sticks," without any compunction whatever.

Refreshed by a short rest, and a cooling draught, we pushed onwards, and reached Kanka Ah Tong about three o'clock. We sought out the old Chinese headman, and through him obtained the loan of a new house, just erected in the centre of the village, so that we were soon established in quarters, and the " boy " then began to cook our evening meal. We were of course soon surrounded by a crowd of villagers; and a paraffin cooking apparatus, which the "boy" had in working order before the door, interested them very much.

I noticed an excellent breed of black and white dogs at this village, in build not unlike a fox-terrier, but larger. These people evidently desired to keep the breed pure; for I noticed that all the dogs in the place were the same. A clear stream ran past the front of our house, and we were glad to get a bath before dinner. In this stream were at least two species of little fish, the largest rarely exceeding three inches in length, being beautifully spotted with dark brown on their sides. We felt deliciously cool after bathing, and ate our dinner comfortably, on seats we extemporised just outside our door.

After a smoke, in the cool of the evening, we prepared our sleeping gear, and turned in for the night. We were up at sunrise, and bathed in the little stream, while my friend's servant and our men prepared breakfast. We left some of our less needful gear in charge of the headman, and then shouldering our guns, we set out for the mountain, a good ten mile walk, over bad roads, and the last three or four miles is stiff climbing most of the way. Altogether it took us about six hours to accomplish, as we started at about seven o'clock in the morning, and reached the hut at the top a little after one P.M.

The first mile or two the path lies through gambier patches; and at one of the clearings we flushed a couple of fire-back pheasants, but we were too far off to get a shot at them. Their plumage shone resplendently in the morning sunlight, as they rose with the " whir-r-r," so familiar to sportsmen nearer home. A tolerably level jungle path succeeds the gambier patches for two or three miles further, and then the path commences, leading up the mountain-side.

Our first stopping place was at some distance up the base of the rise, where a bit of folded paper in a split stick directed us to the " Lady Jervoise Falls;" and, as we stood quietly, the sound of the falling water fell on our ears from the left-hand side of the path. We soon plunged down the slope, and reached them, but were rather disappointed, as all the water visible was a brook rushing down a rocky gully, and falling a distance of five or six feet over into a water-worn basin below. The water was clear and cool, and we took advantage of it to secure a bath in the shade of the tall trees overhead. The rocks were beautifully draped with ferns and mosses; and a small species of anæctochilus grew here and there on the mossy rocks. Its leaves were of a rich velvety-green colour, netted with golden veins.

We sat here, and rested awhile, the cool splash of the water sounding pleasantly as it fell into the spreading limpid pool at our feet. Here, for the first time, I made the acquaintance of the jungle leech, a most energetic thing, which neglects no opportunity of taking its sanguinary toll from the passing traveller. Several of them fixed themselves on our legs, the first notice of their unwelcome presence being the oozing of our blood through our white trowsers. Their first bite is rarely felt; and very often, as I afterwards found, it is only by their gorged bodies feeling cold to the skin, that their presence becomes known.

The road from the falls to the summit is in places very steep, and the muscles of one's legs feel it ere the end of the journey is reached. Many of those who read of jungle travel at home will be sure to imagine it very pleasant to explore a tropical forest, accompanied by a *posse* of native guides and carriers—with gun on shoulder, and luxuriant vegetation on all sides, and an occasional shot at a big monkey or a beautiful bird overhead. So of a truth it is, but in common with all other pleasures it has its drawbacks. After three or four hours hard walking, varied by a rest now and then, and a few stumbles, we reached the summit, and we luckily were rewarded by a most beautiful view. The atmosphere was clear, and in all directions a vast billowy sea of jungle stretched below us—foam-like flecks of white cloud being visible here and there on the top of the low coast hills.

We found the little hut on the summit rather out of repair, but a little labour in strengthening the principal supports of the roof, and the addition of a little palm-leaf thatch, made it more comfortable. We enjoyed a magnificent sunset, and lit our lamps just at dusk, nor were we loath to make a hearty meal of warm soup, rice and tea, which had been prepared while we looked around our camping ground. After a smoke and a chat we wrapped our rugs around us and were soon asleep on the side benches of sticks covered with freshly-cut palm-leaves. We were awoke during the night by the rain dripping through the roof, but managed to keep ourselves dry by suspending our waterproof sheets overhead. We awoke at daybreak, but could see nothing but a mass of snow-white clouds below us on all sides. After breakfast we started on a collecting tour down the mountain side, and soon struck a deep gully, through which a streamlet washed over the water-worn stones and pebbles.

Here we found one or two very interesting aroids (*Schismatoglottis*), and ferns were abundant, notably two or three species of lindsayas, their bold fronds being of a rich green colour, shot with steel-blue. *Dipteris Horsfieldii* clothed the rocky declivities of the gorge here and there, and a large-urned variety of *Nepenthes ampullaria* was strikingly luxuriant, growing along the edges of wet mossy rocks. Tiny plants only three or four inches in height and half buried in wet moss, decayed leaves, and other forest *débris*, bore eight or ten pitchers four inches in height and three inches in diameter. *N.*

Rafflesiana, an allied species, we saw clambering up the thick undergrowth to a height of twenty or thirty feet, but the pitchers were not larger than ordinarily are produced by the plant when grown in our hothouses at home. A large branching species of gleichenia grows luxuriantly near the top of this mountain, and seems to replace *G. dichotoma,* which is so common in Singapore and Pulo Penang. Orchids were sparingly represented by a cœlogyne, and one or two other genera, but nothing of interest was observable. A form of our own *Pteris aquilina* grew luxuriantly around the hut where the forest had been cleared. A dracæna, with green undulate foliage, almost grassy in its tenuity, and the variegated *Cissus porphyrophyllus* were plentiful, and a red-veined echites covered mossy trunks beside the stream.

We returned from our collecting about 5 o'clock, tired and wet through—a very common thing indeed in a tropical forest, so that we were glad to strip to the skin and have a bath, followed by a rub dry with coarse towels, and dry clothes. Our dinner of tinned soup and boiled beef was very acceptable, and our cook made a very appetising curry of dried fish and a few chilies collected from bushes which grew in the clearing around our hut, seeds having been sown either designedly or accidentally by former visitors. A cup of tea and a cigar were deliciously soothing after the rough falls and scrambling of the day. We were disappointed with the place as a collecting ground, and resolved to return to the richer forest of the lower slopes near Kanka Ah Tong on the morrow. Our guides gave us an account of this mountain, and assured us that tigers were not uncommon, and that the Chinamen were frequently carried off by them when working in clearings near the forest. Wild pigs, monkeys, and deer, are plentiful. The Argus and fire-back pheasant are found here, and alligators of enormous size are reported as frequenting the rivers further inland.

After dinner we made up a large fire outside the hut, dragging all the fallen trunks in the vicinity to it, for we scarcely relished the idea of a "man-eater" lurking in the neighbourhood, who might wish to vary his diet. These burned brightly all through the night, although at times it rained heavily, and served for cooking purposes in the morning. We descended about eight o'clock, staying here and there to collect plants and flowers on the way. We reached the "Falls" about 10 o'clock, and I looked around for plants, while my friend bathed, and the men rested themselves awhile. "Shall you not bathe?" he asked me. "I replied, "I'll just wash my face and hands presently, and let that suffice until we reach Ah Tong." We were just about to return to the path when a pretty fern I had not before observed attracted my attention, growing on a bit of jutting rock overhanging the Falls. I borrowed a chopper from one of the men, and clambered up the rocks, but to reach it I had to stride across the stream just where it falls over the boulders. I had secured my prize and was turning to leap back when slip! bump! splash! I went, plants, chopper, and all, into the water-worn basin below. When I regained the surface I was washed down again like a cork by the weight of water pouring down from above, but the next time I struck out for the side and crawled out like a half-drowned rat. My friend and our Malays had a hearty laugh over my misadventure, and I was fortunately not injured in any way. I took off my clothes and wrung them as near dry as possible and then put them on again, and it is astonishing what an excellent substitute wet clothes so treated are when dry ones are not procurable, especially if they can be dipped in sea water and again wrung dry. We walked on rapidly, staying here and there in open places where the vegetation was especially luxuriant to collect such plants as interested us. About 1 o'clock we reached Kanka Ah Tong, and I took the opportunity of at once having another bath—not an accidental one this time—and of getting into dry clothes. I also took a dose of quinine in a glass of brandy-and-water, and felt no ill effects from my accident and long walk in wet clothing.

We stayed here for the night, and the next day we returned to Jahore, and crossing the straits reached Singapore about 6 o'clock. In returning down the Scudai river we saw a slender habited pandanus bearing its crimson fruit in clusters among its long glaucus leaves, and in places on the margins of the stream the beautiful red-sheathed areca palm was very beautiful. Although this journey was a singularly unproductive one so far as the discovery of new plants of horticultural or botanical interest were concerned, yet it had taught me much in other ways, and gave me an insight into the habits and customs of the Malays, whose language I had commenced to learn as soon as I landed in Singapore for the first time.

It is unfortunate that this Puloi mountain is not more readily accessible, seeing that at its summit the air is deliciously fresh and cool, and beautiful views are obtainable. A good road thither, and a bungalow or two, are all that are needed in order to make this a valuable sanatorium for residents in Singapore, who are worse off in this respect than the Penang people, who have a cool health station, with bungalows, &c., on the "Hill," which is only a pleasant pony-ride from the town.

Apart from the Malay and Chinese inhabitants of Jahore, there are tribes of wild men or Jakuns, who are

believed to be the descendants of the aboriginal population. These reside in the interior of the country, some
of the tribes even construct their rude dwellings in the
trees, and wherever land culture is by them adopted it is
of the most rude and primitive description. As a rule,
their life is nomadic. Dr. Maclay visited these people in
1875, and the following are some of his observations
respecting them:—*

"These people are thoroughly disinclined to improvement of any kind in their mode of life, intellectually or
otherwise, although it is not occasioned by want of
opportunity nor from want of brain.

"3. That these tribes are gradually becoming extinct
not only the Malays, but also they themselves are fully
aware.

"This process of extinction is due mainly to the
following causes :—

"*a.* The constant advance into the jungle of the
Malay and Chinese population displaces the
original occupiers of the soil, who retire into
greater solitude.

"*b.* Owing to frequent intermarriages between the
Malays and the 'utan' women, the latter
race is becoming intermixed into the former,
and this mixed race is fast increasing.

"In spite of the almost foregone conclusion with
which I set out upon my journey, and after severely
criticising upon my return the observations I made, I
cannot doubt the fact of the *existence of an aboriginal
non-Malayan population*. Furthermore, previous experience and intimate knowledge of the Papuan race lead me
to the conviction that this aboriginal population is not

* " Journal of Eastern Asia." July, 1875. Trübner & Co.

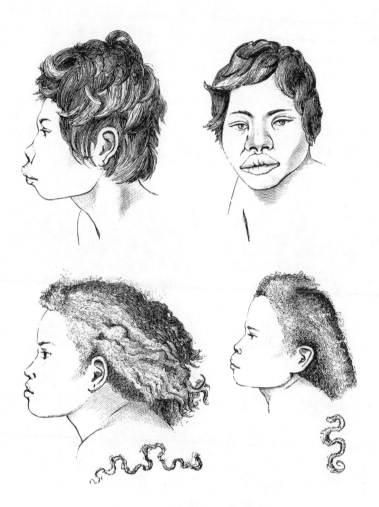

ORANG UTAN OR WILD MEN OF JAHORE.
(Male and Female)

To face page 44.

only *not* of Malay origin, but probably related to the
Papuans. Here and there I came across individuals
whom I could not consider otherwise than as retrogrades
to the main aboriginal type. In most of these cases the
hair, though not absolutely identical with that of the
pure Papuan type, resembled in texture and in growth
that of the Papua-Malay (mixed race) of the west coast of
New Guinea, who are by no means inconsiderable in
number. In these individual cases the hair was quite
different from the curled hair of the other orang-utans.

"My chief reasons for my decision on this point, are
deduced from the existence of these retrograde instances
from the present to the aboriginal type : the fact that
the orang-utans are not easily distinguishable from the
Malays inhabiting the interior of Jahore, does not
diminish this decision, because these Malays gradually
by intermarriages have partly inherited the orang-utan
type. This intermarriage has been in practice for centuries, and is likely to have been occasioned by the flight
into the interior of those of the Coast-Malays, who preferred retirement in the jungle to embracing the doc-
trines of Islam at the time of the Mahomedan conquest
in these parts. To such causes are mainly attributable
the variations in the type, and the diversity in the skull
formations which I met with in my journey. In size the
"orang-utan" are strikingly diminutive. The men rarely
exceed four feet eight inches in height, whilst I came
across many instances of women, mothers of several
children, whose stature was about four feet two inches.
Some allowance in these cases must be made consequent
on the early marriages, and the defective nourishment at
all times.

"Some of the 'orang-utan' whilst preserving their
traditional habits and mode of existence, continue to

dwell in the neighbourhood of the Malay population, selling to them the best-looking and strongest of their daughters. It is rare for the 'orang-utan' to change to Islamism or to adopt the Malay habits of life. In these cases their aboriginal language has yielded to the Malay and become entirely forgotten as if it had never existed. Such are the conclusions arrived at after wandering in Jahore, which I traversed from the Straits of Malacca to the China Sea. In the study of these people I felt as if I were commencing the perusal of an interesting old work, of whose semi-effaced pages some were missing." *

* It is curious to find that in Borneo, and elsewhere in the Malayan islands, the name "orang-utan" (literally "wild man," or, "man of the woods,") is applied not only to the large red monkey, as with us, but also to the aboriginal inhabitants of the interior. The Muruts are frequently spoken of as "orang-utan," not only by the Malays, but also by the Kadyans, a tribe of aboriginals converted to the Mahomedan faith.

CHAPTER IV.

RIVER AND FOREST TRAVEL.

A Sea-snake—A dreary landing—Native dancing—Orchids at home—
Tropical flowers—The jungle leech—A bad dinner—Rough paths
—The blow-pipe—Head-hunting—A Murut reception.

SETTING forth for the first time in a new country, of
which but little is generally known, is always exciting
work, and as a rule things turn out to be very different
to what one had imagined they would be. I had pictured
to myself landing in Borneo beneath a hot sun, and at
one of the trading stations; but, on the contrary, it was a
dark stormy night when I reached its shores amid a perfect
deluge of cold rain; the thunder and lightning was more
impressive than I ever saw it before or since, and the
place where I landed was an obscure little village of
scarcely a dozen palm-leaf huts, and up a river nearly
twenty miles from the coast. It came about in this way.
The Hon. W. H. Treacher, of Labuan, very kindly
undertook to introduce me to the Bornean Kadyans
and Muruts—the last a head-hunting tribe—who had
settlements near the head of the Lawas and Meropok
rivers a little to the northward of the capital. We crossed
in a small open boat pulled by eight Brunei men with
paddles, which is here the usual and best way of making
short sea or river journeys. We started from the fishmarket pier, Labuan, about 9 P.M. on September 7th,

and soon after turned into our rugs beneath the awning
and slept until morning. We awoke about daybreak,
and found ourselves some miles distant from the mouth
of the river; but the heavy swell we had had all night
had now subsided, and the men were making headway
fast. About 7.30 they stopped pulling suddenly, and
pointed to a large sea-snake lying full length on the
surface of the water in the sun. It was about eight feet
in length, and of a blue-black colour, barred with rich
golden-yellow, the belly being dull white. Mr. Treacher
fired at it with a shot-gun, striking it about the centre of
its body; and we could see quite plainly where the shot
had ripped the skin. As it lay quite motionless after
the shot for several seconds, we imagined it to be dead,
but on the men paddling the boat towards it it dived
quite suddenly; and as the water was clear and still, we
could distinguish it at a great depth below the surface.
A week or two before, during my voyage from Singapore
to Labuan, we had noticed a good many of these snakes
on the surface of the sea, but none so large as the one
seen here. The natives say it is a very dangerous kind,
and some strange tales are told of their hiding themselves
in boats and huts near the shore. About ten o'clock we
entered the mouth of the Lawas, the well-wooded banks
of which formed a beautiful foreground to the picturesque
mountains behind, which rise higher and higher right
away into the interior. We soon reached the first cluster
of huts on the right bank, and it is here that one of the
Sultan's relatives, Pangeran Bazar, resides. His house
is built on nebong piles over the water, from which you
climb up a rude ladder on to a spacious platform, on
which are half-a-dozen or more brass swivel guns of
native manufacture. This platform is roofed over, and
an immense wooden drum hangs over the entrance.

This is formed of a hollow tree trunk, over one end of which a deer or goat skin is stretched lightly by means of a rattan ring and wooden wedges. It is beaten in the evening after the old Pangeran has read from the Koran, and sometimes on the arrival of strangers. Beyond the platform is a large public hall, wherein strangers may rest, and where the natives meet to hear the Koran read, or to talk.

The Pangeran's private residence is behind, and differs but little from the other half-dozen palm-leaf houses around it, being merely a superior sort of shed, with mats in place of doors. Duties to the amount of ten per cent. are collected from the natives who bring gutta, rice, or other produce down the river; but by many this tax is evaded, as they drop down the river on a dark night in a prahu, and creep out along the coast, lying up some creek until a favourable breeze enables them to hoist sail for Labuan. I have stayed several times at this place, and always found this river chief obliging and hospitable, but a chronic deafness on his part makes a conversation with him anything but easy. He read from the Koran most evenings when I was there, the choruses or responses being chanted—I ought to say yelled—by five or six wicked young Malay boys, who amused themselves by laughing and talking, except just when their vocal powers were needed.

Two or three hundred yards further up the river is the residence of Pangeran Tanga, and here we went ashore to eat our breakfast of cold fowl and rice, eggs and fruit, followed by coffee and a weed. We bought a dozen new-laid eggs here, also some freshly-plucked bananas, and a splendid durian fruit, nearly as large as a child's head. We noticed a half-finished prahu, or native boat, under one of the sheds, the timbers of which were well

E

modelled, being fastened together with stout wooden
pegs. After our men had cooked their rice and fish, we
again started up the river for Meringit, a Kadyan settlement at the head of the Meropok branch; but owing to
the strong current coming down, we did not reach the
place until after dark, and, as before remarked, in a
drenching thunder-storm. It was so dark that our men
could not find the proper landing-place, and having
ourselves just left a fairly lighted boat, we could not see
a yard ahead in the blinding rain, and so we were soon
drenched as we floundered along up to our knees in the
soft mud of the river bank. At last two boys came down
from the houses in answer to the shouts of our boatmen,
and under their guidance we reached dry quarters after a
few stumbles over logs and through the long grass. Our
first care was to throw off our wet things and get on dry
ones, after a rub with a dry towel, and we then ate our
dinner, surrounded by most of the swarthy-skinned villagers, who flocked in to look at us. Afterwards it
cleared up a bit, and hearing music in a neighbouring
house, we adjourned thereto, and found a few of the
young men and women enjoying themselves. Their instruments consisted of a native-made violin on a European model, a curious kind of native banjo made of a
single joint of a large bamboo, a triangle, or its music
rather, being represented by two or three steel hatchet
heads, which were laid across laths on the floor, and
beaten in time with a bit of iron. The music so produced was of a rather melancholy description, and one
or two of the girls and boys danced a little, a mat being
spread for the purpose; but their dancing is merely
shuffling about in a more or less slow and stately manner,
a singular effect being produced by the graceful way in
which the arms are waved about in all directions. This

was particularly noticeable in the case of one of the performers, who waved a handkerchief about during the dance, changing it from one hand to the other, until eventually it vanished from sight altogether; still the arms waved, and the fingers, in their ever slow changing movement, resembled tentaculæ groping for their prey as they were slowly waved through the air in every possible direction, presumably in quest of the lost article, the ultimate recovery of which terminated the dance. The only light in the apartment was the lurid flickering of a dammar torch, and its reflections on the faces and slightly-draped forms of the performers and lookers-on produced a weird effect, which was intensified by the silence of all present.

The next day " Bongsur," a well-known bird-hunter of the district, and a party of natives, undertook to guide us to the forest we wished to explore, and we set off up one of the largest creeks in a canoe, followed by two or three others containing our men and guides. After paddling about a mile we landed, and after walking through several clearings in the hot sun, the primæval forest was at length reached, where it was much cooler and more pleasant, the sun's rays being screened from us by the masses of leaves, epiphytes, and flowers overhead. After mountain climbing, and the wonders of the sea, perhaps nothing suggests one's own littleness more forcibly than a walk through the old forests which exist in tropical lowlands. There is a comparative dearth of undergrowth, —but a hundred feet or more overhead the birds, insects, and flowers enjoy the bright light and warmth denied to all below. The monkeys and birds too find their favourite fruits aloft, and fling the husks below at your feet.

Nothing can possibly be of more interest to lovers of exotic plants generally, than to be able to form some idea of their native homes, so far as description can possibly supply the place of travel. The earth's surface is like the sea, inasmuch as it is pretty nearly the same all the world over, but in countries where the mean temperature is thirty or forty degrees higher than in England, the clothing of the earth, so far as represented by vegetation, is of a luxuriance we can scarcely imagine, and the variety caused by the addition of such distinct types as tall palms, bananas, grasses, or bamboos and tree ferns to the more ordinary kinds of tree beauty, and the further clothing of these with epiphytes and parasites of the most singular or beautiful description, makes up a scene of immense interest.

Epiphytal orchids are essentially heat-lovers — like palms they are children of the sun. One may often travel a long way in the islands where these plants are most abundant without catching a glimpse of them·; and this is especially true of *Phalænopsis grandiflora,* which is of all orchids perhaps the least obtrusive in its native habitats. This trait is, however, the unobtrusiveness of high birth, they do not care to touch the ground, but rather prefer a sphere of their own high up in the trees overhead. The plants have a charming freedom of aspect, as thus seen naturally high up in mid-air, screened from the sun by a leafy canopy, deluged with rains for half the year or more at least, and fanned by the cool sea-breezes or monsoons, which doubtless exercise some potent influence on their health—an influence which we can but rarely apply to them artificially, and the greatly modified conditions under which we must perforce culti-vate them may not render this one so desirable as it some-times appears to be abroad.

In the lowland forests near the equator a peculiar phase of vegetation is not unfrequently seen. Trees one hundred

GREATER MOTH ORCHID (PHALÆNOPSIS) AT HOME. *To face page* **52.**

feet to two hundred feet in height tower upwards on all
sides; and one walks in the shade—diffused light is perhaps
the more correct expression—the tree trunks being the
pillars of Nature's cathedral, and the leafy branches high
up above represent the roof.   All the vegetation you see
around you on earth, rocks or fallen trunks, is represented by a few ferns, lindsayas, with bright steel-blue
fronds a yard high, broad-leaved aroids, or ginger-
worts; but epiphytes of all kinds seem totally absent :
and the truth is, that, like lovable " Tom Bowling,"
of Dibdin's minstrelsy, they, too, have " gone aloft."
Above you is a world of light and air and sunshine which
birds, insects, and flowers alike enjoy. You feel very
small and helpless as you try to catch a glimpse of the
plants and flowers so high above you, and almost envy
the long-armed red monkeys that swing themselves so
easily from bough to bough.   The monkey, however, has
a rival in the human natives of these forest wilds, and it
would be extremely puzzling to find a tree so thick, or
tall, or otherwise so difficult to climb, that the lithe and
dusky native would fail to reach its summit. The chances
are that he will literally walk up a slender tree in the
neighbourhood with the aid of hands and feet, and then
find a route to the one you wish him to explore by way
of the interlaced branches so high above you. If any
sufficiently stout lianas are dangling near, he ascends
hand-over-hand in a way that would delight the most
accomplished gymnast ; and if the tree so stood that the
ascent could only be accomplished by the direct way of
its own gigantic trunk, then the chances are that a stair
of bamboo pegs would enable the ingenious savage to
effect his object of scouring the branches, and sending
the epiphytes in showers to your feet. Nor does he
neglect to glean such other jungle produce as comes in

his way, such as gutta or indiarubber, camphor, dammar, or forest fruits for food or medicine.

This is in the forest primæval, but near clearings, or on the skirts of the forest near rivers, which let in the light and air, the phalænopsids and other epiphytes are less ambitious, and they may then be found in positions but little above the more plebeian terrestrial kinds of vegetation. This is also the case when, as sometimes happens, they are found on the trees which fringe little islands; and then not only do the plants receive a good deal of sunshine as it streams through the leafy twigs of the branches to which they cling, but it is also reflected back again from the glistening sea. The intense light in which they thus exist, added to the fervent heat and the deluge of rain which falls during six or seven months of the year, accounts for the enormous leaf and root growth made by these plants in their native habitats. The flowering of the plants is not so extraordinary, indeed rather disappointing, after the results which may be seen in English gardens. It is not so much the paucity of flowers produced, however, as their early destruction caused by the " unbidden guests " the orchids are made to entertain.

High up overhead the most lovely orchids hold their court in the sunshine : here they are really " at home " to their winged visitors. Now and then, however, you come across a newly-fallen tree—a very monarch of the woods—which has succumbed to old age and rude weather at last, and has sunk to the earth from which it sprang a seedling generations ago; its branches laden with everything inanimate, which had made a home in its branches. Some of these ruined trunks are perfect gardens of beauty, wreathed with graceful climbing plants, and gay with flowers and foliage. The fall of a large tree, and its smaller dependents, lets in the sun, and so the epiphytes do not suffer much for a time ; and one may thus observe them in all their beauty.

Here, right in the collar of the tree, is a plant of the grammatophyllum orchid, big enough to fill a Pickford's van, and just now opening its golden-brown spotted flowers on stout spikes two yards long.   There, on that topmost branch, is a mass of the moth orchid, or phalænopsis, bearing a hundred snowy flowers at least ; and in such healthy vigour is it, that lovers of orchids at home — supposing it could be flashed direct to "Stevens's " in its present state — would outbid each other for such a glorious prize, until the hammer would fall at a price near on a hundred guineas, as it has done before for exceptional specimens of these lovely flowers.

There, gleaming in the sunlight, like a scarlet jewel, beneath those great leathery aroid leaves, is a cluster of tubular æschynanthus flowers ; and here is another wee orchid, a tiny pink-blossomed cirrhopetalum, whose flowers and leaves scarcely rise above the bright carpet of velvety moss among which it grows.   But what is that attractive gleam of gold and green swaying to and fro in the sunshine ?   Ah ! that is a beauty of another kind ! And a native, to whom it is pointed out, ejaculates, " Chalaka ! ular Tuan ! "—a wicked snake, sir ; and we are content to move on, and leave him alone in his glory.   We tramp on for an hour longer, without even the glimpse of a flower being visible, except here and there a few fragments on the ground, the remnant *spolia* of the flower world which exists on the roof of this grand cathedral of trees.

Half an hour further, and the increasing numbers of ferns and selaginella mosses suggest the presence of water

in the neighbourhood, while the patches of graceful seedling calami or rattan palms increase at every step, the
stones and trunks become moss-covered, and then at
last the "sound of many waters" breaks on our ears
with a cool and welcome noise, and a few minutes later
we have " struck " the stream, as it rushes and sparkles
amongst mossy and water-worn boulders down an open
and sunny ravine. Some of the larger rocks are covered
with a palm-like fern (*Polypodium bifurcatum*); and
filmy ferns, of the most delicate form and texture,
abound on the dripping stones.

As we sit down on the rocks, a small flock of gigantic
hornbills " saw the air " with their great wings far above
us, making a noise almost like a locomotive engine in
their flight. Butterflies come with wobbling motion down
the sunny clearing, formed by the shallow stream; and,
as we are intent on the cold fowl and coffee, which forms
our breakfast, the sanguinary stains on our white trousers
prove that the wily jungle-leech has not been unmindful
of his morning meal. How this little slimy monster loves
to gorge himself with gore ! The wonder, however, is
how they exist when men are absent from the jungle they
infest, as often happens. I suspect that human blood
forms simply an accidental part of their supply. I know
they exact all they can from the water buffaloes ; and
perhaps even the astute monkey is made to pay toll by
these blood-suckers as often as may be. I have often
watched them, when aroused by footsteps, as attached
to a stick, or stone, or leaf, they wave their bodies about,
or walk towards you with a caterpillar-like motion, in
quest of happier hunting-grounds. A squeeze of wet
tobacco juice is the best plan of dislodging them from
your skin; for if pulled off, however deftly it be done,
there is a chance of a bit of their sucker apparatus

remaining in the wound, which will often cause it to become inflamed, and to fester in a troublesome manner.

We suffered a good deal from mosquitoes during the night; indeed sleep was nearly impossible, and in very shaded parts of the forest to-day the little pests fixed on our hands and faces with a persistency that was very annoying. We saw very few birds. A gorgeously attired bee-eater was secured by Mr. Treacher as we paddled up the creek; and "Bongsur," who used an old Tower musket as a fowling-piece, secured a tiny spotted owl and one or two other small birds common to this district. We distinctly heard the whoops and yells of the Muruts, who were out pig-hunting, as we came along, but did not fall in with them. Just as we crossed the stream one of the men picked up a fruit of one of the several varieties of durian, which are here indigenous. It was about the size of a cricket-ball, and only contained two of its chesnut-like, pulp-covered seeds. The seeds were very large in proportion to the quantity of pulp, but the flavour was very delicious.

We had a long walk back to the creek where we had left our canoes, and reached the village about three o'clock, just before the commencement of a heavy shower. As it cleared up a little about five o'clock we took our guns and had a stroll across the padi fields behind the houses, returning to dinner about sunset. I shall not soon forget that dinner. Mr. Treacher had brought his Chinese "boy" who had cooked the previous day. My "boy" was a Madras Telinga to whom, of course, the lard or pork fat which the Chinese use in cooking is an abomination, so that my ingenious fellow, as it was his turn to prepare dinner, made us a fowl curry, using rancid cocoa-nut lamp oil in which to cook the fowl.

We were rather hungry, and tried to get the stuff down, but had to give it up as a bad job. The nasty taste was most persistent, however; and for several days coffee, biscuit, rice, and even fresh fruit, seemed to have somewhat of the offensive cocoa-nut oil flavour about it. I remonstrated with my "boy" about the matter, with the usual result. "Yes, sah, that China boy bad man, sah; he tell me oil very good for curry, sah!" I have no doubt, but that the "China boy" enjoyed the joke with "a smile that was childlike and bland," and doubtless he related the story to his pretty Malay wife on his return, with many "Ah yahs" and inward chuckling. We made shift with biscuit and coffee, and a smoke destroyed the bad taste for the time being.

This was the evening preceding the commencement of Ramadan, the "fast month," observed by all Mahomedans, and there was a great burning of gunpowder in the village. Muskets and small cannon were being discharged all over the place in honour of the event. Salutes of this kind, and the festive firing of shot-guns, however harmless it may seem in print, is in reality sometimes a little alarming. The powder used in charging may possibly be bad in quality; but as a great noise is thought to be the thing, any defect in its quality is pretty well made up for by the quantity used. I am not a very nervous person, but I once or twice felt just a little anxious as the natives amused themselves by firing a charge of five or six inches of powder from a seven and-sixpenny German gun. I once saw some Sulus firing a salute from some old dismounted brass guns which were lashed on the floor of the wharf at Sandakan. They coolly sat down beside the ordnance, waved a bit of rope-yarn until the smouldering fire at one end brightened up into a glowing spark, and then plunged

it into the touch-hole ; nor did they seem in the least
disconcerted as the guns sprang a yard into the air
dragging up the nebong planks with them, the whole
returning with a crash by reason of their elasticity.

In the morning, after breakfast, Mr. Treacher returned
down the river, but could not cross to Labuan until next
day, as a heavy sea was running with much wind and
rain, so he had to put back to Pulo Sirra until morning.
After his departure I had a consultation with " Bongsur"
about the country, and eventually decided to shift my
quarters from his father's house to that of his brother,
from which the forests and hills of the district could be
more readily reached.   A party of natives and one or
two Muruts who had come to the Kadyan's village to
trade, soon got all my traps stowed into the canoes, and
half an hour's pull brought us to the clearing in which
my future head-quarters were situated.   I found here
half-a-dozen palm-leaf houses built on piles six feet high,
a notched tree trunk serving as a ladder by which to
enter.   The largest house was forty or fifty yards long
by eighteen or twenty feet wide, and being nearly new, it
was clean and in good condition.   It was occupied by
" Bongsur's " brother, a lithe and intelligent young
fellow named " Moumein," and three or four other
families.

Within, it was simply one large room open to the roof,
and divided in half by the central path, communicating
with doors at either end.   On the right were the hearths
for cooking, water-jars, bamboos, baskets, and other
simple tools or utensils, the left-hand side being covered
with the sleeping-mats of the separate families.   Two or
three mosquito nets hung over the mats, and at the head
of each hung the parong, spear, musket, or other arms of
the men, other spears, shields, blowpipes, &c., being laid

across the timbers overhead. The floor was of open lattice-work, or rather parallel nebong laths an inch apart, so that perfect ventilation is obtained ; and these houses are always cool. The owner was not at home, but his wife brought a board and desired " Bongsur " to partition off one of the corner compartments for me, which was soon done ; and getting up the boxes, hammock-sleeping gear, &c., the place soon assumed a more comfortable appearance.

As it was a beautiful clear afternoon I left my " boy " to prepare dinner, and started off to the forest with half-a-dozen of the native boys who had followed from the village. I shot a pretty scarlet-breasted trogan with beautifully pencilled wings, in a large fig tree near the houses. We had a rather rough walk through long grass, in which ugly concealed logs were plentiful ; and the only bridges across the streams were formed of a single tree-trunk, often a very slender one not perfectly straight, so that when a particular part of it was reached in one's journey across, it had a treacherous knack of turning round and landing one in muddy water up to the neck. The natives are used to such slender makeshifts for bridges, and, being barefoot, are as sure-footed as goats.

We followed one little stream for about two miles, and reached a rocky hill about five hundred feet high, where rhododendrons (*R. javanicum*) were flowering freely. Hoyas and various orchids were in bloom on the lowest trees ; and it was on bare tree-trunks on this hill that I saw the Veitchian pitcher-plant (*Nepenthes Veitchii*) wild for the first time. It has a singular habit of clasping the trunks on which it is epiphytal with its leaves, and many which bear pitchers have the blade of the leaf much reduced. Four other pitcher-plants grew on this hill, namely, *N. gracilis*, *N. hirsuta*, *N. Rafflesiana*, and the

large-urned variety of the last named, known as " gla-
berrima." A dendrobium bearing clusters of milk-white
flowers was common, as also were bolbophyllums and
several greenish-flowered cœlogynes.

The ground in some places was matted with a very
pretty terrestrial orchid (*Bromheadia Finlaysoniana*)
which has leafy stems two to three feet in height,
terminated by a zig-zag flattened spike of white-petalled
flowers as large as those of the " Spotted Indian
Crocus " (*Pleione maculata*), and having a blotch of
lemon-yellow on the lip and some bright amethystine
veins or streaks. We loaded the men with roots and
specimens, and then returned to the houses just before
nightfall. It was during the wet season, and after dark
each evening the mosquitoes were most ravenous. As a
remedy for this annoyance the women lighted fires
beneath the house, on which cocoa-nut husks were
placed and made to smoulder gradually. This certainly
kept the little pests at bay, but the smoke brought tears
to one's eyes, and was almost as bad to bear as the mosquito bites.

The wild forest fruits were now plentiful in this
district, and, as a natural consequence, birds and
monkeys were abundant also, for they migrate to different places as the fruits begin to ripen. The bird-
hunters were busy, and rarely a day passed but I was
gladdened with the sight of some bird or other animal
that was novel to me. Argus, Bulwer, and Fireback
pheasants and other large ground birds were caught in
snares or springes, while hornbills, owls, eagles, or hawks,
and large birds generally were killed with shot, or very
often small gravel discharged from an old Tower musket.
The smallest birds, especially the brilliant little sweets or
sunbirds, were killed with small arrows from the blow-

pipe or "sumpitan," in the use of which some of the Muruts and Kadyans are especially expert. Even large game was formerly obtained in this way, poisoned arrows being used, in which case the harmless-looking blowpipe becomes one of the most subtle and deadly of weapons. The slightest puncture with one of these poisoned darts is as certain to terminate fatally as is the bite of the cobra; and this, added to the possibility of the arrow being propelled on its journey with lightning-like speed, without the least sound being heard, will give an idea of its deadly power in the skilful hands of savages, to whose ambition the death of an enemy and the possession of his bleached skull for the decoration of their dwellings on feast days, was the all-important feature of their social existence.

I have seen a Murut strike fish after fish with unerring certainty with arrows from a sumpitan, even at more than a foot below the surface of the stream; a much more difficult thing to do than one might suppose, since allowance has to be made for the deviation from a right line which the arrow takes on touching the water. The springes in which pheasants are caught are set in artificial fences half a mile or more in length, and are simply nooses of rattan, although rarely thin brass wire is used. A bent sapling is attached to the noose in such a manner that when the bird runs against a twig in passing through the opening in the fence it becomes disengaged, and flying upwards, draws the noose tightly around the creature's neck.

A device similar in principle, but much more dangerous, is used by the Muruts for capturing the wild pigs. In this case a stout spear of bamboo is made to pass through guiding loops of rattan attached to trees or stakes, so that by the aid of a stout sapling drawn back to its fullest tension it can be hurled right through the body of any passing animal, which unconsciously disengages the apparatus by pressing against or treading on a branch across its track. These pig-sticking contrivances are very dangerous to strangers, and even the Muruts themselves are sometimes injured by them.

One of the Lawas Muruts showed me where the bamboo spear belonging to one of these pig or deer-traps had been driven right through his leg near the knee. His bronzed features underwent the most extraordinary and suggestive of contortions as he explained how it had taken the strength of five or six men to hold him against a tree while others tugged at the bamboo shaft until they succeeded in withdrawing it from the injured limb. In some districts these pig-traps are very numerous, and one has to be continually on the look-out for them. I visited the Lawas district several times, and had good opportunities of seeing the Muruts, and noting many of their peculiarities. Their houses are similar to those of the Dusun, but instead of living in separate houses, one enormous house is built sufficiently large to accommodate from twenty to fifty families. These houses vary from thirty to one hundred yards in length, and, like those of the Kadyans, are built on piles. As the different tribes are continually at variance with each other, and knowing each other's affection for crania, they congregate in one large dwelling so as to be better prepared for resistance in case of a sudden attack. These people, and the Kayans who live in the vicinity of the Baram river, and one or two other tribes of the aboriginal Borneans, still continue the practice of head-hunting, although the custom is now fast dying out here, as it has in the case of the Dyaks of Sarawak, and other places further south. Only a few years back a youth was not allowed to marry until he had taken the head of an enemy, and if any ill-luck or death occurred in the tribe these head-hunting raids were indulged in at once to appease the malignant spirits which were believed to have been the cause; or if a chief's favourite wife or child died, he at once took to head-hunting in a bloodthirsty spirit of revenge.

The desire to shed blood seems inherent in all savage natures, and is adhered to tenaciously even after civilisation has reached them, and so it happens that human heads or skulls are considered the most valuable property of these wild Borneans, just as the Sioux and other Indians of North America still attach a peculiar value to the scalp locks of their foes. Even although head-hunting is gradually becoming a thing of the past in Borneo, still so highly are the old skulls valued even by the now peaceable tribes who have not taken a head for years, that they can rarely be induced to part with them, no matter how much may be offered in exchange. In several Murut houses I visited near the Lawas large baskets full of human crania were preserved as trophies of the prowess of the tribe.

It is very rare that anything like general open fighting now takes place between the native tribes, as was formerly the case, when a party of fighting men would, after marching at night only through the forests for days together, steal up to the house of their foes just before daylight and endeavour to set fire to it, after which the place was surrounded and the men killed as they attempted to escape, the women and children being made prisoners and carried off as additions to the wealth of the victors. Sometimes, however, the besieged were too wary for their foes, and either boldly rushed out and drove them off with loss, or formed ambuscades, into which they unwittingly fell and were annihilated, or perhaps a few would break through and escape to tell the tale. In this way a good many heads and slaves were obtained, but at present the additions to the baskets are more rare, and principally obtained by stealthy murders rather than in warfare. The Muruts and other aboriginals are great believers in omens, and whether on head hunting or pig-killing expeditions they pay great regard to the cries of birds and animals; and if they meet an alligator or a snake, they at once return and wait for a more propitious season.

In travelling with these natives as guides, their careful attention to omens becomes exceedingly trying to one's temper, as they will stop immediately if the omens seen or heard be not good ones, and if anything more than ordinary duties are required of them it is astonishing how soon a bad omen will put an end to all further progress for the day. One place where I stayed for several weeks was within half a mile of a large Murut house, and their gongs could be heard very plainly sometimes all night when they were feasting and drinking a peculiar spirit, which is made of rice and tampoe fruit mixed with water and strained off for use after fermentation. These feasts seemed to be held on the occasion of any good fortune befalling the tribe, such as success in hunting pigs or deer. One night they were gong-beating and shouting louder than usual. I asked the native in whose house I slept the reason of this, and he told me that they had been out head-hunting for a fortnight, but had failed to pounce upon any Murut of another tribe; so to end the suspense they had seized one of their own slaves, who had in some way offended them, and had made a scapegoat of him. I visited this house some days afterwards, and smoked a " roko " with the " Orang Capella," or chief, while three of his lusty followers kept up an incessant din on five gongs which were suspended in the centre of the public apartment. I asked to see his collection of heads, and after a good deal of talking, a few dry old examples were brought; but after we left I was told that they had many more, including the one so recently taken, but that they were afraid to let the fact be known. This tribe had good reasons for secrecy in the matter, since one man had been hung at Labuan for a head-hunting murder a year or two previous to my visit, and another would have suffered the same fate had he not died in jail. They had actually crossed over to the English colony to look out for heads, and ascending a little river on the western side, had shot a man who was coming down in a canoe. The shot, an old nail, struck the shaft of the paddle, and passing through, entered the man's body, after which they made off, but were captured by the Government and tried for the murder. This identical paddle was one of the first things I saw when I paid my respects to His Excellency the Governor of Labuan, and when the story was narrated to me it did not sound very cheering, seeing that I expected to live among these tribes for some months at least. However, I could never hear of a white man being killed, except by the pirates from Tawi Tawi and Sulu, with one exception, which was of a man who is supposed to have been poisoned by his native mistress. St. John mentions one tribe, however, who are peculiarly addicted to poisoning anyone who may be disliked by them. The nature of the poison used is not exactly known, but it is very generally supposed to be a peculiarly irritating fibre or spiculæ derived from some species of bamboo, the effect of which is to cause a chronic state of sickness and depression, followed by death. Whatever it may be, it is a mechanical rather than a chemical irritant. When one travels in such a lovely island, however, as Borneo undoubtedly is, it is extremely difficult to believe half the tales told of the native tribes, and altogether the proportionate number of robberies and murders is not more than takes place in the most enlightened centre of civilisation in the world. The total population of the island is supposed to be from 3,000,000 to 4,000,000, and when we consider that all these unchristianised natives (excepting those in Sarawak and the Dutch territory) live together with no law—nothing in fact but their own sense of right and wrong, and public opinion to keep them in order—the wonder is that, even according to our own standard, crime is so seldom heard of.

The Kadyans are a tribe of peaceable and well-disposed aboriginals, who, living along the coast near to the capital, have mixed a good deal with the Malays and speak their language. It is not uncommon, however, to find the older and more intelligent men of this tribe well acquainted with several dialects of the interior, such as Murut, Dusun, and the Brunei dialect, used by the common natives of the capital. They are mostly Mahomedans, and so are more respected by their Malay rulers than are other of the aboriginals. They form thrifty little colonies on most of the rivers near Brunei, and many have settled in Labuan, where they cultivate their rice fields, and occasionally bring fruit or fish to the markets. They are for the most part a clean and healthy race, and form a great contrast with their neighbours who live in a more irregular manner, and are often troubled with skin diseases, this being in a measure owing to the want of cleanliness and of a regular diet. There cannot be any doubt but that Islam is a great blessing to many Eastern races, especially so far as cleanliness and temperance are concerned.

The Kadyans are very quick in selecting rich bits of
forest and in raising fine crops of rice, which forms the
main portion of their food. Rice and fish from the river
or sea, fruits from their gardens or the forest, and a few
simple vegetables are all the food they require. They
also collect gutta and caoutchouc, camphor and rattans,
from the forest, and the sale of these in Labuan, or to
the Chinese traders who visit the coast, enables them to
obtain cloth, muskets and ammunition, tobacco, and any
other little necessaries or luxuries of Chinese or European manufacture which they may require. Although
less active than the Muruts, yet there are some fine men
among them, and their women, as a class, are perhaps the
most refined and intelligent of all the aboriginals, some,
when young, being singularly attractive. The boys are also
bright fellows, with a keener sense of humour than is
common in other tribes. They live a free and easy life,
contented and happy, and I could not help contrasting
the peace and plenty enjoyed by these people with the
squalor and misery in which the poor of civilised lands
are often plunged. Here, in these sunny wilds, an all-
bounteous Nature, with a minimum of labour, supplies
their every want, and it would be difficult to find another
country where man is more truly the "monarch of all he
surveys"—more truly independent on his fellow-man
than here in Borneo. Although these people are nomin-
ally Mahomedans, still their women enjoy the greatest
freedom and are never secluded, as is the custom of
the Malays of the coast, indeed, many Kadyan houses
consist of one very large room only, there being no
private apartment of any kind. This is a rather singular
trait of these people, since even the Muruts and the
Dusan have one side of their houses partitioned off so as
to allow of a separate private room for each family, the

other half being open from end to end and free to guests
or strangers. The Kadyans take but one wife, and are
apparently good husbands and affectionate parents; large
families, however, are exceptional. This question of
increase of population in the island is one I could not
profess to explain. Here is a rich and fertile island
larger than Great Britain and Ireland, with an entire
population scarcely exceeding that of London. In the
old times inter-tribal warfare may have operated as a
check, and even now whole villages are sometimes carried
off by epidemics, such as cholera or small-pox, yet when
we consider that there are practically none of the checks
on marriage itself as with us, and the readiness with
which food is obtainable in plenty, the easy and natural
way, indeed, in which these people live, it is a puzzle
that they seem scarcely able to hold their own.

In the case of the North American Indians or the
Maories of New Zealand, there is the competition of the
white races, but here they are not crowded out by a
stronger type, nevertheless, the population is supposed to
be less than was formerly the case. If a Kadyan youth
wishes to marry, he has only to select a site for his house,
and clear the ground around it for a garden. He may
take an unoccupied plot anywhere, and there is no
ground-rent to pay, it is freehold so soon as he has in a
manner "staked his claim," by cutting down the brush
and burning the trees, in which the other "lads of the
village" will assist him. The ground is cleared towards
the end of the dry season, and with the commencement
of the first rains a few seeds of Indian corn, cucumbers,
betel pepper, &c., are sown, and yams, kaladi, sweet
potatoes, together with cocoa-nuts, and banana suckers
from his father's or a friend's garden, are planted. Then
timbers, rattans, and nipa leaves for thatch are obtained,

and, with the assistance of his friends, a good roomy
house will spring up, if not quite mushroom-like in a
night, at the least in a week or ten days. A dollar or
two, or the jungle produce he could collect in less than a
month, will enable him to obtain the few articles of furniture, cooking utensils, &c., which he requires, together with a new " sarong " or two for himself and his
bride. And she, the dusky beauty, will have made a few
neatly worked palm-leaf sleeping mats and other needful
trifles, and doubtless looks forward to her wedding with
as much pleasure as her fairer sister of the West. The
actual ceremony of marriage is here very simple. A payment has to be made by the bridegroom to his father-in-
law, and this varies in proportion to the charms or other
good marketable qualities of the girl—an ordinary girl
being worth as much as a good buffalo, or say, £4; as
much as £20, however, is sometimes demanded for the
" belle of the village," but in addition to the first cost
such beauties are apt to give their husbands a good deal
of trouble afterwards, unless, indeed, they be of Cato-like
temperament. Marriages may be dissolved for the
merest trifles by either party, but if by the woman herself,
part of the money or goods paid to her parents is re-
funded. In the case of the Mahomedans, a woman
retains all her real and personal property after divorce-
ment. A native, in whose house I stayed several weeks,
told me that his wife had been married to another Kadyan
before he married her. " And did her husband die ? " I
enquired. " Oh, no," he answered. " Then why did
she leave him ? " " She did not like him," was the re-
joinder. And such cases of mutual separation are far
from uncommon.

These people, unlike the Muruts of the Limbang, had
plenty of rice and other food, the produce of their padi

fields and gardens. In some parts of the island it is extremely difficult to purchase food of any kind, the natives possessing only barely enough for their own wants. Here, however, one could obtain fowls, eggs, rice, and vegetables in abundance. The prices may be interesting. For excellent fowls, from fivepence to eightpence was charged ; eggs fivepence per dozen ; vegetables enough for two or three days' supply for two-pence ; while lodging, fire-wood, and plenty of jungle fruit in season, may be had for nothing. Dollars and cents were current here, but cloth, especially grey shirt-ing and a stout black fabric, were also readily received in exchange at a slight advance on Labuan prices. The men here were willing to act either as guides or carriers for tenpence to a shilling per diem.

When I returned to the house at night from the forest, I generally found a liberal share of the jungle fruit which had been brought home by the men laid on my mats ; and after dinner my own men and the villagers would drop in for a chat by the light of a flickering dammar torch. Twenty or thirty dusky figures smoking or eat-ing betel-nut had a curious effect in the badly lighted hut.

All through the fast month these people never eat or drink anything between sunrise and sunset, but they make up for this between sunset and sunrise, the women being busy cooking rice and fish nearly all night. At the end of the month, too, a great feast was held, at which all in the village and neighbourhood met and smoked the "roko" of peace, all old feuds and wrongs being for the nonce forgiven or forgotten. Everyone came dressed in their best head-cloths and sarongs, being armed with their war parangs, and altogether forming an animated and brightly coloured assemblage. This feast was held at night, and for several days previous the women had been busy bringing in fire-wood and cleaning rice. On the day on which this gathering was held the culinary operations were on an extended scale, and, at the appointed meal time, great heaps of rice, vegetables, fish, and fruit, were piled on fresh banana leaves right down the centre of the house. A dignified green-coated old hadji graced the repast with his presence, and he was pleased to kill the fowl for my own dinner, according to native rite, and evidently liked being noticed as a traveller, for his dark eyes sparkled with pleasure when I asked him of his voyage to Mecca. He complained very much of the insults, losses, and hardships, to which pilgrims were exposed, but his appetite was evidently as good as ever, since the clearance of rice and fish he made around him at dinner was something startling to see.

These people had but few domesticated animals. The Muruts had plenty of dirty, half-starved black pigs running about the jungle near their house, and a few goats. They had also a peculiar race of small, brown dogs, resembling terriers, which are very useful in pig hunting. The Kadyans had cats wonderfully like our own, but with abnormal tails. Poultry are represented only by cocks and hens. Some of the wild birds of the forests are domesticated as pets, the most common being Java and little red sparrows; a beautiful little green ground pigeon; paroquets of two kinds, one very small like a love-bird, the other having two long blue attenuated feathers in its tail. Mino birds are not unfrequently tamed, and they may be taught to speak words or phrases quite readily. Some of the larger hornbills, the "rhinoceros" variety especially, are also tamed, and are most amusing creatures. There was one in a house where I stayed a week or two, and a more voracious bird I never saw. At night it would perch itself on a stick below the house and croak for hours together, but with daylight in the morning it would enter the house to beg for food, and the quantities it could consume during the day were surprisingly large. Everything edible seemed equally welcome — rice, fruit, vegetables, and even the entire bodies of small birds which my boy had been skinning as specimens were gulped down with apparent relish. Any trifles thrown towards it were sure of being caught in its great bill, and then thrown again in the air and caught previous to their being swallowed.

The Kadyans have an ingenious way of capturing the little green or puni pigeons (*Chalcophaps indica*) with a bamboo call, by which their soft cooing notes are exactly imitated. These birds are gregarious, and just before breeding-time they arrive in large quantities.

" The call is formed of two pieces of bamboo, a slender tube, a short piece 3″—4″ in diameter, and a connecting piece of wood. In the short piece is a hole similar to the embouchure of a flute ; and the lower end of the blow-tube is fitted to this in such a manner that, on blowing, a soft, low, flute-like ' cooing' is easily producible; and this can be readily modulated so as to be heard either at a long distance or near at hand. This instrument is figured in Proc. Zool. Soc. 1879, Part II., p. 346. The native, who has taken up his position in the forest or jungle where these little birds are found, blows very softly at first ; but if there be no answering call from the birds he blows louder and louder, thus increasing the radius of sound. If there really be any pigeons of this kind within hearing, they are sure to answer; and then the hunter blows softer and softer until they are enticed into the 'wigwam' of leafy branches which he has erected in order to conceal himself from sight. The door or entrance to these 'wigwams' is partially closed by a screen of palm (*Nipa fruticans*) leaves. This is elevated a little to allow the pigeons to enter, after which it is allowed to fall, portcullis-like, entirely, so as to close the entrance; and the bird is then easily secured. Above the entrance two holes are made, so that the hunter can look out without being seen. These huts are formed of a few poles or sticks, rudely thatched with twigs and palm-leaves, and vary from four to six feet in height.

" This pigeon is migratory, and arrives in Labuan and on the opposite Bornean coast with the change of the monsoon, about April. Many hundreds are then caught by means of this 'dakut,' or 'bamboo call,' and are offered for sale by their captors for a cent or two each. They are also kept by the natives as domestic pets, along with young hornbills, the 'Mino' bird or 'Grackle,' a small species of paroquet, and Java sparrows."

At this season little huts are built in the forest, and the hunter, ensconced within, blows his call, and they will actually run inside the hut, where they are caught. The Kadyans and their Murut neighbours collect a good deal of gutta and caoutchouc in the surrounding forests, which is afterwards manufactured into lumps or balls, and taken over to Labuan for sale. The gutta is obtained from four or five kinds of large forest trees, belonging to the genus isonandra, by felling the trees and girdling or ringing their bark at intervals of every two feet, the milky juice or sap being caught in vessels fashioned of leaves or cocoa-nut shells. The crude sap is hardened into slabs or bricks by boiling, and is generally adulterated with twenty per cent. of scraped bark—indeed, the Chinese traders who purchase the gutta from the collectors, would refuse the pure article in favour of that adulterated with bark, and to which its red colour is mainly due.

Caoutchouc or rubber is in the N.W. districts of Borneo the produce of three species of climbing plants, known to the natives as "Manoongan," "Manoongan putih," and "Manoongan manga." Their stems are fifty to one hundred feet in length, and rarely more than six inches in diameter, the bark corrugated, and of a grey or reddish-brown colour; leaves oblong, and of a glossy green colour; the flowers are borne in axillary clusters, and are succeeded by yellow fruits, the size of an orange, and containing seeds as large as beans, each enclosed in a section of apricot-coloured fruit. These fruits are of a delicious flavour, and are highly valued by the natives. Here, again, the stems are cut down to facilitate the collection of the creamy sap, which is afterwards coagulated into rough balls by the addition of nipa salt.

It is most deplorable to see the fallen gutta trees lying about in all directions in the forest, and the rubber-yielding willughbeias are also gradually, but none the less surely, being exterminated by the collectors here in Borneo, as, indeed, throughout the other islands and on the Peninsula, where they also abound.

It was formerly thought that gutta was the produce of one particular species of tree—*Isonandra gutta*—but that from the Lawas district is formed of the mixed sap of at least five species, the juice of ficus and one or two species of artocarpeæ being not unfrequently used in addition as adulterants. The Bornean "gutta soosoo," or rubber, again, is the mixed sap of three species of willughbeias, and here, again, the milk of two or three other plants is added surreptitiously to augment the quantity collected. The gutta trees are a long time in attaining to maturity, and are not easy to propagate, except by seeds. The willughbeias, on the other hand, grow quickly, and may be easily and rapidly increased by vegetative as well as by seminal modes of propagation, hence the latter are more especially deserving of the attention of our Government in India, where they might reasonably be expected to thrive.

No doubt there are yet many thousands of tons of these products existing in Bornean woods, but as the trees are killed by the collectors without a thought of replacement, the supply will recede further and further from the markets, and so prices must of necessity rise as the supply fails, or as the collection of it becomes more laborious.

The demand for caoutchouc from Borneo is a very recent one, yet in many districts the supply is practically exhausted. In Assam, Java, and also in Australia, rubber is supplied by *Ficus elastica*, which is cultivated for the purpose. There are many milk-yielding species of ficus in the Bornean forests which might possibly afford a supply in remunerative quantities as the result of careful experiments. The Malayan representatives of the bread-fruit family also deserve examination, as excellent rubber is yielded by *Castilloa elastica*, a South-American plant of this order.

CHAPTER V.

KINA BALU, OR CHINESE WIDOW MOUNTAIN.

ON the 29th of November, just as the dry season was
commencing in Labuan, Mr. Peter Veitch (who had a
few days before joined me after his travels in Australia
and the Fiji Islands) and myself started off on a journey
to Kina Balu, which we intended to reach by way of the
Tawaran river. We had with us twenty-six men and two
bird-hunters, so that we formed a rather imposing party
of thirty, all told. The men were armed with native
parangs or swords; some had krisses, and eight or ten
carried muskets with which we had provided them. We
embarked our men, stores, and travelling gear on board
a little coast-steamer bound for Sulu, and the following
morning we arrived at Pulo Gaya, and the captain
lowered another boat in addition to the one we had
brought with us, and put us all safely ashore near

Gantisan in Gaya Bay. We waited here at a Roman Catholic Catechist's Station for some time, and I ascended to the summit of the grass-covered hills northwards. These are forest-covered below, the nebong palm being very abundant, and attaining large dimensions.

The hill-tops above, which look so smooth and green when seen from the sea, are found to be clad with coarse "lallang" grass a yard high, among which the men who accompanied me pointed out several deer lairs. Fresh green tufts of *Cheilanthes tenuifolia* grew in the crevices of the decomposed sandstone, and among the clumps of nebong palm; a singular fern, *Schizæa digitata*, was very plentiful.

Returning, we re-arranged our baggage, and sending our boat round to Pangeran Rau's place at Kalombini, by sea, we and the majority of the men started over the ridge of the wooded hill on foot. It was a stiff climb in the hot sun, the path being both steep and rough. In descending to the plain on the other side we shot three large swallows and a crimson and blue-painted barbet; we were also fortunate in finding a pretty pink-flowered zingiberad in bloom. The flat plain into which we descended was partly cultivated, and the rice especially looked strong and healthy. Fine buffaloes were also grazing here.

We reached Pangeran Rau's house at three o'clock, and had the usual *bichari* or talk, arm-chairs and mats being at once brought into the head-house on our arrival. Some of the women were busy pounding the rice to separate it from the husk; and one or two ran away shrieking at our approach—it was simply affectation, and not fright. We found the Pangeran rather reserved, but hospitably inclined. He was a gray-haired old fellow of over sixty, and spoke but little, asked no questions, and spent most of his time sitting cross-legged on a mat drinking tea, chewing limed " sirra " leaf and betel, or smoking long cigarettes of tobacco rolled in nipa leaf, all being brought to him from time to time by little Malay boys. The head-house was soon filled with men from the other houses, who flocked in to see us and to hear the news from Labuan of our followers. We rested a little, and then walked out to obtain a bath before dinner. Some natives directed us to a spring about half a mile off across the plain, which here, near the houses, is of sand covered with coarse sedges and scrub. We passed two or three palm-leaf cottages on our way ; and here I noticed the first implement of agriculture I saw in Borneo. It was a wooden harrow; and a native seeing me interested in it, pointed to a rude iron-shod plough which hung in a large mango tree near one of the huts.

A good many of the people who live here are Badjows or " sea gipsies," so called from their habit of wandering about from place to place in boats, in which they seem more thoroughly at home than in the wretched huts they now and then build on shore. They are essentially lazy, and will not walk a yard if they can get a buffalo or anything having four legs to carry them. We saw two Badjow boys going to the spring for water, and they both rode on a buffalo calf, which seemed used to its mischievous load. We returned to dinner at dusk, and managed to get a good night's rest here, as the houses were cool, being built over the water, and the mosquitoes were not nearly so bloodthirsty as usual.

Our boat did not come round until nearly ten the following morning. We had been up since sunrise, and had our breakfast ; so, when our craft appeared, we borrowed a boat and a couple of men from the Pangeran, and left for the Badjow village on the Menkabong. We reached that place about noon in a drenching shower, and our guides assured us that further progress that day was impossible. We therefore had our things brought up into the head-house and soon made ourselves comfortable. We had brought two dozen fine pomoloes with us from Labuan, and the ripe ones were now really excellent in flavour; and we thoroughly enjoyed this delicious fruit for dessert after a frugal luncheon of bread and dried fish. About four o'clock the rain ceased, and the sun shone beautifully, so we took our guns, and went ashore for an hour to shoot. We secured a few pigeons and other birds, returning to dinner at sunset. Mr. Veitch lost his watch among the long grass, but was fortunate enough to find it on retracing his steps.

We arose at day-break the following morning, and started off, reaching the market-place on the Tamparulie plain about seven o'clock. A large market of fruit, fish, vegetables, rice, and other native produce, was being held, and on landing we met with the Datu in whose village we had remained last night. We told him the object of our presence in his territory, and found him agreeable, although not nearly so dignified as Pangeran Rau. He sent off one of his men to fetch us some fruit, and he soon returned with a basket of fine langsat, in return for which we gave him a couple of pomoloes, and we afterwards smoked a cigar together while our men unloaded the boats. We tried to hire two or three men from him; but as he was very extortionate in his demands as to payment for them and a buffalo-sledge which we wished to load with rice for our men, we cut the matter short by refusing his assistance at any price.

We sent back the Pangeran's boat, and giving our men as much rice each as they could carry, we returned the rest to the other boat and left two men in charge until our return.   I am inclined to think his greed was excited by seeing the cloth and goods we had as the men unloaded the boat.

We now found out the value of the man "Musa," whom we had engaged to superintend our men.   He was an old man, but still powerful and active, and he possessed the secret of persuasion to the utmost degree. Under his direction the men were all loaded equally, and to their individual satisfaction, and we set off towards Tamparulie.   We saw a pretty white-flowered cucurbit growing over bushes here and there, and bearing spindle-shaped fruits of a scarlet colour and about two inches long.   Here and there also the red-berried spikes of an amorphophallus were seen among the tall grass.   I and Veitch shouldered our guns, and pushed on across a low grassy plain inhabited for the time by a few black water buffaloes, and then came a long march in single file across a series of wet rice or padi fields, the paths through which were scarcely a foot broad, very uneven, and being of pure clay, the last night's rain had made them as slippery as wet soap.   We who had only our guns to carry found it rather hard work floundering about on the greasy tracks ; but the men were in good spirits, and a march of about two hours brought us to the Tawaran, close to the village of Tamparulie which stands on its banks.

The plain we had just traversed was well cultivated, and very fertile, rice, bananas, cocoa-nut trees, and other vegetation being most luxuriant.   Buffaloes were employed to draw the rude ploughs through the rich, moist earth.   We saw immense flocks of white "padi birds," and here and there a crane, majestically stalking among the crops. At our halting-place the river is very shallow, its high banks being fringed with groves of cocoa-nuts and bananas; and in one or two places I noted neatly-fenced and well-kept gardens descending nearly to the water's edge. In these were sweet potatoes, cucumbers, maize, and "kaladi," or *Caladium esculentum.* The women seemed to be the principal cultivators of these little plots, and we could see them at work among the garden crops here and there as we passed along.

Here we noticed a lovely palm for the first time—a caryota—having dark green plumose foliage, the pinnæ abruptly jagged, and notched along its margins. As we partook of our luncheon, an intelligent old native came along, and sent our men to his garden, which he pointed out to us, for some green cocoa-nuts, so that we obtained a delicious draught, which we found very refreshing after our hot walk. He was very talkative, and begged a little brandy; and he also gladly accepted the seeds of a fine pomolo (*Citrus decumana*), to plant in his garden. We did not cross the stream here, but plunged on beside the river, following a narrow, muddy buffalo track, which in places resembled a tunnel, being completely embowered with tall grasses, bound together with large convolvuli and other creeping and climbing plants.

A heavy walk of a couple of hours brought us to the first group of Dusun houses, which stood on a bit of rising ground close beside the stream, being surrounded by a grove of cocoa-nut palms and other fruit-trees. We stayed here to rest our followers, and while waiting shot several birds on the surrounding trees. Let not the gentle reader blame us for wanton destruction! There was " method in our madness;" we did not "kill for sport," but only for the advancement of learning, or for food.

About half a mile beyond we came to a fording-place in the stream, and descending the slippery clay banks, we crossed the river, which in places reached up to our waists; and in one place the current was rather too strong to be pleasant. Reaching the other side, our way lay along an abandoned bed of the stream for some distance. The old shingly bed was in some places quite thickly covered with *Celosia argentea*, forming compact little bushes, two feet high, every branchlet terminated by a rose-tipped spike of silvery bracts, forming, as seen here, a very pretty object.

We reached the Dusan village of Bawang (*bawang*, in the Dusun dialect = river) about four o'clock, after fording a creek up to our necks, and indeed we were both tired and hungry. We took refuge in a house, which stood on the bank, quite close to the river, and our men soon had several fires ablaze on the pebbly beach below. We pulled off our wet things, and enjoyed a bath in the bubbling stream, and then a nice rub, dry and clean clothes, made us quite comfortable by dinner time. " Bongsur," one of the bird hunters, brought in two or three very pretty birds here; and Mr. Veitch added a black, red-bellied squirrel (" basing ") to our collection.

We slept the sleep of the weary; and the following morning pushed on up the slope beyond the village. The shady jungle through which we passed ere we began to ascend was thickly carpeted with selaginellas, *S. Wallichii* being especially luxuriant. *S. caulescens* drooped from the moist rocks here and there very gracefully. We found the climbing rather arduous work, and but for the shade of the overhanging bamboo, which grows here plentifully, we should have fared worse.

On reaching the crest of the hill, an altitude of say 800 feet, we got along better. At this height we found our first nepenthes, a pretty green-pitchered form, swollen below, and having a broad, flattened red rim to its mouth (*N. Phyllamphora*). We rested an hour on the top, but could procure no water, excepting a few drops from the cut end of a climbing plant, which the natives call "kalobit," and of which they sometimes form rough cordage, by rending it into long strips. The juice of this plant is intensely bitter; but the water which distilled itself slowly from the cut end was quite pure and tasteless.

We ascended about 1500 feet to-day, and the views from the summit of the range between Bawang and Si Nilau were very satisfying, all the intervening country to the sea being plainly visible, as well as the whole coast-line, as far as Gaya Bay. We walked along quicker than usual, for the sky became very black, and it was evident that we should soon have a drenching shower. Our guides had forgotten the way to Si Nilau, and so there was nothing for it but to push on, in the hopes of meeting with a shelter by the way.

At length we suddenly came upon the site of a deserted village, and took shelter in a hut—a little better in repair than the rest—while from the trees near both langsat fruit and cocoa-nuts were procurable. Here we waited until the rain abated, when we took up our quarters in the house of a Dusun man, near the site of the old village, which had, as we afterwards heard, been deserted on account of the death of the headman.

We had previously met our Dusun landlord about two

miles from this village, in some patches of rice and gourds, but he had been too frightened to answer our inquiries as to the route, and rushed down the hill just as the first few drops—big, heavy, solitary drops—fell from the black rain-clouds over head. Fortunately, I had struck the right road a few yards further on, and followed it up, when in turning a rocky corner, where two roads merged into one, I came across the man again

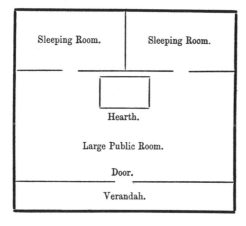

PLAN OF A DUSUN COTTAGE, N.W. BORNEO.

face to face. He was so surprised at my sudden reappearance, that he fairly shook with terror, and he rushed down the rocky ledge, which served as a path around the hill-top, with the speed of a startled deer. I had yelled after him to stop, but he ran all the faster; and when afterwards we entered his house, our men had a little trouble to reassure him that we meant him no harm.

We soon put the old boy at his ease, however; and

then a fowl for our dinner was caught and killed. For this and the fruit we had stolen we paid him a fathom and a half of grey shirting, with which he was very pleased. His house was a very neat one, having a large public room in front, with a stove, hearth, or fire-place opposite the door, and two little sleeping rooms behind. Like all Dusun houses the floor was elevated four feet from the ground, level on piles, so that the pigs and fowls had shelter beneath. The side walls and floors were of bamboo, beaten or pressed out flat, like boards, and being of a clear, yellow colour, they had a warm and comfortable appearance as the fire glowed on the hearth, above which was a rack for the storage of fire-wood, or on which clothes could be dried.

After dinner we lit our lamp, and made ourselves as cosy as possible over our post-prandial cigar, after which we were not loath to turn in. Up by daybreak, and snatching our morning meal, we were soon *en route* for Kalawat Peak, and thence we descended to Kalawat village by a rocky mountain-path, fringed with bamboos, large ginger-worts, and ferns of various kinds.

A strong growing species of bauhinia was very showy here, overrunning the branches of bushes and low trees beside the path, and bearing its pale, yellow flowers in large clusters very profusely. As seen at a distance it has a pleasing effect in the landscape—a rare thing with Bornean flowers; and a nearer sight of it is suggestive of our native woodbine.

Selaginellas were plentiful near the streams, and near the crest of the Peak (alt. 2000 feet) we saw a dainty little bertolonia, rarely exceeding two inches in height, having pearly-spotted leaves, and terminal clusters of rosy-pink flowers. A stately habited nephrodium, with gracefully arching light-green fronds, nearly a yard

long, a zingiberad, with richly barred foliage (*Alpiniá
sp.*), two or three species of gleichenia, and now and
then an inconspicuous epiphyte, orchid, or fern occurred, to add variety to
our route.

We were puzzled to-
day by seeing horizontal
bamboo-stems fixed in the
trees over our path, but
we eventually discovered
that they were intended
to serve as bridges or
paths to rats or other
animals, traps being set
to catch those who were
unwary enough to avail
themselves of the con-
venient crossing.

A curious custom of
the Dusun is to entrap
and eat the common field
rats, wild cats, &c., of
the country. Beside all
the little paths through
the forest, near Kina Balu,
wooden rat-traps (see Fig.)
are set in the herbage
through which the animals
have made their tracks.
A form of this trap,
slightly modified, is hung
on the branches of trees
for the capture of squir-
rels, and other fruit-eating

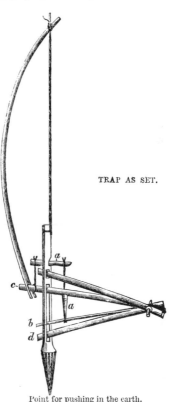

TRAP AS SET.

Point for pushing in the earth.

BAMBOO RAT-TRAP, USED BY DUSUN,
N.W. BORNEO.

a a, Pegs connected by rattan for setting the trap ; *b,* catch, anything
touching this liberates the pegs,
and the bamboo forces *c* tightly
down on *d,* thus securing any
animal that has touched *b.*

rodents. I asked Kurow how long the Dusun had eaten
rats? His reply was that, "Once upon a time," a
horde of rats, far more than ever followed the 'Pied
Piper,' I should judge by his adjectives, came and ate
up all the rice and kaladi. A conference was held by
the then reigning chief in the head house, and his advice
was of the stern, practical kind. "Talking is of no
use," said he; "the rats have eaten all our rice: we
have no other food left to us; *ergo*, we must eat up
the rats!" "And so it was, and is to this day," said
Kurow; but I fancied I could see a sly twinkle in his
bright eyes—just the same merry twinkle one expects to
see in anyone's face, after having related a palpably
improbable story with all due solemnity!

We pass several very pretty little rills, at which
drinking or washing was facilitated by spouts, made
of the leaf-stalk of the sago palm, and placed so
as to conduct the cool sparkling water on a level
with one's face. Flourishing rice and kaladi fields
became more plentiful; and the tree ferns, which we
had first sighted after leaving Si Nilau, now became
more numerous. Just ere we reached Kalawat, we
noticed some splendid specimens in the jungle; and now
and then even out in the clearings their great crowns
of fresh green plumose fronds being fully exposed to
the sun, and in some cases borne aloft on slender black
trunks, 20 feet or more in height. At the village of
Kalawat the houses are in one place backed by an
immense grove of these feathery plumed tall tree ferns,
above which the white stemmed betel-nut palm towers
aloft, its dark green foliage and pendent clusters of bright
orange fruit standing out clear and bright against the
cool blue sky.

At Kalawat we rested awhile. The straggling dwell-

ings were built on piles over the muddy ground, and a
few ill-fed black pigs were rooting up turf in all directions
in quest of food. Here, for the first time, along this
route, we were pleased to see tame bees hived in sections
of hollow tree trunks, about two feet in length, the top
and bottom being stopped up, and a hole burnt in the
centre as an entrance for the busy workers. In one or
two cases separate little huts were erected especially for
the bees, but as a rule the hives were placed on a board
beneath the overhanging eaves of the houses. The kind
of bee kept is very small, much smaller than that common
in England, and I was struck at the peculiar manner in
which they wriggled their bodies simultaneously as they
congregated in groups on the hive near the entrance.
These tame bees, as well as their wild brethren, who nest in
the tall forest trees, make but little honey in proportion to
that of our northern kinds, and are especially kept for
the wax they yield, this being used occasionally by the
natives in the form of rude candles, and it is also an
article of export from Borneo.

Being in advance of our followers we waited here an
hour. It is a singular trait of the Borneans to show no
curiosity when strangers pass through their villages. We
sat here on a rock for some considerable time, and yet,
not even the children came out to look at us. Two men
sitting outside on a verandah, basket-making, and an old
woman, were all the inhabitants we saw, but doubtless
many a pair of bright eyes watched us secretly through
the cracks of the bamboo houses. As it came on to rain,
however, we entered one of the houses, in which were
seven or eight young men and several women. We tried
to get some fruit here, but the langsat were not ripe, and
cocoanuts were scarce owing to the flowering stems being
cut off and the exuding sap collected in a bamboo vessel

to be made into toddy, a drink of which the hill villagers
are very fond. At last a couple of young nuts were forthcoming, and a dash of brandy in each gave us a most
refreshing draught. As the rain ceased, we decided to
proceed to Bungol, the next village along our route. To
this one of our guides, Pangeran Raman of Labuan,—
an artful old sweep—loudly objected, urging that the
Tawaran would be flooded—that we should not reach
Bungol at all that night, as it would be dark long ere we
could do so—adding, that there was no intervening resting-place. I was used to these excuses, and determined
to go on, to which Mr. Veitch also agreed. Our guides,
who had come here from Si Nilau, refused to go further,
nor would any of the Kalawat people go to Bungol with
us as guides, but at last one of them pointed out the
right road for us to take, and I and Mr. Veitch set out
along the rocky path alone. We rested on the hill above
the village, and then Pangeran Raman and our two servants, or " boys," joined us, and said the men refused to
come on. This did not deter us, and we plunged down
the hill-path and through one or two clearings, in which
sweet potatoes, maize, and tobacco grew luxuriantly.
Then down a greasy clay path, embowered with bamboos,
tall canes and jungle, until at last the Tawaran was
reached in the valley below, rushing and boiling among
the smooth boulders in its bed.

We sat on the banks of the stream to rest. Here a
pretty little palm about a yard high formed strong tufts
and patches, its roots being laved by the stream below.
Its pinnate leaves were graceful, and had a distinct
grassy appearance. Draping trees close by the river
also we found a species of vanilla in bloom. It had
large waxy flowers of a creamy white colour, the lip
having a five-lobed hairy crest of a dark purple-brown

colour. As many as twenty buds were counted in a
cluster, but the flowers expanded one at a time. We
crossed the river, which nowhere exceeded our knees in
height, and pushed on up the next hill. The mist was
gathering thick and white in the valleys, and it began to
rain in torrents. In a very few minutes the path up the
hill-side became a brook, and the rain beat in our faces
so that we could scarcely see our way. Added to this
inconvenience was the thought that we might not be in
the right track, and of this our worthy "guide," Pangeran
Raman, could tell us nothing. He was a very good fair-
weather traveller, and the biggest man in our party when
all was well around a good camp fire ! At a pinch, when
most wanted, he was perfectly useless—indeed, in the
way. I am afraid I did not pity him as he stood shivering in the cold, and begging piteously of us to return to
a miserable little hut beside the river for the night. This
was out of the question, as we had not a dry thread on us
and no food, so I pushed up the hill to reconnoitre.
Just at the top I met a Dusun man who had come from
Bungol, and who was going to Kalawat, and when Mr.
Veitch and the old Pangeran came up, we induced the
native to return with us to Bungol. We now felt more
at ease, and splashed down the hill-side merrily, and
after crossing the Tawaran four times, in one place nearly
to our necks, we reached the cocoanut-crested hill on which
the village of Bungol stands. Our "boys" had lagged
behind and only reached the houses just before night-fall,
having been mainly guided by the accidental discharge of
our guns, which we had let off in order to dry them soon
after our arrival. Our guide had brought us to his own
house, and we soon had a good fire, and took off our wet
clothes, after which we sat by the fire clad in native
sarongs which our host lent us. We soon wrung out our

clothes, and hung them on a beam over the blazing fire to dry, and then came the question of dinner. At last we procured a fowl and a bowl of rice, and my Chinese "boy," Kimjeck, who was a good cook, soon had these on the fire.

After it was dark we heard shouting, and soon after six of our men who carried the food, clothes, and sleeping gear came in, being afraid, as they said, that we should want food. We were soon all as jolly as sandboys. The fowl was cut up and boiled with a tin of julienne soup and three or four chilies, and this and a nice white bowl of steaming rice formed a dish which to us, tired and hungry as we were, seemed "fit for a king." A cup of chocolate and a cigar followed by way of dessert, and all our troubles for the time being vanished in smoke! We paid our guide a fathom of grey shirting, and gave him a looking-glass for our night's lodging. The fowl and a couple of cocoanuts also were paid for with a fathom of shirting, and everybody was thus easily satisfied.

Having only a sleeping-rug each, we found it rather chilly, and I could not sleep well. I rose about 11 o'clock, however, and made up a good fire, and then lay down beside it and slept well until daybreak. We had breakfasted in the morning and were outside ready to start, when our laggards of yesterday came in, and they looked sheepish and crestfallen when they found that we were really about to start on and had not intended to have awaited their coming. Two Dusun men now accompanied us as guides, and after crossing the Tawaran several times, we mounted the hill to the left, crossing the ridge and descending towards Koung. The way to the village was down rocky gutters seemingly worn by heavy rains, and the hill-side paths in the kaladi gardens were very bad to traverse, and we were thoroughly tired out ere we reached the grassy flat on which Koung is built, indeed, this was the most toilsome day's work we had hitherto had, although, perhaps, our long tramp yesterday had something to do with its being so.

We found the Koung people peaceably inclined, although we did not forget that it was here that Mr. Low and St. John had some difficulty with the natives the first time they came this way. We slept well, and in the morning after breakfast we retraced our steps by the river to examine a scarlet flower which we had seen from the opposite bank yesterday. It turned out to be *Bauhinia Kochiana*, or an allied species. Mr. Veitch shot a fine white-headed hawk, which was on the look out for a breakfast of fresh fish from the river. We also secured several other birds we had not before seen. The red-fruited *Rubus rosæfolius* was very pretty here among the rocks, and we observed one or two orchids of interest on the trees overhanging the stream. The river is very pretty as it passes the village, and as the water comes from the hills above, it is deliciously clear and cool, quite a luxury, in fact, either for drinking or bathing. We enjoyed our morning ramble, and on returning to the house wherein we had slept we found all the men ready to start for Kiau. On our crossing the ford at the end of the village we met a large party of natives laden with baskets of tobacco and a little beeswax, going on a trading expedition. There were some women among them, who, of course, carried the heaviest loads. Several of the men were tattooed on the breast and arms, and all were armed with brass-handled parongs and slender-shafted spears. They showed no surprise at seeing us, and passed on apparently unconcerned as to our object. Our way now lay up the valley, first on the right and then on the left of the river, but there was no great difficulty in crossing, the water being rarely as high as the hips. We passed huts here and there, and irrigated patches of rice. Maize and sweet potatoes grew around the houses, and almost all had a clump of big-leaved bananas near the door. The rice land was irrigated by a ditch cut from the river, a little dam being made so as to direct the water into it as required. We noticed several fish-traps set in the river to-day. These are made of a bamboo stem six feet long, split lengthwise and made into a long basket-like shape with rattans, so that it is wide at top and narrow at the other end. In order to set them effectively, an oblique dam of stones and earth is made so as to direct a large body of water through an aperture, and in this the basket is placed. A fish once washed into it has no chance of escape, and large quantities are caught at times, especially after the river is freshened by rains. Occasionally we saw men or women working on the rice-land, and I was very much struck at the care taken in planting and cultivating the crop, not a weed being anywhere visible in the rice-patches. The planting was extremely regular, each tuft or stool being about eight inches from its neighbours, so that all obtained their due amount of earth, light, and air, a lesson indeed for some of our own cultivators of cereals here at home.

We passed immense clumps of bamboo, the feathery wands rising in masses to a height of fifty or sixty feet. From one of these clumps our men secured some of the young crowns, which are white and tender, and by no means despisable as a vegetable when boiled with salt. At Bawang I had noticed them eating boiled fern-tops with their rice, and on asking for a little I was surprised at its delicate spinach-like flavour. We met a boy at one of the crossings with a basket of fine langsat fruit, some of

which we purchased, giving him a Chinese looking-glass
in exchange.

At length, crossing the river for the last time, we
rested in the shade of a huge sandstone rock for a
luncheon of cold rice and fruit. Our path then lay to
the left through low jungle, and on one or two of the old
remaining trees we noticed masses of *Grammatophyllum
speciosum* with stems eight feet in length—each plant a
good cartload, and evidently in the most luxuriant health,
with foliage fresh and green, although fully exposed to
the hot sun. Cœlogynes were plentiful on the lower trees
and rocks by the river. One sandstone boulder was
entirely covered with *Davallia ciliata,* and some fine tall
grasses grew among the pebbles of the old river bed.
The rocks bordering the river are of sandstone, and yet
at Koung and along our route to-day we continually met
with boulders of granite sometimes in the present river
bed, sometimes on the old dry bed, and sometimes, as on
the green Koung, immense pieces, a hundred tons weight,
lie isolated on the plain. Half an hour's walk from our
resting-place by the river brought us to the clearings and
the hill or dry rice-fields of the Kiau villagers. The
crop was ripening fast, and the whole hill-side, as well
as the one opposite beyond the river, looked very flourishing. Here and there were green patches of kaladi,
and around the field-huts of bamboo, cucumbers clustered,
and sweet potatoes, maize, and occasionally bananas,
looked prosperous. We followed a narrow footpath
through the rice, which was kept from injury by a little
fence of bamboo, and in places the earth was prevented
from washing down by a few large stones laid in line.
We reached the village about two o'clock, the journey
from Koung having taken us about five hours. The
people here did seem to feel more interest than ordinary,

and we soon had a tolerably good audience around us. One by one our followers came in, and we soon availed ourselves of the comfort of a rub over with a towel and dry clothes, after which we arranged the various plants collected during the day, and continued our journals. " Bongsur " brought in a fine brown owl and a pretty scarlet bird with black wing-tips, neither of which we had

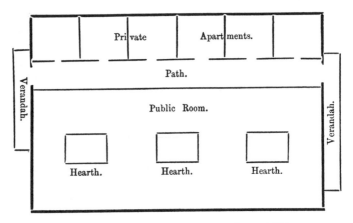

PLAN OF LARGE DUSUN HOUSE AT KIAU, N.W. BORNEO.

seen before. For dinner we had boiled fowl and rice, followed by coffee and a cigarette of native tobacco wrapped in maize-husk. We lay on our mats and rugs at one end of the large public room, all our men being cooking and jabbering away to their hearts' content, the Babel of sounds, partly Malay and partly Dusun, being deafening. Tobacco was brought in for sale soon after our arrival, and one man brought a fowl, but as he asked double its value we refused to buy it.

The greatest interest was shown in all we did, more

especially by the boys and young girls who crowded on the pathway just in front of where we lay. When we extinguished our lamp and turned into our blankets they soon became quiet, the people of the house retiring to their private apartments, and the others to their houses in the village. It was a wet night, and we felt chilly, but slept well. Our first task after breakfast in the morning was to overhaul all our stores, arranging those we wanted on the mountain so that they could be easily carried, and packing the rest so that they could be left with safety. Our stock of rice was so low that we were rather alarmed, but "Musa" assured us that he should be able to buy some in the village. After re-arranging all our things, we took our guns and walked over the hill. We saw very few birds, nor were the plants we discovered of any particular interest, with the exception of a large white-flowered arundina, having a rich amethyst-coloured lip. We saw some immense gingerworts, having leafy stems ten or twelve feet in height; also large ferns of the angiopteris type, while *Mikania volubilis* overran the bushes along our route.

Returning to the house, we engaged Boloung and Kurow, the acting head men of the village, and six of their followers, to take us up the mountain on the morrow. "Musa" and Pangeran Raman did most of the bargaining on our side, and at length concluded the matter by paying over the amount of cloth and brass wire as agreed. Next morning we selected sixteen of our men and started for the mountain. In a rich bit of shady forest on the other side of the Kiau ridge we found the evergreen *Calanthe macroloba*, bearing spikes of white flowers much larger individually than those of *C. veratri-folia*. A foliage plant marked with silvery blotches above and crimson beneath was also collected. Our road was a

H

rough and tiring one of sloping hillside paths very wet
and slippery, and in places blocked by fallen trees. About
one o'clock we reached a rushing stream, and our guides
brought us to a large overhanging rock, where they said
we must pass the night. It now began to rain heavily,
so we at once told the men to cut sticks and palm-leaves
to lay on the ground where we were to sleep, and over
which we could spread our waterproof sheets and rugs.
This was soon done, and meanwhile our "boys" prepared luncheon. We were disgusted at stopping thus
early in the day, and wished our guides to proceed when
the rain abated, which however they determinedly refused
to do. To make the best of a bad bargain, I and Mr.
Veitch explored the forest above our camp, where we
found a pretty aroid with white blotched leaves, and
another marbled with silvery grey; also a variegated
plant resembling an anæctochilus, but which Professor
Reichenbach tells me is the *Cystorchis variegata* of
Blume. This plant I had previously gathered in another
locality further south; indeed, it seems pretty generally
distributed along the north-west coast. Specimens of
two or three delicate filmy ferns were found near the
streams; and at our camping-place, which we named the
"Sleeping Rock," the pretty little *Adiantum diaphanum*
was plentiful, and living plants were brought to England
from this habitat.

About seven o'clock next morning we started on our
upward journey. It was hot work at first, but we could
feel it perceptibly get cooler after the first two or three
thousand feet. At about four thousand feet mosses are
very plentiful, the finest species gathered being *Dawsonia
superba*, which fringed the path, but nowhere in great
plenty. A new white-flowered species of burmannia was
also gathered, and small-flowered orchids were seen. In

one place a shower of small scarlet rhododendron flowers covered the ground at our feet, the plant being epiphytal in the trees overhead. It was very misty, and the moss which covered every rotten stick, and the vegetation generally, was dripping with moisture, and every sapling we grasped in climbing upwards was the means of shaking a shower-bath on us from the trees above. At about five thousand feet a dead and broken pitcher of *Nepenthes Lowi* lying in the path led to the discovery of the plant itself scrambling among the mossy branches overhead, its singular flagon-shaped ascidia hanging from the point of every leaf. It is a vigorous-habited plant, with bright green leathery leaves, the petioles of which clasp the stem in a peculiar manner. The only plants we saw were epiphytal on mossy trunks and branches, and we searched for young plants diligently, but without success. All the pitchers hitherto seen are cauline ones, and as the plant has never yet been seen in a young state, it is an open question as to whether the radical pitchers differ in shape or size, as is the case with most other species. As we ascended higher, epiphytal orchids, especially erias, dendrochilia, and cœlogynes became more plentiful, and we came upon a large-flowered rhododendron, bearing rich orange flowers two inches in diameter, and twenty flowers in a cluster! It grew on a dangerous declivity, and not one of our lazy men would venture to get it for us. Such a prize, however, was too lovely to forego, and after a wet scramble among the surrounding bushes, I secured it in good condition. Two or three other species were seen in flower, but none equal to it in its golden beauty. Casuarina trees became common, and higher up these were joined by two or three species of gleichenias, and a distinct form of dipteris. Phyllocladus also appeared, and a glaucus-leaved dianella (*D. javanica*).

Here also were two of the most distinct of all rhododendrons, *R. ericifolium* and *R. stenophyllum*. On open
spaces among rocks and sedges, the giant *Nepenthes
Rajah* began to appear, the plants being of all sizes, and
in the most luxuriant health and beauty. The soil in
which they grew was a stiff yellow loam, surfaced with
sandstone-grit, and around the larger plants a good deal
of rich humus and leaf debris had collected. The long
red-pitchered *N. Edwardsiana* was seen in two places.
This plant, like *N. Lowii*, is epiphytal in its perfect state,
and is of a slender rambling habit. Highest of all in
the great nepenthes zone came *N. villosa*, a beautiful
plant, having rounded pitchers of the softest pink colour,
with a crimson frilled orifice, similar to that of *N. Edwardsiana.* All thoughts of fatigue and discomfort
vanished as we gazed on these living wonders of the
Bornean Andes! Here, on this cloud-girt mountain
side, were vegetable treasures which Imperial Kew had
longed for in vain. Discovered by Mr. Low in 1851,
dried specimens had been transmitted by him to Europe,
and Dr. (now Sir Joseph) Hooker had described and
illustrated them in the Transactions of the Linnæan
Society, but all attempts to introduce them alive into
European gardens had failed. To see these plants in all
their health and vigour was a sensation I shall never
forget—one of those which we experience but rarely in a
whole lifetime!

We reached the cave (altitude 9,000 feet) about three
o'clock, wet and hungry, but far from unhappy. Our
first care was to light a fire, which was not at all easy to
do, since everything was dripping wet. We secured a
bit of dry wood at last, however, and by whittling thin
shavings from it with a knife, we managed to start a
good fire, and some of the men were directed to cut fire-

wood; but so paralysed were they by the wet and cold, that it was with the greatest difficulty that we could persuade them to do this. Poor old " Musa " cut some wood and made a floor to the cave, after which some brushwood and leaves formed a substitute for a mattress. The next difficulty was to obtain water, since the men we had sent to search for it returned empty handed, having failed to find any. As a last resort I had to undertake this duty myself, and, descending the hill-side, I found a tiny pool in a gully, from which I procured a little in our cook-pots. It was not near enough, however; and in wandering in search of more, I came upon a patch of the large nepenthes, from the old pitchers of which I was able to augment my supply by carefully pouring off the rain water from a rather liberal under stratum of flies, ants, and other insect *débris*.   Our guides slept under a rock a little further on and higher up the mountain side, and they found a stream from which good water was procured by our men in the morning and during our stay here.

It commenced to rain heavily at nightfall, and we found it very cold, although we kept a good fire burning nearly all night, one of the results being that we were nearly blinded by the smoke, there being a draught towards an opening at the hinder part of the cave.   The wet dripped from the roof all night, and the walls were also wet and slimy; indeed our quarters were neither extensive nor luxurious; still we made the best of them, and, after all, were rather sorry to leave them at last. We arose at daybreak to collect plants and roots, in the which we were tolerably successful; and before night we had secured all our collections in baskets and bundles ready for the men to carry down.   It was very cool and misty in the morning, but about noon it became clearer, and it was hot indeed, the rocks and old trunks reeked in the sunshine. A slender-growing species of calamus was very common in the low forest below the cave, and it supplied "rattans" of excellent quality for tying up our plants. At least three showy species of cœlogyne grow on the rocks and mossy banks here, at 9,000 feet elevation; and a dainty little plant with reddish pseudo-bulbs in clusters, each bearing a single spathulate dark green leaf, is common. This last has erect spikes of pure white flowers and buds, reminding one of the lily of the valley in cool, fresh purity, an effect partly due to its column being of a soft green tint, like a speck in the interior of the blossom. The cœlogynes are very distinct and beautiful as seen here blooming among the coarse sedges and shrubs. One has white flowers with a blotch of gold on the lip, eight or ten of its waxy flowers being borne on an erect scape. Another has yellow sepals and petals, and a white lip corrugated with brown warts. Another, not so showy, has a nodding spike of white and brown flowers.

We ascended about 9,000 feet, and were delighted with the charming views obtainable during clear weather. The whole upper portion of the mountain along the south and south-eastern slopes is nearly devoid of vegetation, except where there are streams and rather sheltered gullies up which the stunted trees and a few other plants struggle up near to the summit. On the north-western side the rocks rise very precipitous; and here vegetation fails to gain foothold. Looking upwards in the early sunlight, we had clear views of the shelving granite slopes, on which are numerous shallow channels down which streams of water pour during misty and rainy weather. When we gained the top of the great spur the morning after our arrival at the cave, we were delighted at the immense panorama which lay at our feet as we looked back. Looking away south-west we beheld the coast-line from the mouth of what our guides said was the Tampassuk river right down to Gaya Bay and Pulo Tiga, which was distinctly visible, the many-mouthed Menkabong river glistening like a silver net quite close to the coast line.

Looking south-east over a billowy sea of silvery clouds we saw a gigantic range of mountains, and from this the conical peak of Tilong rises through strata after strata of cloud, or stands out on a clear blue background of pure sky, according to the state of the atmosphere. This claims our interest as the beacon of a land unknown ; and this magnificent peak, Tilong, is by repute as high, or even higher, than Kina Balu itself. Altogether we spent three days on the sides of Kina Balu collecting plants, flowers, and seeds ; and after a life on the plains and among the coast mountains—hills compared with this grisly giant—we found the climate most deliciously cool and invigorating. Rain generally commenced about 3 P.M., and continued until eight, the remainder of the night being clear, bright if moonlight, and cool—so cool, indeed, as to make a good camp fire and woollen shirts two or three-fold and blankets very desirable. The mornings were generally misty, every leaf and branch dripping with the rain and heavy dews common here at night, especially during the wet season. About noon the sun was warm, and the temperature at 9,000 feet rises to 758 if the day is fine and dry.

As I have elsewhere said, our Malay followers suffered much from what to them was bitter cold ; indeed they seemed perfectly helpless, with scarcely energy to make a fire and cook their food. They have no notion of actively bestirring themselves in order to keep warm.

Our food supply, too,—that is, the rice—ran short, and so the men were reduced to live on kaladi and sweet potatoes roasted in the embers and eaten with a little salt. Our Dusan guides also complained of the cold, and tried to hurry us in our descent; indeed at last they would wait no longer, and they slipped away, leaving us to reach their village alone as best we could. We were fully determined not to be defeated in our object, however, and keeping ahead of our own men we descended leisurely so as to gather plants by the way, until all had as much as they could possibly carry down. I carried my servant's load in order that he might carry a lot of rare specimens which I had secured for him in a hand-kerchief. The descent after the rain of the night before was difficult and dangerous, and we had a good many falls. Once I fell down a steep place a depth of about twenty feet, among shrubs and creepers, which saved me from serious injury. Mr. Veitch and myself, my " boy," and a solitary Labuan man, went on a-head of our main party, and just at nightfall discovered that we had lost our way. The right path lay across a clearing down which we turned instead of pushing across and striking the path beyond.

We floundered along in the gloaming down several dangerous steeps and across a rocky stream, in crossing which I stepped incautiously on a slippery water-worn boulder, and became thoroughly submerged in the water, which being from the heights above is icy cold, at least it seems so after one has been used to the heat of the tropics. This increased my discomfort, and poor Mr. Veitch was but little better. Here we were at dark lost and benighted beside the rocky declivities of this moun-tain stream; but there was no help for it; and after vainly trying to strike a path, we gave up at the base of

a large tree, and putting down our burdens, we resolved
to pass the night here. To mend matters, it commenced
to rain heavily about seven o'clock, and I am afraid we
were not so happy as the mere possession of health and
strength ought to have made us. We had no food
except a couple of wet biscuits and about half a glass of
brandy in a flask. These we shared, and perhaps they
were sweeter than the choicest viands would have tasted
had we been in dress clothes and in comfortable quarters.
Then Mr. Veitch had a great find in his bag—a couple
of cigars and a box of matches. Sitting in the smoking-
room of a comfortable club, or in the billiard-room at
home, one may smile at such a discovery; but, situated
as we were, cold and wet, a cigar added much to our
comfort. Our two followers tried to make a little shelter
from the rain for themselves, but failed miserably.

About ten o'clock the rain ceased, and we then tried
to improve our position; for hitherto all we could do
was to walk about around a large tree—a distance of a
few yards only; for in the darkness we knew not what
ugly falls might not await us if we strayed from our
wretched camping-ground, which was wet and spongy
under foot; and the leeches crawled up our legs and bled
us to their hearts' content. We noticed luminous fungi
on the rotten sticks at our feet glowing quite brightly,
and the effect was weird and ghostly in the extreme.
My "boy," quite by accident, had placed a couple of dry
flannel shirts, a pair of trowsers, and a blanket, in the
other man's basket, and so, after the rain ceased, I was
able to put on a dry warm shirt and trowsers, a luxury I
had not expected, and also to give Mr. Veitch a dry
shirt and a share of my rug. We now sat down on some
brushwood, and leaning back against the tree, fell asleep,
and we did not wake until near sunrise. Thus ended

one of the most dreary nights I ever spent in the Bornean woods.

In the morning we retraced our steps across the rocky stream, and soon struck the right path for Kiau, but we had not gone far before we met "Kurow," the chief of our runaway guides, in a great state of excitement, coming in search of us. He brought us some fine langsat fruit in his bag—presumably a peace offering—and seemed rather surprised that we did not chide him for his desertion of the day before. As we arrived nearer the village we came across our men, armed with muskets, also in search of us, and the hilltop was covered with Kiau people, who appeared greatly concerned, and doubtless glad to see us safe and well.

When we reached the house, everybody seemed glad to see our safe return, and sweet potatoes, maize, rice, and kaladi, were readily brought in by the villagers for ourselves and our men. "Musa" and the rest of our followers had arrived at Kiau soon after dark the night before. One man brought a basket of excellent langsat fruit, and a woman gave us two beautiful oranges from a tree near her door. They were quite yellow, with tender skins and sweet pulp, similar to those of the south of Europe, not green skinned, with tough desepiments, as are those of Labuan. I was much surprised at the oranges having grass-green skins when perfectly ripe in Singapore, and even the brittle skinned Mandarin variety had this peculiarity.

Our guide, "Kurow," was twitted pretty much by his neighbours for having left us the day before, and at last he retired to his house evidently not well pleased with himself, and, I believe, not a little surprised at our treating the matter so lightly.

We went out to a shady spot near the house to
examine our plants and see that they were in good
order, and we then rested all day. We were not altogether satisfied with our trip to the mountain, and
resolved to start off to it again in the morning, but
this time taking another path so as to reach the "Marie
Parie" spur. We sent off for "Kurow," and, telling
him our intentions, asked him to collect his followers
and be in readiness to accompany us. The poor fellow
was delighted at this sign of our confidence in him, and
helped us zealously, enduring cold, rain, and waiting—
to him meaningless, weary waiting—without a murmur.
In the morning we crossed the hill behind the village,
and fording the "Haya-Haya," "Dahombang," "Pino-
Kok," and "Kina Takie" streams, we reached the foot
of the "Marie Parie" spur.

Now came a climb up a rocky pathway, besides which
we noticed fine plants of *Cypripedium Petreianum, Cystorchis variegata,* and a lovely yellow flowered terrestrial orchid belonging to the genus *Spathoglottis,* but quite
distinct from *S. aurea.* As we ascended, our path lay up
through a belt oftall bamboos, and here two species of
nepenthes were seen. One was the long, green pitchered
kind, covered with purple blotches (*N. Boschiana var.
Lowii*), and the other a tall growing species, bearing
beautiful white pitchers, elegantly ewer-shaped, diapha-
nous like "egg shell" porcelain, and most daintily
blotched with reddish crimson in a way quite unlike
any other variety. This grew on both sides of the path,
and climbed the trees to a height of forty or fifty feet.
We reached the crest of the ridge about three o'clock, in
a heavy drenching shower, the climate being similar to
that of a warm autumn evening in a Devonshire wood.
We slept under some overhanging rocks at an elevation

of about 4,000 feet, having an under stratum of sticks and brushwood to keep our water-proof sheets off the wet ground. The air, even at this low elevation, was chilly during the night, and we found a fire and blankets acceptable comforts. *Melastoma macrocarpa*, bearing its large, rosy flowers, formed a large proportion of the brush around our camping ground. Here the large nepenthes were very fine; and a beautiful white flowered dendrobium grows among the bushes. It belongs to the nigro hirsute section, and has pseudo-bulbs five or six feet high. The blossoms are described by Mr. Low as being similar to those of *D. formosum giganteum*, but with a deep orange red blotch on the lip.

Just above our camping ground, the long, red, pitchered *Nepenthes Edwardsiana* was very beautiful, growing up through the low jungle, its pitchers contrasting with the tufts of rich green moss which draped trunks and branches everywhere. *N. Rajah* was also abundant; and we noticed some immense urns depending from its great broad leaves, far finer, indeed, than those found at 9,000 feet elevation, on the more southern spur. That distinct and curious fern, *Lindsaya Jamesonioides*, grew here and there in the chinks of the serpentine rock, and a long-leaved insect-catching sundew (*Drosera*) was common in most places among the stones and herbage.

After collecting what plants we desired, we had breakfast, and then commenced our return. We reached Kiau in about five hours, but some of our men did not come in until long after our arrival, as they had heavy loads to carry, and the clay paths were very slippery. At Kiau village, and on the slopes of the mountain itself, we spent eight days, and then came the weary march back to Gaya Bay, which, however, we accomplished in six days. When we reached the Datu's village, he gave us a fine goat, which our "boys" promptly slew for dinner, and, being young, it had a delicate mutton-like flavour, and we thought it a great treat after our hard fare.

A present of a revolver and some cartridges delighted our host; and the next morning, having obtained another boat, and loaded the one we had, we pulled to Pangeran Rau's place, where we hired a prahu, and two days afterwards reached Labuan safely.

During our journey to and from the mountain, we met occasional parties of natives from the far interior on their trading excursions, the women, as a matter of course, carrying the heaviest loads, while the men carried nothing, save a little food in a bag behind them, and their arms. Some had buffaloes with them. The women, as a class, are strong and healthy, with small hands and feet, and well-proportioned features—indeed, in many cases, the young girls are very pleasing in face and figure, and have lovely black hair, and the brightest of expressive black eyes. Early marriages, childbearing, hard labour, and exposure in the fields, however, soon make shrivelled leather-skinned old hags of them. Their drapery is nothing worth mentioning, and in such a climate but little is required. Their manners are gentle and dignified—often when we met them quite suddenly they showed no surprise, even though they had never seen a white man before. They make affectionate wives, and tender mothers—indeed, I never saw a child beaten or chided roughly during my stay in the island.

In the capital and elsewhere on the coast, young Malay women are almost invariably kept secluded from the gaze of strangers ; but here among these hills inland, as elsewhere among the aboriginals proper, we found the women enjoying perfect freedom with the men.

While staying at these villages, all the women and girls flocked to see us, and watched us eat and drink with evident interest. The young girls were especially confident, and formed laughing groups around us, chatting to each other in low, modulated tones, and evidently comparing notes on their observations. They frequently brought us little presents of fruit, and eggs, or fowls, and were delighted with the needles and thread, looking-glasses, and white cloth which we gave them in return. Some of the younger girls were much handsomer than the Malays, and stood lovingly together as they quizzed us, often resting their plump little arms or their cheeks on each other's necks or shoulders as they watched our every movement.

Looking-glasses were considered fashionable at the time of our visit, and we could have disposed of many more with advantage had we had them with us. Combs were not so desirable, since these are made by their husbands or sweethearts ; and they are often very prettily decorated with carved work.

Some of the men seem "thoroughly domesticated," and I saw them affectionately nursing their naked little babies at night, or in the daytime, while mamma had gone to the field for food, or the forest for fuel. I particularly noticed the younger married men standing behind their nice little wives at night when we were at dinner. They folded their brown arms around their necks, and whispered loving gossip into their ears, evidently well contented with themselves and with each other ; and, perhaps, their love is as real and as ardent and as true here as it is in high places where dress clothes are worn. The farther one travels, the more plainly

does one see how deep rooted and how world-wide are
all the springs of human feeling, whether of love and joy,
or death and sadness; in every land and in every breast
is written the great truth, "One touch of nature makes
the whole world kin."

One night after dinner a bevy of dusky beauties had
gathered around our mats, and to afford some amusement, I showed them several *carte de visite* portraits of
friends which I had with me. They were particularly
interested in that of one lady, and examined it very
attentively; not a bead or button escaped their quick
eyes; but they soon began asking questions. Was she
married? How many children had she? Was she a
good wife? I asked what they meant by the last question. "Well," they answered, "did she bring plenty
of firewood and kaladi in? and could she clean padi
(rice) well?" Thus a woman among these thrifty villagers earns her good name as a wife by her capacity
for physical labour. This is also so among other savage
races. The Indian girls on the north-west coast of
North America in like manner endeavour to excel each
other in the quantity of quamash (*Camassia esculenta*)
roots they collect, their fame as future good wives depending on their activity in the Quamash plains. They
were much interested in all particulars of dress as shown
by the *carte;* but one girl regretted the absence of rattan
coils around the stomach and "chawats" of thick brass
wire on the wrists, and more to the like effect, all from
the Kiau standpoint—for Kiau and its simple fashions
are held to be inviolable. Kiau is all the world to
them!

The morning we left, I believe all were sorry to part
with us, and they came to the top of the hill to see us
off. On loading our men, we found that we had four

men's loads of plants more than our men could carry, and so we engaged some of the Kiau villagers to carry them for us as far as Bawang. We had a good deal of talking, and a grand display of red cloth and brass wire on the hillside, but eventually "Musa" concluded the bargain, and paid over the goods in advance, as is the general custom here.

After receiving the goods, they coolly told us they should not go on with us, as we walked very slow, but that they would start next day, adding, that they should reach Bawang before we did. We showed no signs of wishing otherwise, but passed on with our followers, after having told the Kiau men to water the plants well as they crossed the streams, and to protect them from the sun by means of large leaves, all of which they did ; and when we reached Bawang, there, sure enough, were our plants, all safe and in good condition.

After reaching Labuan, both Mr. Veitch and myself had bad attacks of intermittent fever, the result of chilling exposure in wet clothes, and ill-cooked food, accompanied by more than ordinary exertions. Fortunately our long and difficult journey had been interrupted by nothing serious, and we were glad to see our native followers safe home again. Certainly one of them had a nasty fall from a rocky path near Bawang and cut his head badly, but he was a plucky Brunei man, and soon overgot his trouble. Another of our fellows who had been trusted with a musket tried to fire it off after he had blocked up the barrel by pushing it into the ground accidentally ! He succeeded in exploding the thing, and one of the fragments cut open his forehead, while another piece struck one of the bird-hunters on the arm. No serious damage was done. The road from Gaya Bay to Koung is so hilly and difficult for loaded men to traverse, that I determined

that if ever I went to Kina Balu again I would take the
Tampassuk route.	This I did on a subsequent occasion,
but during the wet season, when fording, the swollen rivers
presented great difficulties and dangers.	During the dry
season, or say, in January or February, this route would
be by far the best to follow.

CHAPTER VI.

LABUAN is one of the smallest and least well known of
all British Colonies.

This island was ceded to Great Britain by the Sultan of
Borneo in 1847, and the year afterwards a settlement was
established here, the late Sir James Brooke, K.C.B.,
being the first governor. Its area is 19,350 acres, and it
is situated in lat. 5° 20′ N., being about six miles off the
nearest point of Borneo, and about 700 miles from Singapore. When ceded it was uninhabited and very unhealthy.
but now contains about 5,000 inhabitants, mostly Kadyans and Malays, and by clearing and draining the
climate is improved. The principal traders and artificers
are Chinese. Chinese coolies are imported as labourers.
A few Klings or Bengalees also live here. The main
object of the colony was the suppression of piracy once
rife along the coast, and the working of the coal measures which exist at the northern point of the island.
The quality of the coal obtainable here is very good, but
the output hitherto has been comparatively small, owing
to a series of adverse circumstances. At present the

TANYONG KUBONG OR COAL POINT, LABUAN.

To face page 114.

mines are deserted, the company having discontinued mining operations. There is a good harbour at the only town, Victoria, and this place forms a convenient coaling station for H.M. gunboats on the China station, which cruise in these seas. The trade is mainly in the hands of the Chinese, who purchase the native products of Borneo, Palawan, and the Sulu Archipelago, which is brought hither in native prahus or boats. Some of the traders also make voyages to different parts of the Bornean coast to collect sago, gutta, beeswax, edible swallows' nests, camphor, trepang or beche de mer, mother-o'-pearl shell, and other produce, in return for which they barter cloth or cotton goods, opium and tobacco, muskets, ammunition, gongs, and crockeryware, spirits, tea and provisions, mostly derived from Singapore. The ss. " Cleator " carries the mails and most of the imports and exports between Singapore and this port, and affords the only regular means of transport. This vessel makes the voyage between Labuan and Singapore every twenty-one days, calling at this port on her way to Brunei.

The main industries of the colony are the coal-mines, sago-washing factories, and the culture of rice, fruit, and other food products. The mines were leased by the Government to the Oriental Coal Company of London and Leith, at a yearly rental of £1000 a year for mining privileges and the right of cutting timber free of duty. £50 annually was also paid for a wharf and store sheds at the harbour, a distance of nine miles from the mines. The coal was brought down in large sailing boats or lighters, manned by Malays. In 1876 only 5824 tons were obtained, but additional workings have been opened and alterations were made by the Company's manager, Mr. A. Boosie, which it was thought would have facilitated a much larger output. The greatest drawbacks to successful mining operations were the enormous rainfall and its effects on the workings, and the inefficiency of native labour. Chinese coolies have now, however, been to a great extent substituted for the Malays previously employed. The ships of H.M. Navy have a prior claim to coal at £1 0s. 6d. per ton, ordinary trading vessels pay a trifle more. The revenues of the Colony are derived from various monopolies, such as the sale of opium, tobacco, spirits, fish, arms, and ammunition, the rental or sale of lands, and a per centage on all timber cut in the Colony.

In 1876 the opium farmer paid £2,687 10s. for the exclusive right of importing, preparing, selling, or exporting opium in the island. Tobacco produced £750; spirits, £300; fishmarket, £550; pawnbroking, £112 10s.; licences to sell arms and ammunition, £65. A duty of ten per cent. is payable on the value of all timber cut on crown lands, except by the Coal Company, who, as already stated, have the right, free. The estimated acreage of the colony is 19,350 acres, of which 1,738 acres are supposed to be cultivatable, and 17,612 uncultivatable. Field labour, the felling of timber, &c., is carried on by Chinese and Malays, who receive 25 to 30 cents per day; carpenters, 50 cents; blacksmiths, 60 cents. The land under padi (rice) cultivation is about 11,000 acres, and consists of well watered alluvial plains near the centre of the island. Cocoanut palms and other fruit trees, 550 acres; sugarcane and vegetable gardens, about 50 acres. The Chinese here, as elsewhere eastward, monopolize the vegetable-growing industry. The largest cocoanut plantation and oil factory is on Pulu Daát, a large islet lying between Labuan and the Bornean coast. The total number of cocoanut trees in the colony is estimated at 200,000. The nuts, retail, either green or ripe, fetch two or three cents each, and the oil obtained from them fetches the uniform price of £33 per ton. A young plantation of the African oil-palm (*Elæis guineensis*) has been established on Pulu Daát, and the experiment promises to be a successful one. The little coarse un-crystallised sugar made in the colony fetches about 50 cents per gantang, a measure holding about 7lb. Padi, or rice in husk, fetches about £1 10s. per 100 gantangs (6 cwts.). There are three sago washing works near Victoria Harbour, where the raw pulp, as brought from the Bor-nean coast, is hand-washed and sifted into the dry sago-flour of commerce. Some of the low-lying well watered or marsh-land has been planted with the sago-palm.

A new fishmarket has been erected, and this building, together with the right of buying and selling all the fish caught, is let annually to the highest bidder with the other farms. No regular fisheries are organised, nor is any record kept of the quantity and description of fish supplied. It is estimated at about 1000 piculs. In the capture of fish along the coast, seine nets and "kelongs" or bamboo traps are used. In deep water a baited hook and line.

An oil-spring exists in the forest, near the mines, at an elevation of 130 feet above the sea, the yield during wet season being about 12 gallons of petroleum every twenty-four hours. The highest land in the island is Bukit Kalám, 280 feet above sea level. The total area in scrubs and fern is 1000 acres, timber or forest about 300 acres. The quit-rents on lands sold for 999 years produce about £230 annually. It not being consi-dered advisable to alienate any further crown lands at present on account of the low prices obtainable, the Government rice lands are let annually for prices varying from two to four shillings per acre. The edible fruits cultivated are fine oranges of several kinds, excellent

pomoloes, Durian, mangoes, tarippe, rambutan, jack fruit
and champada, rose apples (jambosa), cocoanuts, mangosteen, rambi, bananas in variety, limes, guava, papaw,
cashew nut, and several others, including the bread-fruit,
baloonas, mambangan. The total revenue in 1877 was
£7,490, the expenditure being £7,995. Imports, total
value, £126,594, exports £112,996. Cattle and ponies
are cheap—thus, good cows are worth £2 to £4 each;
Shanghai sheep, £1 to £2; goats, 10s. each; ponies, £4
to £10. These last are imported from the Sulu Islands.
Water buffaloes are generally used as draught animals,
and are worth from £4 to £6 each.

The whole island is tolerably flat, and at one time
was entirely covered with forests, yielding fine timber.
Of late years, however, jungle fires have been frequent
during the dry season; and at the present time but little
old forest remains. The climate is now generally supposed to be drier and more healthy than formerly; but
the flora has suffered much, many orchids and other rare
plants, formerly found here in abundance, being now
quite extinct. After the rains a lovely little blue burmannia (*B. cœlestis*), and a tiny sundew become very pretty
on the plains. Yellow flowered xyrids and eriocaulons
grace the wet ditches, and the orange orchards are
redolent with perfume, the trees being then in bloom,
and at night the gardens are illuminated with fire-flies.

I resided for some time in a house which had been
occupied by Mr. Hugh Low, the garden and fruit orchard
of which afforded the most delightful walks morning and
evening. I never saw the elk's-horn fern (*Platycerium
grande*) so luxuriant anywhere as it was on the boles of
some large orange-trees here. The barren fronds were
broad, like the horns of the giant Irish elk; and the
more slender fertile ones drooped on all sides from the

base of the nest formed by the leafy expansions.   I
measured some of these fertile fronds, and found them
fully seven feet in length.   These splendid ferns (one of

ELK'S-HORN FERN.

which is here represented in my sketch), and the choicest
of epiphytal orchids, which had been planted among the
branches of the trees, made a walk amongst them most
enjoyable.   I thought at the time I should never like to

see orchids, and other rare exotics stewed up in a glass shed again, after seeing them thus luxuriant in the open air.

The flowering trees, many of which have been introduced into the gardens, are very lovely a week or two after the rains. *Poinciana regia,* two or three species of cassia, and *Lagerstrœmia regina,* and *L. indica,* with white lilac or rosy flowers, are common. Different kinds of jasmines, ixoras, and hibiscus flower freely nearly all the year, as also does *Thunbergia laurifolia,* which drapes trees, and fences, the fire-blossomed pomegranate, the fragrant oleander; there are also pools filled with the sunshade-like leaves and rosy flowers of the Sacred Lotus, the beauty of which rivals even the celebrated Lotus pools of Japan. One or two honey-suckles and *Jasminum grandiflorum* form tangled masses in the hedges, the pearly flowers of *Pancratium zeylanicum* spring up from the grass, sheltered here and there by caladium leaves, and a scarlet hippeastrum forms glowing masses in old gardens, and on waste places where houses have once been situated.

Where many indigenous plants have died out, this hippeastrum has become naturalised: the light sandy soil and hot sun seem to suit its requirements; and it increases so freely, that a barrow-load of bulbs might be dug from a square yard of earth. Another introduced plant, perfectly naturalised here, as also in Penang and Singapore, is the dwarf and acrid *Isotoma longiflora,* which bears snowy-white long-tubed flowers. The purple-flowered "Mudar" (*Calotropis gigantea*), and the glorious mauve wreaths of *Bougainvillea spectabilis,* are in places very beautiful. The climate is hot, especially during the dry season; but about five o'clock P.M., when the land breeze sets in, it is cool and agreeable.

Mangoes, especially the fine Manilla varieties, and pomoloes, grow well in the gardens and orchards, as also do oranges of various kinds. The soil is so poor, however, that in order to obtain fine fruit, it is necessary to keep a herd of cattle, and to fold them at night, for the sake of a good supply of manure. Where the trees are planted on the grass, a circle beneath each is cultivated with the " chunkal," or heavy iron hoe ; and this is regularly manured and watered. It is quite usual to see the boles of mango and some other fruit trees gashed with blows from a chopper at intervals, an operation analagous to the ringing or strangulation formerly practised in English gardens before root-pruning came into fashion. This is done to induce the trees to bear fruit earlier, and more abundantly.

There is only one species of bird endemic, a lively black and white one (*Copsychus amœnus*), which frequents gardens near the bungalows, and sings very sweetly during wet weather ; indeed, it was the only Eastern song bird which reminded me of our dappled thrush at home. Of eagles and fish hawks there are several species. Tern are seen in flocks on neighbouring sand-banks. Golden plover and snipe abound on the plain near the shore, and there two or three sand pipers and rails. The white crane, or " padi bird," is common ; and the long-pinioned frigate bird wheels overhead, far out of gun-shot, diving now and then into the sea after food with wonderful velocity. The mellow whistle of the mino bird is one of the most familiar sounds of the forest, especially when the fruit of the wild figs ripen, and then white, large blue, and pretty little green tree pigeons of many kinds appear, attended by flocks of glossy, red-eyed starlings.

The " chuck, chuck " of the goat-sucker (*Caprimulgus*

macrurus) is one of the most familiar sounds during moonlight nights. At daybreak the chatter of the Java sparrows
assures one of its being high time to rise. Cuming's
mound bird (*Megapodius Cumingi*) is found in **Labuan,**
but is more common on the islets of **Kuraman,** where its
nests are met with in mounds of earth, three to four feet
in height, and twelve feet in circumference.

Even the Nicobar pigeon visits this island; and a
solitary hoopoo was shot there during my visit. Two
species of great beaked hornbills inhabit the forest; and
there are three or four species of swallows. One of the
prettiest of all the small birds is a long-tailed green and
brown fly-catcher, which might easily be mistaken for a
swallow, so swift and graceful is its flight. A large
red kingfisher (*Halcyon caromanda*), found here, builds
its nest in a peculiar manner, as described by Mr. Sharpe,
in Proc. Zool. Soc., 1879, part ii., p. 331:—

"The nest is said to be pendulous, and invariably to
be accompanied in the same mass by a bee, which is
peculiarly vicious, so that the nest can only be robbed
after destroying the bees."

The interior of the island is flat and marshy; and
here the soil being deep and alluvial, it is well adapted
for rice; and the wet patches beside the streams suit the
sago palm well. In the patches of low jungle beside the
roads three or four species of pitcher plants abound,
rooting into the wet, sandy peat earth, and climbing up
the shrubby undergrowth in the most luxuriant and
graceful manner. These nepenthes stems are wonderfully tough, and are used as withes, and as a substitute
for rattan cane in tying fence timbers together. More
rarely they are used in basket-work. The kinds most
common in Labuan are *N. gracilis*, several varieties,
N. nivea, and *N. ampullaria*. There are five or six species

of terrestrial orchids ; and from trees on Dr. Ley's estate
plants of the new genus astrostruma (*A. spartiodes,* Benth.)
were gathered for the first time.

Alligators infest the streams, and shallow sea, near the
town of Victoria; and now and then a native is carried
off. One of these large brutes actually tried to carry
off a pony one night during my stay. Snakes are plentiful. A deadly green snake is common on the Bird
Island, just off the mouth of the harbour, and great
brown rock snakes abound. One night a Kling man
brought a black snake, six feet long, tied to a stick,
which he said he had caught up a cocoa-nut tree, and
added that it had just swallowed a bird. It was purchased ; and in the morning, when it was being skinned,
the " boy " came to say that it had young ones inside it.
This we did not believe; and, on going to see it, we
found that the " young one " was a snake, two feet
long, of another species, very common in the island,
which had been swallowed head foremost, as usual, and
was in part digested. The large snake was so fat, that
hunger could not have prompted it to swallow a smaller
brother ; and so I more than suspect that Malaysia can
now boast of a snake-eating snake, as well as British
India, whence one of these cannibals, the *ophiophagus,*
was introduced to the Zoological Gardens a few years
ago.

A large boa, ten to twenty feet long, and as thick as
one's arm, is common in the jungle, and often commits
depredations amongst badly-housed poultry, as also does
the iguana. A singular sluggishness characterised all
the snakes I saw ; and as many of those said to be deadly
by the natives rest on the trees, rather than on the
ground, this may account for the extreme rarity of
death from snake-bites in this part of the East.   A

slender green species, nearly six feet in length, infests the fig-trees when in fruit; and, twisting its tail around a branch, it coils itself up ready to spring at any bird unwary enough to venture sufficiently close. One of these I saw shot; and it had a double row of hooked fangs in its wide set jaws, admirably adapted to hold anything once within its grasp.

Perhaps the most lovely and interesting of all, however, are the sun-birds, which are here in the East the representatives of the true humming-birds of the Western tropics. " They are ethereal, gay, and sprightly in their movements, flitting briskly from flower to flower, and assuming a thousand lovely and agreeable attitudes. As the sunbeams glitter on their bodies, they sparkle like so many precious stones, and exhibit at every turn a variety of bright and evanescent hues. As they hover around the honey-laden blossoms, they vibrate their tiny pinions so rapidly, as to cause a slight whirring sound, but not so loud as the humming noise produced by the true humming birds. Occasionally they may be seen clinging by their feet and tail busily engaged in rifling the blossoms of the trees. I well remember a certain dark-leaved tree with scarlet flowers, that especially courted the attention of the sun-birds; and about its blossoms they continually darted with eager and vivacious movements. With this tree they seemed particularly delighted, clinging to the slender twigs, and coquetting with the flowers, thrusting in their slender curved beaks, and probing with their brush-like tongues for insects and nectar, hanging suspended by their feet, throwing back their little glossy heads, chasing each other on giddy wing, and flirting and twittering, the gayest of the gay. Some were emerald-green, some vivid violet, and others yellow, with a crimson wing."

Sir Jas. Emerson Tennent describes them as being common in Ceylon, where they frequent the gardens, and rifle the blossoms of the passifloras, and other flowers; at other times searching for small insects and spiders, and again pluming themselves, and warbling their pleasing songs on the pomegranate-trees. " If two happened to come to the same flower—and from their numbers this has often occurred—a battle always ensued, which ended in the vanquished bird retreating from the spot with shrill piping cries, while the conqueror would take up his position upon a flower or stem, and swinging his little body to and fro, till his coat of burnished steel gleamed and glistened in the sun, pour out his song of triumph." The rich plumage of the dainty little male birds is only seen during the breeding season, after which they moult, and are as unattractive as their mates. Two tiny eggs are laid in a wee nest, which is suspended from a twig, or sometimes the stout web of a large spider is made to bear the little shelter for eggs and young.

The spiders in the jungle, and old buildings of the East, are numerous; and some are of an alarming size, but of beautiful colours. One large, black, yellow-spotted species measures six or eight inches across its extended legs, and its web is held in position by grey lines, almost as stout as fine sewing-cotton, and strong enough to pull one's hat off. It is a very disagreeable sensation to feel them across one's face, as often happens in a little used jungle-path. Ants are particularly plentiful; and the white termites throw up mounds of red earth, five or six feet in height, and often do much damage by burrowing into the piles of houses, and other buildings. The species of ants vary much in size. One is a tiny red fellow, but little larger than a cheesemite, and scarcely visible; others are black, their bodies being an inch in length. Some species bite very sharp if disturbed, as I found to my cost, when scrambling about over the branches of trees after orchids, and other plants. There is one species of nepenthes (*N. bical-carata*), having large red urns, the stalks of which are invariably perforated by a species of ant; and I found a flowering shrub on the Tawaran river, the stems of which were swollen and hollow just below the flower-heads, this being due to the punctures of ants; a remarkably curious gouty-stemmed plant, parasitical on low jungle-trees in Labuan—myrmecodia—actually depends for its existence on the bite of a species of ant. The seed germinates on the bark of the foster-tree; and when the seedling has attained a certain height, the growth ceases, and it remains stationary, until the necessary bite is given, when the stem swells out at the base, and leaves and flowers are produced in due course. If not thus punctured, the young plant dies. The gouty or swollen stem is hollow, and forms a refuge for the ants, which in their turn may afford it some needful protection, since they rush out boldly to attack trespassers who disturb the tree on which their fostered-shelter plant grows.

One day, as I emerged from the forest on the western shore of the island, I came across a young Kadyan engaged in making salt. The process, as carried out by him, was very simple. A heap of drift wood is collected, and of this a fire is made, so as to secure a good supply of ashes. The ashes are placed in a small tub, and sea-water is filtered through them, so as to catch up whatever salt they contain. It now remains for the water to be evaporated, so as to leave the salt. To this end evapo-rating-pans, or rather receptacles, are neatly made from the sheaths of the nebong palm, fastened into shape by slender wooden skewers. Two logs are then laid parallel to each other, and a foot or fifteen inches apart, and over these the pans are placed close together, so as to form a rude kind of flue, in the which a fire of light brushwood is lighted, and very soon afterwards the salt may be observed falling to the bottom of the evaporators. It was a very hot morning, and the heat in the close forest where I had been exploring was so intense, that I was thankful to reach the coast and feel the delicious breezes which came from the open sea. The beach to the westward of the island is mainly of firm yellow sand, but here and there paved more or less thickly with honeycombed coral rocks and pebbles. The outer edge of the old forest nearest the shore is fringed with tall casuarina trees, here called " Kayu Aru." The Malays have some legends connected with this tree, and can rarely be induced to cut it down, although the tough light timber is well suited for some particular purposes.

Under a group of these trees a large company of Kadyans were encamped, and busily engaged making " Pratchan." This is a reddish product made of prawns. Some of the men were out in canoes just beyond the shallow reefs catching the tiny fish, while others and the women and girls were preparing them on shore. The fish are jammed up in troughs formed of hollow trunks of trees by beating wooden pestles, and when finished resembles a stiff red paste, which is afterwards packed in circular palm-leaf bags or baskets for the Chinese markets. Some of the fish were being dried by being spread out in the sun on mats. They were bright as burnished silver, and in flavour reminded one of whitebait. The price of the red paste, or prepared " Pratchan," is about three dollars per picul, and the dried article fetches ten or twelve cents per gantang. Their encampment of yellow palm-leaf mats and bamboo poles formed a pretty rural scene beneath the tall trees which overhung the yellow sands, and the dusky limbs and faces, and the bright-coloured "sarongs" worn by the women of the party, added much to the picturesque view as seen beneath a blue and cloudless sky. I and Mr. A. Cook visited the oil springs, which are situated in a shady glade in the forest two or three miles from the coal-mines. All the evidence of the old borings we saw was an old door and a rude trough, into which the oil-surfaced water rises as it wells up slowly from the rocks below. No use is now made of this oil, except by the Kadyans and other natives, who utilise it now and then in the manufacture of torches. The odour of the oil is distinctly perceptible near the spring, and the oil itself covers the surface of the little stream as it flows seawards. Before the spring was reached we passed through an open clearing of a hundred of acres or more covered with grass, on which a few milch cattle belonging to some of the Kling residents were grazing. We were surprised in one place to come across an old garden, of several acres in extent, containing mango, banana, and other fruit trees, with here and there native huts, houses, and rice-barns all going to decay. A Kadyan, who overtook us just before we entered the forest, told us it was an old village belonging to his tribe, adding that they had abandoned it after their headman had died there. It is by no means unusual to find localities abandoned in this way in Borneo owing to the death of the principal man in the village, and when the rotten old palm-thatched houses have been eaten up by the luxuriant jungle which springs up around, the fruit-trees prosper and serve to mark the localities of former villages long after they themselves have vanished for ever.

Here, as elsewhere in warm climates, the mosquito is of all animals the smallest and most troublesome to the weary traveller. Large moths flutter about the ceilings, especially on cold wet nights, and insect life of many kinds is attracted to the lamplight. In every house there is a colony of lively little drab-coloured lizards. They run very nimbly up the sides of the room and on the ceiling, keeping a sharp look-out the while for their supper of moths and flies. The Malays have a proverb, " That even a lizard gives the fly time to pray." This has been derived from the peculiar manner in which this tiny Saurian " goes for " its quarry. On seeing a fly it darts at it swiftly, but when within an inch or two off it suddenly stops itself and pauses several seconds ere the fatal spring is made and the fly seized. Now and then the lizards lose their hold of the ceiling and come on the table with a " flop," but this is a rare occurrence. One of the most common and interesting of the domestic insects is the " mason wasp," a large yellow species which constructs a series of mud cells or a gallery of earth against the woodwork of the verandah or roof. In each cell, as completed, an egg is deposited, and ere closing up the cavity it is stuffed full of green caterpillars, which are then sealed up alive to serve as food for her larva when hatched out. The big black carpenter bees are also often seen examining the woodwork of the house or verandah, and on finding a piece in suitable condition they bore a clean hole into it in which to deposit their eggs. These two insects are highly interesting—a mason and a carpenter—and both do " worke moste excellently well." Native houses and gardens are dotted pretty freely about the island, and there are some interesting

K

walks. I was enabled to explore the island pretty well, in which work the Hon. Dr. Leys very kindly assisted me by the loan of his favourite horse "Joseph." This animal was the most gentle and tractable creature imaginable, and admirably accustomed to jungle travelling, since he would go anywhere among trees or bushes, and

MASON WASP.

might be trusted to stand quietly if tied; or he would follow one like a dog if loose. He was of Australian breed, and had his faults too. At the "whish" of a whip or stick he was inclined to bolt, and once threw me pretty heavily when frightened in that way. Another trick he had was to stop suddenly at any place where he had turned off the road, or had been tied before, and as he would stop short or turn off thus suddenly when at full gallop, the consequences which sometimes resulted from such freaks may be readily imagined. With all his

vagaries, however, he was a sleek and loveable creature ;
and I once saw the little daughter of the Doctor's Malay
syce or groom lift up one of his hind legs when in the
stable, at the same time telling her little group of dusky
playfellows how very vicious he was (eine kudah jahat—
jahat banyiak skali, etu lah !). "Joseph" was the
swiftest animal in the island, and rigorously excluded

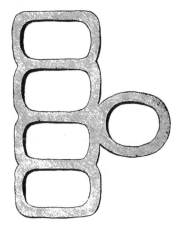

SECTION OF ITS NEST.

from competing at the races held on the plain by the
shore every New Year's Day. These annual races and
sports are much appreciated both by Europeans and
natives, and they afford the only general holiday in which
both natives and Europeans mingle during the year.

The native canoe races in the harbour are a speciality,
the Malays and Brunei men being here seen in their
native element. The "tug of war" between Malays and
Chinese is also an amusing feature, while all are interested in the performance of the ponies and in the

European athletic sports. A palm-thatched erection beneath the casuarina trees, near Ramsay Point, does duty as a grand stand and refreshment bar, and from the slight elevation, it affords an excellent view of the dusky but smiling faces and parti-coloured costumes of the natives and Chinese. All the native beauties are present, and glimpses of bright expressive eyes, coal-black hair secured with silver pins, and brilliant sarongs beneath neat cool-looking sacques meet one at every turn. Here and there the sparkle of jewellery and the glitter of bangles meet the eye, and on all sides the lavish display of pearly teeth and the ripple of merry laughter is seen and heard. A dinner at Government House, to which almost all the Europeans in the island, or from the gunboat which may happen to be in harbour, are invited, winds up this gala day of the opening year.

There is a neat little wooden church here on the hill behind Government House, and there is a service once or twice every third year, when the Lord Bishop of Sarawak visits this part of his diocese. From some of the elevated portions of the island beautiful views are obtainable, with the blue mountains of Borneo towering skywards in the distance ; and from the verandah of the manager's house at the coal-mines at the northern end of the island, Kina Balu may be seen quite plainly at sunrise and sunset during clear weather ; and although more than a hundred miles away, its topmost crags stand out clear and sharp, and are tinged with the most beautiful tints of purple and gold by the rising or the setting sun.

It was from Labuan that my visits to the Bornean coast and to Sulu were made. Some of these adventurous wanderings were pleasant, others the reverse. The following is a short account of a boat journey made by myself and Mr. Peter Veitch, its object being to obtain pitcher plants (*Nepenthes bicalcarata*), *Burbidgea nitida*, *Pinanga Veitchii*, *Cypripedium Lawrenceanum*, and other beautiful fine-foliaged plants and orchids :—

"Towards the noon of a hot day in January 1878 —a day hot even for the tropics—two Veitchian travellers in North-western Borneo, with their native contingent of guides, boatmen, and carriers, were descending one of the most lovely of all the rivers in the island. The water was clear and smooth—so clear and so smooth that the great nipa leaves, which arched gracefully out from the banks and laved their ends in the stream, were reflected in the water as clearly as if in a mirror. The boatmen were in good spirits, for there was but little work for their paddles, so they chewed their betel-nut and limed pepper leaves contentedly, or rolled up a little tobacco, cigarette-like, in wrappers made of the young leaves of *Nipa fruticans*, and smoked in a silence only broken by low laughter and sentences murmured in the most musical of tongues. The river banks were clothed with forest trees, as also was the rising ground behind, and where the river was shallow mangrove trees, thickly interlaced, took the place of the big fruited nipa. On the lower trees near the fringe of the forest cœlogynes, dendrobes, bolbophyllums, and other orchids—not often beautiful as that word is too often understood—clothed the branches ; the tiny *Davallia parvula*, *D. heterophylla*, and *D. pedata*—all modest little species of ferns—were also seen on tree trunks or on rocks, and on the outer branches far overhead *Platycerium biforme* made itself a home, its fertile fronds drooping four or five feet below the cluster of barren ones. For company, but never at so great a height, varieties of *Neottopteris nidus avis*, or an allied species, were seen forming nests of glossy broadly strap-shaped fronds often of great length. Of

palms the 'Nebong' (*Oncosperma filamentosum*) and the
unique red-stemmed 'Malawarin' (which long defied
Eastern collectors who wished to introduce it to Europe)
were most beautiful. The former produces an excellent
'cabbage,' as good as seakale when well cooked, and its
old stems are generally employed as piles by the Malays,
who almost always erect ther palm-thatched 'atap'
houses over the water of river or sea.

"Bird-life generally was dozing—the birds were enjoying
their noontide siesta in the shady trees. The handsome
Bornean pheasants, the 'Argus,' the 'Fireback,' and
the 'Bulwer' with its pure snowy tail of blackcock-like
shape, were alike unseen and unheard. Now and then
the deep rich and mellow whistle of the 'Mino' bird or
Javanese 'Grackle' reached us, and a whole colony of
large blue, and of pretty little greyish green, yellow-
winged pigeons—Carpophagi—were surprised on a fig
tree in fruit as the canoe shot around a sudden bend in
the stream. Of the seven or eight species of hornbills
known to inhabit these groves we saw not one—indeed
our view of the birds would have been but meagre but
for the apparition of a black darter with only its head or
neck above the water, in which attitude its resemblance
to a snake is well nigh perfect. A few kingfishers braved
the sun and flitted alongside the nipa leaves, or flew
rapidly across stream like clusters of jewels endowed with
life and motion. Scarcely a sound disturbed the quietude
and beauty of such a tropical scene, except that now and
then for no very apparent reason the boatmen made a
spurt with their paddles, any little extra exertion in this
way being often accompanied by a plaintive song in
chorus—melody in perfect keeping with a wildly natural
albeit lovely spot. At one well-remembered bend of the
glassy stream the men had been directed to stop awhile,

and a few dexterous strokes of the paddle on the part of a handsome young Kadyan man named ' Moumein,' who acted as steersman, sent the canoe beneath the arching nipa plumes to a bare spot where it was possible to land. The wet branches of a low mossy tree were covered with the elegant little *Davallia parvula,* among which grew a cirrhopetalum only about two inches in height, and bearing little purple flowers in semi-circular whorl-like tufts at the apices of tiny scapes. On sandstone rocks near at hand the handsome *Dipteris Horsfieldii* was abundant, its stout rhizomes creeping over the nearly bare wet rock, and adhering so firmly by its tiny rootlets that it was difficult to displace.* Above one's head grew the great glossy green umbrella-like fronds, borne aloft on stipes varying from two to eight feet in length. Truly a noble fern—alas ! how difficult to cultivate. At the time I lived in the locality in which it is found in the utmost luxuriance, I read of the plant being exhibited in London and elsewhere, but each successive report of it unfortunately recorded its decadence. This and the glorious *Matonia pectinata*—also Bornean, although first found together with our old friends *Cypripedium barbatum, Nepenthes sanguinea,* and *Rhododendron jasminiflorum,* on Mount Ophir, in Malacca—are two of the most noble of all ferns, rivalling the palms indeed in stately beauty and substance of frond-tissue. How unfortunate, then, is it that both so persistently resist the efforts alike of collectors and cultivators. As one of the two travellers beforementioned I had previously visited the spot where we had

---

* On mountains in Borneo above 7000 feet a form of *Dipteris Horsfieldii* grows freely among dacrydiums, droseras, dianella, dawsonia superba, a tiny umbellifer, and other Australian types. It is dwarf, rarely above two feet high, with glaucous leathery and brittle fronds, almost silvery below.

now landed, and after a long walk through the tall forests, which are carpeted in moist places and near streams by lovely steel-blue aspleniums and lindsayas, and also by the freshest and most luxuriant of selaginellas, had, after ascending a sloping and rather dry hillside, come upon a plant which I saw at a glance was zingiberaceous, but it was so distinct in port and flower to anything that I had previously seen that I sent roots of it to Chelsea, and a few of these fortunately survived. Its fate was not known to us at the time we again visited the spot, and so the object in again running the canoe among the nipa plumes at this place was to obtain a fresh supply. I shall long remember this second journey to collect *Burbidgea nitida,* since I was ill with fever at the time, and on Mr. Peter Veitch devolved the duty of a long tramp through the tall forest; past numerous felled gutta-yielding trees (*Isonandra sp. ?*), and up the hill slope beyond, until just below the rocky summit, this plant is found at a place called the 'Devil's House' ('*Satan punya ruma*') where are some dark deep holes in the face of perpendicular rocks, frequented by the swallows which build the edible nests so highly valued by the rich Chinese. The burbidgea grows on low wet sandstone boulders, on which their rhizomes and roots form a perfect mat, and among the plants as thus elevated decayed leaves and other forest *débris* is blown by winds or washed by rains. Although growing in rich shady forest, and subjected to a heavy rainfall, and high, albeit fresh and often windy atmosphere, the plants rarely exceed a yard in height. To this place Mr. Veitch went with a body of trusty natives, and many bundles of the plants were brought back, some of them fine masses of twenty or thirty stems, each having recently borne a large cluster of its rich, orange-coloured flowers.

" While Mr. Veitch was away, my Chinese boy, ' Kim-jeck,' got out the cooking utensils to prepare dinner on the shore, and the men who stayed behind amused themselves by looking for flowers (' cheri bunga ') in the low forest and on the sandstone rock near our landing-place. I had to lie in the boat beneath the awning, feeling very sick, and with a splitting headache—feverish symptoms which all travellers in tropical forests alike must suffer. I was just dozing off to sleep when I heard much yelling, and my boy, who had joined the men, returned down the jungle path at full speed, shouting ' Ular! Ular! Tuan! Sayah mow etu snapang lakas skali! ' ' Trima kasi! ' he ejaculated, as he snatched my gun and disappeared with the agility of a young goat. The gist of the matter was, he had seen a snake and was off to shoot it. After listening for ten minutes to the most deafening shouts and yells, mingled with many ejaculations of advice and caution, and the reports of both barrels echoing through the forest, I was rather disappointed to see them return with a small snake, not larger than the English viper. On my expressing my surprise, and observing that, by the noise, I thought it was a snake big enough to swallow a buffalo, the men all agreed that what it lacked in size was amply compensated for by its fatal bite —or, as they expressed it, ' if that snake bit a man he need not trouble about food any more, as he would have no time to pray.'

" The Muruts have a great love for gong music; and now and then a cheap German gun, or old Tower musket, is obtained from Chinese traders. Spears, blow-pipes, krisses or parongs (swords), and their ghastly baskets of human skulls, form their only accumulated wealth. These heads are used to ornament their dwellings at their periodical seasons of feasting, and when illumi-

nated by the flickering glare of ' dammar ' gum torches
the effect is melodramatic in the extreme.   It was rather
difficult to make any use of these Muruts as collectors—
they showed no powers of discrimination whatever, while
the Kadyans, on the other hand—who are also aboriginals, but have mixed much with the dominant Malays, by
whom they were years ago converted to the faith of Islam
—showed great aptitude, and were of real service ; and I
shall long retain pleasant memories of some of the Kadyan
villagers, especially ' Moumein,' of Meringit, who received
me into the little village he had founded with every de-
monstration of friendship, and rendered me much intelligent assistance for many weeks.   Of Malays generally one
may say that they live by lying and thieving in one form
or another, but the aboriginal races of Borneo, like the
Papuans whom Goldie met inland in New Guinea, are
gentle and hospitable to peaceably disposed strangers,
and it will be a great pity to see them exterminated in
the way their prototypes, the Incas of Peru, and the Red
Men of the West, have been."

CHAPTER VII.

BEAUTIFUL BORNEO.

Borneo—Wild animals—the Malays—Poetry—Romances—Dewa Indra
—Native government—Pile dwellings—Intermarriage—Language—
Clothing — Courtship — Marriage — Inland tribes—Land culture—
Native villages—Food products—Textile fabrics—Bark cloth—Native
women — Climate — Native produce— Kayan weapon — Rivers—
Gambling—Opium smoking.

BORNEO, the beautiful—the "garden of the sun"—is
the third largest island in the world, and boasts a much
larger area than that occupied by the British Isles. The
equator divides it, and the climate is, perhaps, that most
suitable for vegetation of any other, being uniformly hot
and humid all the year round. There are no volcanoes,
the tiger is unknown, and it is the only habitat of the
wild elephant in the Malay Archipelago. It is also remarkable as being the home of the wild man of the
forests, or the "orang utan" of the Malays. Alligators
abound in the rivers, and are the most dangerous of the
wild animals. Snakes exist plentifully, and in great
variety, but death from snake-bites is very rare. The
two-horned rhinoceros, wild cattle, pigs in abundance,
and several species of deer are known.

The human inhabitants may be roughly divided into
two races, the Malays and the Borneans, or aboriginals.
The origin of both types is obscure. The Malays, however, are immigrants who inhabit the coasts of all the
large Malay islands where, as here in Borneo, they have

long held the dominant power. Some believe them to have originally been the descendants of Arabs who settled in the Celebes long before the Dutch became rulers in these seas, and this view gains some support from the fact of the Arabic character being used in writing, and their titles as Sultan, hadji, and sherrif, are of Arabic origin. They all profess Islam. The Bornean Malays may be said to have but little literature : the Koran, a few MS. poems, prayers, and tales are the only books generally seen in the island; but the people possess a vast amount of traditional lore, and many of their songs refer to the history of the country, the beauty of their women, or to the personal attributes and prowess of their former rulers.

The following may be taken as a fair sample of Malayan poetry, and was originally published in the *Asiatic Journal.* Many of the tales and legends of the Malays are in blank verse, with a good many repetitions; and choruses, are extremely popular, as also are extemporaneous vocal performances :—

> " Cold is the wind, the rain falls fast,
> I linger, though the hour is past.
> Why come you not ? whence this delay !
>   Have I offended—say ?

> " My heart is sad and sinking too ;
> Oh ! break it not ! it loves but you !
> Come, then, and end this long delay,
>   Why keep you thus away !

> " The wind is cold, fast falls the rain,
> Yet weeping, chiding, I remain,
> You come not still—you still delay !
>   Oh, wherefore can you stay !"

Malayan romances and minstrelsy are alike rich in imagery, as the following examples from Marsden's Malay Grammar will suffice to show :—

PASSAGES EXTRACTED FROM A RO-
MANCE, CONTAINING THE ADVEN-
TURES OF INDRA LAKSANA, MA-
HADEWA, AND DEWA INDRA.

PŬNGUTIB SAGALA REMAH DERI-
PADA HIKAYAT INDRA LAKSANA,
DAN INDRA MAHADEWA DAN
DEWA INDRA.

" THE prince then smiling (at
the defiance sent by the enemy)
went to soothe the affliction of his
wife, and addressed her thus : ' O
my love, thou who art to me the
soul of my body, farewell ! If perchance it should be thy husband's
doom to fall (in the approaching
battle), wilt thou cherish the memory of him with some degree of
fond concern ?   Wilt thou wrap
him in the scarf that binds thy
waist ? Wilt thou bathe his corpse
with thy tears pure as the dew
that hangs at the extremity of the
grass ? Wilt thou bestrew it with
the flowers which now adorn the
folds of thy hair ? '   The princess
upon this wept the more abundantly, and embraced the neck of
Indra Laksana, her arm enfolding
it as the muskscented epidendrum
entwines the *angsuka* tree (Pavetta
indica).   Such was the picture
she exhibited, whilst *Indra* wiped
away the tears from her eyes."

" MAKA baginda pun tŭrsŭnyum
sŭraya pŭrgi mŭmbujok istrinya
itu, katanya, ' adoh adinda ting-
gallah tuan nyawa dan badan kakŭnda, jikalau kakŭnda mati kŭlak,
maka tuan kŭnangkanlah kasih
sayang kakŭnda yang sŭdikit itu,
dan tuan slimutilah kakŭnda dŭngan kain yang dipinggang tuan
itu, dan tuan mandikanlah mayat
kakŭnda dŭngan ayer mata tuan
yang sa'pŭrti ŭmbon yang dihujong
rumpot juga adanya.   Dan tabori-
lah mayat kakŭnda dŭngan bunga
yang dalam sangol tuan itu.' Maka
tuan pŭtri itupon makin sangatalah
iya mŭnangis sŭraya mŭmŭlok leher
Indra Laksana.   Adapun tangan
tuan pŭtri mŭmŭlok itu sapŭrti
gadong kasturi yang mŭlilit pohon
angsuka itu dŭmkianlah rupanya,
maka sŭgralah disapunya ulih Indra Laksana ayer matanya tuan
pŭtri itu."

" UPON the arrival of *Indra Mahadewa* at the palace, he seated
himself by the side of the princess
(his bride) and said to her, smiling,
' My love, my soul, what manner
is it your intention to dispose of
yourself, as I am obliged to proceed
in the search of my brother ? If it
be your design to accompany me,
you should lose no time in giving
orders for the necessary prepara-

" ADAPUN Indra Mahadewa sŭtlah iya datang kamahligie itu,
maka lalu iya dudok dŭkat tuan
pŭtri sŭraya tŭrsŭnyum katanya,
' ya adinda tuan nyawa kakŭnda,
apatah bichari tuan skarang ini,
kŭrna kakŭnda ini akan pŭrgi
mŭnchari saudara kakŭnda? Dan
jikalau tuan akan pŭrgi bŭrsama
sama dŭngan kakŭnda, maka baik-
lah tuan mŭnyurohkan orang bŭr-

tions, as my departure must be immediate.' When the princess *Seganda Ratna* heard these words, she held down her head, and with glances sweet as the blue lotos flower in the sea of honey, replied, What plans, my love, am I, a young female, to pursue but those of my lord alone ? For is not a wife under the guidance of her husband? *Indra Mahadewa* showed his satisfaction at hearing these expressions from the princess, embraced and kissed her saying, ' Thy good sense adds grace to thy lovely features ; thou shalt be the soother of my cares, my comforter, my companion.' "

simpan simpan, skarang ini juga kakŭnda ini akan bŭrjalan.' Sŭtlah tuan pŭtri Seganda Ratna mŭnŭng ar kata Indra Mahadewa itu, maka tuan pŭtri itupon tundok, maka ekor matanya spŭrti sruja biru yang didalam laut mŭdu, rupanya manis bukan barang barang, sŭraya bŭrkata, ' ya kakŭnda apatah bichara kapada anak prŭmpuan, mŭlainkan lebih bichara kakŭnda juga ? Kŭrna prŭmpuan itu didalam maalum lakinya? Maka Indra Mahadewa pun tŭrsŭnyum munŭngar kata tuan pŭtri itu, maka lalu dipŭlok dan chiyumnya sluroh tubohnya, sŭraya katanya, ' Pandienya orang yang baik paras ini bŭrkata kata,' dan tuanlah akan pŭmadam hati kakŭnda yang mŭshgol dan yang mŭnjadi panglipur lara hati, dan tŭman kakŭnda."

" HAVING spoken thus, *Indra Mahadewa* bent his course wherever his uncertain steps might lead. With an anxious heart and suffering from hunger and thirst, he penetrated into forests of great extent, ascended high mountains, and crossed wide plains. The sun was now set, and the moon rose in all her splendour as if to serve him for a torch. The prince, although fatigued, proceeded towards the hills of *Indra Kila*, and as he passed, the tender branches of the climbing plants waved with the wind and seemed inclined to follow the beautiful youth. As the dawn gadually arose, the clouds in the border of the sky assumed a variety of shapes, some having the form of

" SUTLAH sudah iya bŭrkata dumkian itu, maka Indra Mahadewa itupun bŭrjalanlah dŭngan sapambawa kakinya, dŭngan rawan hatinya, dŭngan lapar dahaganya, masok hutan rimba yang bŭsar bŭsar, dan mŭlalui gunong yang tinggi tinggi, dan masok padang yang luas luas. Maka mata hari pun masoklah, maka bulan pun tŭrbitlah spŭrti orang mŭnyulohkan Indra Mahadewa itu, chayanya pun tŭrlalu trang tŭmarang. Maka baginda pun lalu mŭnuju gunong Indra Kila dŭngan lŭlahnya, maka sagala puchok kayu yang mŭlata ditiup angin mŭlambie rupanya, spŭrti handak mŭngikot orang baik paras lakunya. Maka fajar pun mŭnyensenglah bŭr-

trees, and some resembling animals ; but the trees of the forest were still obscured from sight by the dense vapour rising from the dew. The light of the sun now began to appear, glancing from the interstices of the mountains like the countenance of a lovely virgin, whilst its beams shooting upwards exhibited the appearance of flags and banners waving in front of an army marching to battle."

pangkat pangkat, maka awan ditŭpi langit itu bŭrbagie rupanya, ada yang spŭrti pohon kayu, dan ada yang spŭrti binatang rupanya, maka sagala pohon rimba itu pun tiadalah klihatan kŭrna kabot ulih ŭmbun. Maka chaya matahari pun tŭrbitlah mŭmanchar manchar deri chŭlah chŭlah gunong, spŭrti muka anak darah yang elok rupanya, dan rupa sinarnya yang mŭmanchar kaatas spŭrti tunggol dan mega dihadapan lawan akan prang."

" THE king was highly pleased with the manners and disposition of *Dewa Indra*, as well as with his graceful person and superior understanding. He said to him, ' Partake of betel, my son.' *Dewa Indra* having accordingly partaken, returned the betel-stand to the king, who thus addressed him : ' I have sent for you, my son, in order to make known to you a resolution taken by me some time since ; that to the person who having counted out ten large measures of sesame seed and as many measures of sand, thoroughly blended together, should be able to separate the grains of the one from the grains of the other, and to complete the performance of the task in the course of a day ; to such person alone should I give the hand of my daughter in marriage.' *Dewa Indra* smiled on hearing the king's words, knowing them to proceed from the artful suggestion of the princes (his rivals), and bowing replied, ' whatever may be your majesty's injunctions, your servant

" MAKA baginda pun tŭrlalu sangat bŭrkŭnan mŭlihat lakunya dan pŭkŭrtinya Dewa Indra itu, tambahan pula dŭngan baik rupanya, dŭngan arif bijaksananya. Sŭraya katanya, 'Makanlah sireh, ya anakku.' Maka Dewa Indra itupŭn lalu makan sireh sa'kapor, maka dipŭrsŭmbahkaneya kapada Dewa Indra, katanya: ' hie anakku, adapun ayahanda mŭnyuroh mŭmanggil tuan kamari ini, kŭrna ayahanda ini sudah bŭrtitah dahulu ; shahadan barang siapa dapat mŭmbilang biji lang yang sa'puloh koyan, dan pasir sapuloh koyan juga, maka dichamporkan antara kaduanya itu, kŭmdian maka dipilehnya pasir dan biji lang itu, shahadan maka habislah dŭngan sa 'hari itu juga, atau kapada malam, maka iyalah akan suami tuan pŭtri.' Maka Dewa Indra Kayangan itupun tŭrsŭnyum, dan taulah iya akan tipu itu deripada anak rajah rajah itu juga, maka Dewa Indra itupun mŭnyŭmbah sŭraya kaatanya, 'mana titah deri bawa duli tuanku, patik junjong.'

is ready to execute them.' The sand and the sesame seed being then provided and mixed together in the court before the palace, *Dewa Indra* made his obeisance, descended to the spot, and as he stood beside the heap, silently wished for aid from the king of the ants; when instantly the monarch made his appearance, followed by his whole army, consisting of the population of nine hillocks. Upon receiving the directions of *Dewa Indra* for separating the grains, each individual ant took one seed in his mouth, and in this manner the separation was presently effected and the grains laid in distinct heaps, not one being wanting. This done, the king of the ants and all his train disappeared, and returned to the place from whence they came. *Dewa Indra* reascended the steps of the palace, and having taken his seat and made obeisance, said, 'Your Majesty's commands for the separation of the sand and the sesame seed have been obeyed by your mean and humble slave.' The king expressed his amazement, and all the ministers of state, the warriors, and the people in general were astonished at witnessing this proof of the supernatural power of *Dewa Indra;* but with respect to the princes, some of them shook their heads, some bent them down, and others turned them aside, being unable to support his looks."

Maka pasir dan biji lang itupŭn sudah sŭdialah dichamporkan orang ditŭngah miedan itu dibalerong itu, maka Dewa Indra itupun mŭnyŭmbah, lalu turon bŭrdiri dihampir lang dan pasir itu, maka dichitanya rajah sŭmut; maka dŭngan skutika itu juga rajah sŭmut itupun datang dŭngan sagala blantŭntaranya, yang sambilan timbunan itu. Maka disurohnya ulih Dewa Indra mŭmilih pasir dan biji lang itu, maka ulih sagala tŭntara sŭmut lalu digigitnyalah sa'orang satu biji lang, itupun dilainkannya, maka dŭngan skutika itu juga pasir dan biji lang itupun masing masing dŭngan timbunannya, maka barang sa'biji juga pun tiadalah kurang. Maka rajah sŭmut dan sagala blantŭntaranya itupun raiblah kŭmbali katŭmpatnya, maka Dewa Indra itupun naiklah ka'atas balerong itu lalu dudok mŭnyŭmbah baginda sŭraya katanya, 'Sudah tuanku turpilih biji lang dan pasir itu ulih patik yang hina papa ini.' Maka baginda pun hieran dan tŭrchŭngang chŭngang, turmangau mangau dŭngan sagala pŭrmantri, hulubalang, pahlauan dan rayat skalian, itupun hieranlah iya mŭlihat kasaktian itu, maka akan anak rajah itu ada yang mŭnggrakkan kapalanya dan ada yang tundok, dan ada yang bŭrpaling, tiada mau mŭlihat muka Dewa Indra kayangan."

The Malays of Borneo acknowledge the rule of a Sultan, who is assisted by various Ministers of State, who are principally his own relations. The Court at

Brunei is kept up by taxes imposed on the few Chinese merchants, and on the native Borneans who live inland beside the rivers on the north-west coast from the Baram to Kimanis. A yearly payment is also made to the Sultan by the Rajah of Sarawak. Many of the Malays are traders. The poorer classes are sailors, fishermen, or engaged in simple domestic industries.

The true bred Malay has a penchant for building his pile dwelling over the shallow water near the mouth of or beside a river wherever such a site is procurable. The Borneans, on the other hand, prefer a clearing near the streams, and some tribes, especially the Dusan, build their huts high up in the hills.

Intermarriages with native women have helped to identify the Malays with the Borneans, and especially with the Kadyans, a tribe who live near the capital, and who long ago embraced the faith of Mahomet. The language of the Malays is soft and pleasing in sound— the "Italian of the East"—and very expressive. It is readily acquired by strangers, and forms the medium of commercial communication throughout the Straits Settlements and Malay Archipelago. Like our own tongue, Malay seems to be a conventional blending of several other languages, Arabic, Sanscrit, and the languages of the aboriginals with whom the Malays were first thrown into contact. At the present day many English and Portuguese words find their way into it but little disguised by pronunciation. Malay is the Court language at Brunei, but the inhabitants generally use a dialect similar to that of the aboriginals who live near the capital.

The clothing of the Malays of high rank is often very lavish and showy, consisting of fancy head-cloths and short jackets, often highly embroidered with gold buttons

L

and wire or lace. White trowsers, similar to those worn by Europeans, and patent leather slippers are also affected by the rich Malays, and all, rich or poor, wear the national "sarong," a sort of chequered petticoat wound around the waist, and allowed to fall to the feet in graceful folds. When trowsers are worn a shorter "sarong" is worn kilt-fashion, barely reaching as low as the knees. The Malay Hadjis or priests wear long green Arab coats, and green or white turbans around their shaven heads. The women when engaged in their household duties wear nothing but a "sarong" reaching from the breasts to the feet. When abroad, however, neat print sacques reaching as low as the knees are worn, having long and tight sleeves. This dress opens in front, and is fastened by a set of three silver or gold brooches. Below this a chequered, or Javanese sarong reaches from the waist to the ankles. Beautiful sarongs are made by the Brunei ladies. They are richly embroidered with gold wire, and are worn by the well-to-do women along the coast.

Slippers of European or Chinese manufacture are sometimes worn. Their black hair is oiled profusely, and secured behind with silver pins. It is often perfumed by tying up in it flowers of the champaca, jasmine, gardenia, or other scented blossoms over night. Both men and women bathe at least twice daily, morning and evening, and the women dye their nails with a mixture made of the red stems of a common balsam, mixed with lime juice, as a substitute for the henna so largely used in Persia and Egypt.

There are some very singular liberties allowed to loving swains in out of the way places in Wales and Cornwall, but those allowed by the Malay and native girls of Borneo to their favourite lovers are of a yet more faithful kind.

A Bornean youth may enter the house of his loved one's parents and awaken her if she be really sleeping, to sit and talk with him in the dark, or to eat betel-nut and the finest of sirih-leaves from his garden. A similar custom, so far as nocturnal visits are concerned, formerly

COURTSHIP.

existed in the country districts of Scotland. It is but seldom that immorality results from this custom in Borneo, even according to European ideas on the subject, and the parents think no more of putting a stop to these nightly meetings than do those of our own fair daughters in the case of the "morning call" of an eligible suitor at home. There was a grand wedding at the capital during one of my visits there, the bride being a relation of his Highness the Sultan. There was a grand procession of boats on the river, and a large lighter had been decorated with parti-coloured flags and streamers, and in the centre a raised daïs and a canopy overhead of red cloth had been erected for the parties mainly concerned.   In the case of the Malays there is the usual religious ceremony, at which the " hadjis " appear and chant the prayers in gorgeous apparel of green Arabic coat and ample turban.   There was much firing of cannon throughout the town, the whole event lasting nearly a week, and there was a grand reception, the bride and bridegroom being seated in state on a raised daïs, and covered with finery and gold ornaments, mostly borrowed for the occasion.   In the interior, where nearly all enjoy " liberty, equality, and fraternity," in a way one can only dream of in civilised " society," marriage is very simple, and monogamy the rule.   The celebration of a marriage consists of a notification of the fact, and it is acknowledged by all in the village, who meet for feasting.   A couple of fowls or a goat is killed, and the appearances presented by these after death furnish auguries of good or ill fortune for the newly married pair.

The native Borneans proper are sparsely scattered over the whole country, and are divided into various tribes, each inhabiting a particular district, and speaking a dialect peculiar to itself.   These tribes have been compared with the natives of our English counties, but they are much more distinct, each having its own customs, dress, mode of life, weapons, and in many cases a language unknown to the tribes only a few miles distant.   The Dyaks, Kayans, Muruts, Kadyans, Dusun, and Lanun, are a few only of these tribes.   Another peculiar race are the Badjows, or " Sea Gipsies," common to all the islands of these seas.   They are nomadic—water rovers—and engaged in diving for pearls, or pearl shell, fishing, or in

MARRIAGE.

To face page 148.

petty trade.   They rarely settle down on shore, or remain
long in one place, but live in their boats.   Indeed they
are the gipsies of the sea in every sense of the word,
and given to pilfering like their namesakes on shore.
The Badjows, Lanun, Balagnini, and Sulus, who inhabit
the north of Borneo and the islands to the north-east are
an adventurous people given to piracy, and, of course, excellent sailors.   The Muruts are the only existing race
of head-hunters north of the capital.   The Dusun and
Kadyans, although formerly head-hunters, have now taken
to agricultural pursuits, and are well fed and prosperous
compared to the Muruts, who, although they clear and
plant the land around their immensely long pile dwellings,
still depend much on their skill in hunting wild pig, deer,
and other game for food.   The Dyaks of Sarawak, although formerly fierce and warlike, are now peaceful and
industriously engaged in seafaring or agricultural pursuits.   The Kayans are still warlike, and a fine race of
straight-limbed powerful people.   They formerly inhabited the country inland near the Limbang and used
to plunder the villages of the Muruts and Sabayans,
killing the men, and taking the women and children into
slavery.   Of late years, however, they have migrated
further south, and their head-quarters are now on the
Baram river.   The Lanuns live on the coasts north of
Menkabong, and are petty traders or cultivators.   Like
the Badjows, however, they have a lingering affection for
the sea.   The Dusun, who live in the hills further from
the coast, give them a bad character and assert that formerly they used to steal their children.

   Land culture is becoming much more general among
the natives inland than formerly, security of life and property having also increased.   Rice, kaladi, sweet potatoes, and Indian corn and sago are the principal food

products cultivated. Tobacco, cotton, sugar-cane, tapioca, and fruit are also grown here.

The implements used for purposes of land culture in the island are of the most rude description. On the plains of Menkabong, Tawaran, and Tampassuk, near the coast, ploughs and harrows drawn by buffaloes are employed, and their produce is carried to market in light bamboo sledges. Further inland, however, the implements are yet more primitive, nearly all the necessary labour of cultivation being performed with a blunt-pointed iron chopper, or a sharp-pointed bamboo.

The hoe, another implement used, may be taken as the type of that adopted by the Chinese emigrants in the Straits Settlements and Eastern Archipelago generally; indeed, wherever a Chinaman sets his foot in a new locality for cultural purposes, a chopper and a blade or two of his national " chunkal " or spade-hoe are sure to form a part of his extremely small belonging. He sets to work cutting the brushwood and small timber on his future clearing, and piling this at the base of the large trees, he fires the whole until only a few great black stumps, and here and there a gaunt leafless durian or dryobalanops remains of the old forest. Now, the " chunkal" is used to stir the virgin soil by chopping it up, a much quicker process than digging; indeed, a spade would have no chance in a competition where, as in this case, the soil is full of roots. If desirable, the soil can be thus chopped up to a depth of 12 in. or 14 in., the only drawback being that the operator stands on the freshly cultivated land. Armed with a chopper and one of these spade-hoes, a solitary Chinaman will not unfrequently build a miserable little palm-leaf hut on a well-watered bit of forest near a river, and in a month or two he will have cleared several acres, to which, when planted with gambier or pepper, he looks for a fair return. Here, alone in the forest, or at the best with a companion or two equally poor as himself, he subsists on a little boiled rice, until his crops of sweet potatoes, bananas, sugar-cane, egg fruit, maize, and yams, are fit for use ; for one of his first cares has been to clear the bit of land around his hut, on which to plant the few roots and seeds which he has brought with him, most probably the gift of one of his richer countrymen, perchance of the trader of whom he bought the bag of rice, which with a little freshly caught fish from the river, are the only " stores " which stand between him and starvation, until his garden pro-duce is available. I have often come across these clear-ings right in the heart of the forest, miles away from any other human habitation, and have been as much aston-ished at the amount of labour performed with such a simple tool, as the thrifty labourer himself was to see me.

The Dusun villagers keep bees and export wax in quantity, and most of the tribes collect the varied natural products of the sea or of the forests in their respective districts. The Sulus were until quite recently a warlike race inhabiting the large island of Sulu, between Borneo and the Philippines. They were independent and ruled by a Sultan, who held Sulu, Tawi Tawi, and the north of Borneo, including the fine harbour of Sandakan. The Sulus, however, are now practically under the Manilla Government. Slavery, although not yet abolished in Borneo, is not nearly so common as was formerly the case. The native government at Brunei is practically under the eye of the British governor of Labuan, and thus many former abuses have become mitigated merely by the moral influence of a British colony being located thus near to the capital.

It must not be imagined that either the Malays or the native Borneans are the bloodthirsty savages they are sometimes made out to be. The Malays generally are courteous, dignified, and hospitable. Many of them have made long journeys for purposes of trade, and have a tolerably good idea of the manners and customs of Europeans. Others have taken to the use of European commodities after observing them used by the Chinese traders and settlers, and one can rarely visit a native of any consideration without finding him the hospitable possessor of a chair or two, plates, dishes, water bottles and glasses, and very often of excellent brandy and cigars. They are most sensitive, innately polite and gentle in manners, and very quick to understand and appreciate any little courtesies or civilities one may offer them. All but the poorest carry their national weapon, " the murderous crease," a sort of long sinuous-edged dagger, generally as sharp as a razor, and most deadly when wielded by a skilful hand. In many cases where the owners are rich or of high rank these weapons are beautifully finished—rarely damascened—and the handles of ivory or gold set with pearls, diamonds, and other precious stones. The running "amok," so often cited as an instance of their savage bloodthirsty nature is really a very rare occurrence, and is generally attributed to the excessive use of opium, or to some great disappointment or dishonour having befallen the frantic creature who, drawing his kriss, rushes at friend and foe alike until either shot down like a mad dog or run through the body with a spear. Jealousy is the main cause of all the bloodshed of which the Malays are guilty. The co-respondent in Borneo must either have a tacit understanding with the husband or rather proprietor of the frail one, or his adventures may end very suddenly. I saw one man in the hospital at Labuan who paid the penalty of his indiscretion. One night a kriss or spear had been driven into his thigh through the interstices of the floor of the house in which he was sleeping with his Helen, and with such force that the bone was completely severed. It is possible the weapon was poisoned, at any rate he died some little time afterwards, notwithstanding all that surgical skill could suggest. In the case of the Malays their women are, as a rule, secluded from the gaze of strangers in private apartments, but in the interior the women of the aboriginal tribes enjoy equal freedom with the men, and often join in discussions and trading difficulties with great tact. Monogamy is the rule with the Borneans and polygamy with the Malays. In Borneo, as in Europe, the female exceeds the male population, and here, too, the women do a large proportion of the field labour in addition to their domestic duties.

Some of the little villages of the native tribes inland present a pleasant and prosperous exterior. Little palmleaf houses stand here and there beneath groves of cocoanut trees, betel-palms, tree-ferns, or graceful willow-like bamboo. Breadths of fresh greensward occur among the clumps of low brush or scrubby vegetations, the remains of the old jungle, and here buffaloes or goats, and occasionally other cattle, browse around the houses. Pigs, bees, and poultry are domesticated, and are often very abundant. The houses are built on piles, and a sloping hill-side or knoll is generally selected as a site, so that all superfluous surface water may readily escape. The fowls are caught every evening and placed in open-work baskets of either rattan or bamboo, suspended beneath the eaves of the houses. This care is essential in order to guard them from the attacks of large snakes and iguanas, or other poultry-stealing saurians.

The main food product is rice, of which two distinct races are grown. One kind only prospers in the rich alluvial deposits of the valleys near the streams, where it can be irrigated at particular stages of its growth. The other kind, or "hill-rice," will grow on the hills up to 3000 feet elevation, and prospers in dry red earth, and when growing it closely resembles a barley-field at home. One of the most important of the women's duties is to clean and prepare daily the "padi" or rice in the husk, which, with fish and fruit, forms the main food supply of these islanders. The "padi" is placed in large wooden mortars and beaten with wooden pestles a yard or more in length. This beating or pounding separates the husk from the white grain within. It is a very pretty sight to see the girls of the villages inland thus engaged. As many as three may sometimes be seen beating the rice in one of these large wooden mortars. With one hand they grasp the pestle about the centre, while the other hand is rested on the hip. One woman commences to beat the rice with a steady, regular stroke, then another one joins her, and then a third. Of course, the most exact time has to be observed, and the graceful motions of their slightly-draped figures, the dancing pestles, and the regular thudding sounds produced, are very interesting to a stranger. After the rice has been sufficiently beaten, one of the girls scoops it out of the mortar with her little hands into a shallow tray of closely-woven rattan work of circular form and about two feet in diameter. Standing on the verandah or platform between the houses so as to catch the breeze, the rice is sifted, and now and then dexterously thrown up into the air so that the chaff and refuse is blown away, but the rice falls back into the tray. When finished the rice is as clean and as white as that dressed by the finest machinery in England. Two or three girls will soon clean the day's supply, and by the laughing and gossip indulged in one may infer that the task is not a very unpleasant one to them.

The farther one proceeds inland the more extensive are the clearings devoted to rice culture. This is accounted for by the fact that near the coast rice is often imported in exchange for jungle produce, but far inland the natives are obliged to grow all the food they require, and in some cases as in the district to the south of Kina Balu most of the hills up to 3000 feet are either under rice culture, or are lying fallow, covered with low brushwood or jungle. Virgin land or old forests are rare here, unless on the slopes of the great mountain itself. The clothing of the aboriginals is in most cases very scanty, now and then " sarongs " and white calico are obtained from the coast in return for wax, gutta, tobacco, or other produce of the hills, but, as a rule, the clothing of the native tribes of the north of Borneo inland is a short " sarong " made of a strong indigo-dyed cloth, which is woven by the women from the strong fibres of the " Lamba " (*Curculigo latifolia*), a yellow-flowered broad-leaved weed, often seen in great abundance on old cultivated plots near the houses. Many of the men, especially those of the Murut tribes, who are perhaps the most primitive of all the northern Borneans, wear nothing but a strip of bark-cloth or " chawat " around the loins, and I have no doubt but that this was the first clothing ever worn by the natives of the island. This bark-cloth is the produce of *Artocarpus elastica*, a tall tree with a trunk two feet in diameter, and leaves closely resembling those of the bread-fruit, but rough instead of glossy. The inner bark is stripped off and soaked in water, being afterwards beaten to render it soft and pliable. Of this " chawats " or loin-cloths and jackets are commonly made by the Muruts on the Lawas and the Limbang rivers, and it is also still used by the Dusan villagers on the Tampassuk, notwithstanding their skill in preparing, weaving, and dyeing the "Lamba" fibre.

The native women inland wear short "sarongs" of "Lamba" cloth reaching from the waist nearly to their knees, and a profusion of stained rattan coils, brass wire, coloured beads, and other trinkets around their waists, and heavy rings of brass on their legs, or coils of brass wire on their plump and dusky arms. The younger ones wear a strip of dark cloth across the breast. All have glossy black hair and dark eyes. Some of the Murut women are fine muscular creatures, and either in boats or afield they appear to be as strong and active as the men. Their hair is often very gracefully wreathed up with a string of red or amber-coloured beads, sometimes with a strip of the pale yellow nipa leaf in its young state, and the colour contrast is then very effective. The physique of the inland tribes, especially of the Dyaks, Kayans, and Muruts, is superior to that of the Malays. The Kayans and Muruts are especially lithe and active— bronzy, straight-limbed, and statuesque. This is the result of an active life spent hunting in the forest, climbing after gutta, rubber, jungle-fruit, or beeswax, or in cultivating the clearings around their dwellings, or in fishing in the rivers. The aboriginals are active, while, as a class, the Malays are lethargic and luxurious, and rarely exert themselves or make long foot journeys unless actually compelled to do so, and the richer ones spend much of their time in opium smoking or with their women instead of trying to ameliorate the condition of their poorer neighbours, who in one way or another have to "pay the piper."

It is sad to see such a lovely and fertile island impoverished to a great extent by the avaricious Malays, who ought to encourage the natives to improve themselves and the country in which they live, instead of which they wring their property from them whenever possible under all manner of pretences. The harsh treatment to which the aboriginals, and even the poorer of the Malays, were formerly subjected by the petty chiefs and Pangerans, is now much moderated, as many natives have visited Labuan, and it has now become known as a sanctuary from their unjust oppressors.

The climate of Borneo although hot and wet, is fairly healthy, especially on the hills inland, where the air is much fresher and cooler than on the lowlands near the coast; the mean annual temperature is about 84°. The hot and dry monsoon lasts from December to May, and the cool and wet one from June to November; the rainfall is very heavy, especially on the hills. The economic products for which the soil and climate are suitable are coffee, cinchona, cocoa, cotton, tobacco, sugar-cane, indigo, gambier, cocoa-nuts for oil, and manilla hemp. Fine timber, gutta, caoutchouc, rattans, and camphor, are the indigenous products of the forests primæval. Among the introduced fruits which succeed well are oranges, limes, pomoloes, mangoes, pine-apples, and bananas. The animal products are edible swallows' nests, ivory, sea-slug or *beche de mer*, (Holothuria), fine fish of many kinds, pearls, and pearl-shell. Among minerals, coal, antimony, cinnabar, and gold seem the most promising; diamonds, tin, copper, plumbago, and iron are reported; and if one may judge of the iron by the old weapons, such as krisses, parongs, and spears as made by the Bruneis and the Kayans, it must be of excellent quality.

I made a pen and ink sketch of a Kayan war knife which I saw in the collection of native weapons in the possession of Mr. Treacher at Government House, Labuan. Of this sketch Mr. Cooper has made me this careful fac-simile on wood. It had a finely-tempered blade, ornamented along the back for about half its length. One side of the blade was flat, the other rounded; the sheath was elaborately carved and, as is generally the case in Borneo, made of two flat pieces of wood bound tightly together by neatly worked rattan cane; the hilt was ornamented with tufts of red and black hair, and it was furnished with a girdle of rattan plaited — altogether a most handy and formidable implement in the paw of a lusty naked savage.

KAYAN WAR KNIFE.

Gold, diamonds, and antimony have been obtained in remunerative quantities at the Sarawak mines, which were originally worked by the Chinese settlers, but are now in the hands of a company. Mining operations are very difficult owing to the enormous rainfall; and it is only the abundance of cheap Chinese or native labour which renders it possible in such a climate.   Coolies from Hong Kong may be obtained for seven to eight dollars per month, or for less if their food is provided; and natives will work sometimes for five to seven dollars per month.   A good Chinaman as a labourer, is however worth two Malays.

The largest rivers in the island are supposed to be the Kinabatangan and the Pontianak; the former is said to be navigable over two hundred miles from its mouth, and at the farthest point reached it was fifty yards wide, and there was seven fathoms of water.   Dutch steamers have ascended a long way inland up the Pontianak which lies south of Sarawak.   Most of the rivers on the north-west coast are very shallow, having dangerous bars at their mouths; and that at the mouth of the Brunei was partly blocked by large rocks about the time of the siege of that city by the English.

Gambling and opium smoking are the bane of the Chinese settlers and of many of the well-to-do Malays; and of all forms of intemperance surely this last must be the most degrading and otherwise hurtful in its effects. The manufactured drug as imported from Benares and other opium producing districts, is in the form of balls six inches in diameter, covered with the dried petals of poppy flowers.   This product is the inspissated juice of the opium poppy (*Papaver somniferum*), and is of a dark brown or black colour.   Before it is used for smoking, however, it has to be still further prepared by boiling and stirring in shallow pans over a bright fire; and as the pure product is very high in price, it is often subjected to adulteration.   In our eastern colonies it is usual to let or farm out the right to prepare and sell or export opium to an enterprising native or Chinese merchant, and the revenue thus obtained is often enormous as compared with that on spirits and tobacco, or other duty-paying goods.

An opium-smoking establishment consists of a few gloomy rooms furnished with cane-bottomed couches, and on little stands are the pipes, tiny lamps, and other implements used by the smokers. The smell is generally sufficient to deter Europeans entering an opium-smoker's haunt from motives of curiosity; or if under guidance one does venture into the ill-ventilated and mal-odorous apartments behind, it is with feelings of relief that the sweet outer air is again gained. The smokers lie on the bamboo couches, and a little stand is brought, on which are one or two flute-like pipes, a pill or two of the drug, and a little glass lamp. In some cases an attendant manipulates the drug and fills the pipes; as a rule, however, this is done by the smokers themselves. There is no mistaking an habitual opium smoker; his eyes are dull, his complexion sallow, and in general a listless bearing, with a frame more or less emaciated, betokens his being a degraded victim. Without a supply of his favourite drug he is miserable; and when under its influence he is useless. Here he lies holding a morsel of the black drug on a needle over the flame of the lamp, twirling it round and round, and toasting it in the flame until the proper consistence is attained. It is then introduced into the pipe, and the needle, on being withdrawn, leaves a tiny air-hole through the mass as it fits like a plug in the bowl. The smoker now holds the bowl to the lamp, and obtains a light, and then he draws a long whiff or two as the burning morsel of opium rapidly decreases in the bowl.

CHAPTER VIIl.

A CITY OF LAKE DWELLINGS.

BRUNEI, the capital of Borneo and the seat of the government, is a water-city of about twenty thousand inhabitants. The palm-thatched houses of which it for the most part consists, are built on piles so as to be above the river at high tide. From one of the adjacent low hills the view of this " Venice of the East " is a most novel one—indeed, unique in its way ; and although the town is nearly fifteen miles from the mouth of the river, yet a moderate-sized gunboat can anchor in the broad water-way in the very centre of the city, and within a few yards of the Sultan's Istana. There is a rather awkward bar at the entrance to the river. A trading steamer from Singapore calls here once a month to bring letters and goods for the Sultan and a few Chinese merchants, and to take back sago, which is the main export. In some cases the blocks of houses are connected by bridges formed of long palm stems lashed together with rattans ; but, as a rule, all general communication

M

must be carried on by boats. Some of the inhabitants grow a few flowers and herbs in boxes of earth ; and occasionally papaw trees and gourds of different kinds are thus cultivated. Little rafts, or floating tree-trunks, are moored to the piles which support the houses for the accommodation of ducks and fowls.

The market held on the river every morning is one of the most singular sights of the place. Here you may see a hundred or more little boats containing fruit, fish, rice, and other produce, for sale or barter. Among the petty traders the Brunei women are most prominent, and many of them present a most singular appearance, the hats they wear being made of neatly plaited Nipa leaves, and being from two to three feet in diameter, they serve the purpose of both head covering and umbrella, and they screen the whole body of the wearer from the hot sun. Most of the women to be seen in the market are old and coarse featured—in many cases positively ugly— reminding one of the orang utan as they glance at you from beneath their wrinkled foreheads, their mouths overflowing with betel nut-juice the while, their repulsive black teeth being worn off level with their gums ; their more beautiful sisters are secluded according to the etiquette of Islam; the nobles and richer Malays have wives and slaves in abundance. A European lady who visited the court here and was admitted into the women's apartments, tells me that some are passing fair, with tiny hands and feet, straight noses and liquid eyes, prototypes of those black-eyed damsels who are to attend all true believers of the Prophet in the gardens of Paradise.

The principal traders are Chinamen, who have floating warehouses singularly like the Noah's arks of early memory. Brunei is the Sheffield of north-west Borneo, the manufacture of knives, parongs and krisses being largely carried on ; and on one of the little islands is a primitive foundry where gongs, brass guns, cooking-pots, betel boxes, &c., are cast. Some of these articles are ornamented with well-designed figures in relief, and would not be any disgrace to a European manufacturer. The models and methods of casting are singularly like those of our own artizans. I visited one rude armourer's shop, and much admired the exquisite finish of some weapons he had made. The peculiar long swivel guns or small cannon cast here are now rarely used, except as currency, being valued at about thirty dollars per cwt. In the good old times slaves could be purchased here at thirty dollars, or a picul of gun-metal each; but at the present time the Malays complain of the low purchasing power of money—*i.e.* of brass guns—just as do most people nearer home.

The Sultan's palace or Istana, like nearly all the other dwellings here, is built on piles over the water, and is a shabby, tumble-down looking establishment. In front is a large audience chamber, containing a few old gilt framed mirrors and silvered globes, and there are, on occasion, a round table and a few rickety chairs. The Sultan himself is now an old man, over eighty, and so avaricious that he will do anything for the sake of a few dollars.

The Government here is corrupt, and, indeed, but little more than nominal; and if his people of the out-lying districts refuse to pay tribute, or to obey his mandates, he has no means of enforcing his demands. He has a good many wives, and female slaves or concubines, but no children. I visited the palace in company with Mr. Peter Veitch and Inche Mahomed, the British Consular agent at this port. We were honoured with an audience by His Highness. His two nephews, Pan-geran Matassan and Pangeran Anak Bazar, were present, and welcomed us before the Sultan appeared. They were intelligent men, and it was a pleasure to hear Malay spoken by them in all its purity. Tea was offered us, together with the long Nipa leaf cheroots so largely smoked by Malays and Borneans of all grades.

In about five minutes His Highness appeared, dressed in a long Arab coat, a sarong, and having a small black cap on his head. That the portraits of Pope Pius IX. resemble him very much has repeatedly been observed by visitors here. He walked slowly, bearing rather heavily, as I thought, on a long staff, which had two short prongs at the lower extremity. He came forward, and we shook hands, after which he sat down in an arm-chair on the opposite side of the table. He told us that he was now a very old man, and that every day found him weaker. I thanked him for a passport he had given me some months before for the journey inland to Kina Balu.

He seemed interested in hearing of the great mountain, and asked several questions. He appeared astonished to hear it was so cold there; and inquired as to the tobacco and rice crops. He also expressed his regret that being now old and infirm, he could not undertake a journey to the mountain himself, of which, he observed, he had heard several accounts derived from natives who had accompanied Mr. Low and Mr. St. John.

On leaving the Sultan's, we visited a foundry situated near the house of the minister of war or the Tumongong; also the house of a gold worker, who made most of the trinkets, rings, and ear ornaments worn by the Brunei ladies. The proprietor, an old man, showed us some prettily designed specimens of native gold work, the ear ornaments being especially singular. It is the fashion for many of the ladies of Brunei and the interior to cut

a large gash in the lobe of each ear, and in these holes
are inserted gold or silver ornaments, as large as a wine
cork. If of gold, they are mostly made of beaten work ;
the highly decorated convex ends, however, are generally
cast in little moulds formed of clay and wax, or dammar.
The crucibles used for melting the metal are of the size
and shape of half a hen's egg, being formed of fine
porous clay. These are heated over tiny charcoal fires,
the heat being augmented with a blow-pipe.

In some of the ornaments we observed rudely cut rock
crystals, or Bornean diamonds ; and part of a waist-belt
contained a dozen fine pearls, but most of their beauty
was lost by bad setting. The stock in trade of a gold-
worker here is of the most simple description. A rough
block of hard wood serves as a bench or anvil, and is
perforated with large and small holes, into which iron
pins of various sizes are inserted for various uses. Ham-
mers of iron and wood, a chisel or two, a pair of shears,
wax and clay for models, or matrices and earthen crucibles for melting up the Spanish gold pieces, are all the
plant he deems necessary.

There is not much originality in the designs used.
Some of the Brunei ladies must have fingers of the most
delicate proportions to be able to wear some of the rings
I saw here for repair. Smiths' shops are pretty much
the same all over the world. We visited one here, and
except that iron and tools were less plentiful, it was
pretty much like a village smithy in England. Sheffield
files and rasps are used even in this out-of-the-way part
of the East. Most other tools were of Brunei make.
Choppers, knives, parongs, and krisses represent the
manufactures. A Bornean bellows is peculiar, being
made of two upright wooden cylinders four or five feet
high, and connected at the bottom with the iron pipe

which enters the fuel. In each cylinder is a wooden disk edged with soft feathers stuck on with glue, and to each a piston rod of wood is attached. A man standing behind the cylinders works them up and down alternately, and in this way a constant current of air is supplied to the fire. The old smith was much struck with a breech-loading Reilly shot gun Mr. Veitch had with him, and he took the trouble to go across a rickety bridge of bamboo into his dwelling-house to fetch a parong, or Brunei sword, of which he asked our opinion. Considering the rude appliances of this primitive smithy, the sword, in fine damascene work and finish, was perhaps as wonderful in its way as the gun. On returning to the ship, which was anchored in the river below the town, we saw a gathering of natives on a grassy knoll a little above the old ruined Consulate, and were informed that a public execution was going on. It appears a China trader had been murdered and robbed on the Trusan river, and two of the Trusan Muruts had been arrested, and were being executed for the crime, although it was by some thought that the murder had actually been committed by Brunei men. At any rate, of these poor Muruts scapegoats were made. A grave was dug beneath a tree, and a noose connected with a bit of board was passed over their heads. A stout stick was now inserted in the rope, and two or three turns—Spanish winch fashion—finished the poor fellows' existence, whether innocent or guilty. We did not land, but watched the proceedings as well as we could from the bridge of the vessel with glasses. Summary justice is the rule here.

Just afterwards a ship came here and anchored in the river. It was very hot, and at night the ports were left open to secure ample ventilation. In the morning a gold watch and a revolver were missing. The thieves had dropped down the river silently in a boat and taken advantage of the darkness to put their hands in at the ports and take all they could reach. A complaint was made to the Sultan at once. In a few days the goods were recovered, and word was also brought to the effect that each of the offenders had lost one of their hands for the offence. Of course nothing so severe as this was anticipated when the charge was made, and no one more regretted the cruelty than those who were so near being losers by the dishonesty of the maimed sufferers. The principal export product is sago, of which large quantities are brought down from the Limbang and other rivers in the interior. There are two large sago-washing establishments in the town, both the property of intelligent and hospitable Chinamen. Gutta-percha, caoutchouc, edible birds'-nests, camphor, rattans, and fine timber are also obtained in small quantities from the forests of the country behind. Fine fish is obtained from the river by the natives, and fruit is very plentiful in season. Excellent drinking-water is obtained from some rocks beside the river between the town and the old Consulate. It is pure, cool, fresh, and abundant, inestimable qualities in such a hot and thirst-producing climate.

We visited one of the sago factories, and found their water remarkably good; and when I and Mr. Veitch went out one evening snipe and pigeon-shooting on a plain behind we came across an aqueduct formed of large bamboo stems, in which this water was conveyed from a spring nearly a mile away. I was very much interested in the old Chinaman's garden, which contained a fair assortment of fruits and flowers. The lively white-flowered *Pancratium zeylanicum* was blooming beautifully in one of the well-watered beds. The mangoes were large, and of excellent flavour. In exploring the garden behind the

house I came across our host's coffin standing on supports in one of the sheds. It was large and curiously
shaped, and made of some dark durable wood highly
valued by the wealthy Chinese. Most Chinese settlers
here, when sufficiently wealthy, send to China for one of
these coffins, which is preserved until their death. Nearly
all the Chinese settlers here in the capital are married to
Malay women, and healthy children generally result from
these unions. On the other hand, the Malay or Bornean
women rarely bear children when married to Europeans,
and if so, the children are generally unhealthy, and they
themselves rarely have offspring. No doubt the Malays
of the capital are gradually becoming absorbed by inter-
marrying with the native Bornean women of the Murut,
Kadyan, and other inland tribes. Many of the Malays,
so called, closely resemble the aboriginals in physiognomy,
and the common people or Bruneis may be characterised
as an ugly and immoral lot of mongrels. Now and then
traces of African blood are seen.

Nowhere else in Borneo are the men such liars and
thieves as here, and the Brunei women have been described by a former writer as being perhaps "the most
immoral in the whole world." Of classical celebrities,
Cato and Phryne are certainly well represented in this
great water city of the far East. The climate is sultry.
A large upas tree is pointed out to all comers, and it is a
fine specimen, standing on the right bank of the river,
just below the town, near some ancient tombs. A burial-
ground, indeed, occupies nearly the whole right bank of
the river from just beyond the Consulate as far as the
sago factory. One or two of the tombs are large, and
built of stone, with entrance gates; but most are small,
with perhaps only a large stone to mark the spot.

The capital, as also the towns all along the coast, suffer

now and then from epidemic diseases, cholera and small-pox being the most common. Senõr Quateron the old padre, now resident in Labuan, formerly had a mission here, and the remains of his chapel still stand on the left bank of the Brunei river, a little below the town. As seen coming down the stream, it forms a picturesque object, a white campanile standing on a grassy knoll, the blue peaks of Molu towering up into the sky behind. I should think that Brunei, of all other places in Borneo, is the last at which missionaries of any denomination would be likely to succeed. Their sphere is not with Mahomedans, whose faith is good, so far as it teaches cleanliness and temperance; but with the aboriginals of the interior, who are thrifty, honest, and truthful to a fault, and who have no systematic faith unless their belief in the cries and motions of birds and animals, and other omens can be so called. With these people missionaries would doubtless be successful, but they must be hard-working men who could teach these gentle savages the benefits of civilisation without introducing its vices.

A missionary has thus recorded his impressions of life among the natives near Sarawak :—" A message came to me from one of the Christians on the Kabo, asking me to go up and see them. Accordingly, as soon as I could get a boat ready we were on our way down the Sebetan river . . . . the wild, sombre, solitary feeling of the primeval forest, the easy motion of the boat, the cheeri-ness of the paddling Dyaks, united to produce a sensa-tion of repose and awe. . . . . Next morning we soon came to the first waterfall rushing and roaring over the rocks. Here we had to halt and stow away the palm-leaf awnings, and pull the boat over the fall. Then one could not help feeling the charms of tropical scenery,—the clear stream running over a pebbly bottom, rocks here and there with occasional tufts of vegetation forming little islets in mid river, hills on each bank running down perpendicularly to the water's edge and covered with creepers, moss, wild palms, and ferns, magnificent trees on either side stretching their branches into triumphal arches over head. Soon the whole scene was changed, clouds gathered, and thunder rumbled, and down came the rain in a continuous torrent. Towards evening we arrived at our destination like so many drowned rats. In the evening I held service under difficulties, there being no prayer-house, and the long public verandah of the house being the only available place. The dignity of worship suffers terribly in such circumstances. No sooner do we begin than dogs begin to fight, or a child to cry, or an unsympathetic heathen at the other end of the house to make some discordant row, or a fighting cock will fly right into the midst of the kneeling assembly, and distract everyone's attention."

The condition of the natives near the capital is not nearly so good as at Kina Balu, a hundred and fifty miles away, if we except the Kadyans, who being Mahomedans, and having powerful friends in Brunei, are able to resist many of the taxes which the Muruts of the Limbang and elsewhere are called upon to pay. I made two visits here to the capital, and made a boat journey up the Limbang and Pandarowan rivers as far as Bukit Sagan. This trip was made in the wet season, and took twelve men three days, owing to the heavy freshes against which they had to pull. The Pandarowan river is small compared with the Limbang, of which it is a tributary; but it is, without exception, the loveliest river I ever saw· At the end of the second day after leaving the capital we reached a large house belonging to the Muruts of this district. It stood in a little clearing close beside the

stream, and was nearly a hundred yards in length. A
rude pathway of tree trunks lay on the muddy shore
reaching to one end of the building. We landed here to
cook our dinner, and clambered up into the house by a
rude stair formed of a notched tree trunk. The Muruts
looked rather surprised to see such visitors, but spread
mats for us, and gave us some firewood and water. After
dinner we had a smoke with the head-man, a fine muscular old fellow, nearly six feet high. About fifty men,
women, and children swarmed round the circle, of which
a wood fire was the centre, to get a peep at us. The
head-man's wife was a young and rather handsome girl,
having a fine dusky little baby swung behind her, and
several other of the younger married women and girls
were comely, with dark eyes and luxuriant hair. Others,
however, were less attractive, and many of both sexes
were troubled with peculiar skin diseases. We engaged
two men of this tribe to go with us as far as Bukit Sagan,
as our men did not exactly know the best place at which
to land. We slept by the fire until about two o'clock,
when the rain, which had been coming down heavily all
day, ceased, and the silver moon being nearly at the full,
it quite illumined the stream as it sped past the house.
The mosquitoes became very troublesome, and so I called
the men and went down to the boat. After shouting for
about half an hour, the Muruts came down and took their
places; and pulling across the current, we crept up stream
beneath the arching plumes of the Nipa palm, which is
here abundant. It was hard work for the men, although
we had now fourteen paddles. A sharp look-out had to
be kept for snags and floating trunks of trees, several of
which we saw shooting past us mid stream. Our Labuan
men were rather afraid, and several times wanted to make
fast until daybreak. At one place the boat struck heavily

and keeled over in an alarming way, but we found the obstruction was a raft of the stems of the sago palm, which some Muruts had felled and lashed near the bank ready for floating down to their rude washing-sheds below. This heavy bump woke up our men, several of whom had previously been dozing, although paddling the while, and we got along for a mile or two in first-rate style. Then, in crossing the current, at an awkward bend we were well-nigh washed away; indeed, had it not been for the silent but strenuous exertions of our Murut guides, the alligators would possibly have had a feed. The stream for the moment got the better of our men, but by a clever touch of the paddle our guides steered us through safely, and a steady pull for an hour longer brought us to the foot of the hill where we were to land. We made our rattan-rope fast to a tree, and slept until nearly daybreak. One man told us in the morning that he had not slept a wink all night, as he was afraid our "painter" would part; but it stood the strain well, although the boat had swung about and tugged a good deal, owing to the swift current running down. The scene at sunrise was lovely; every stem and leaf was covered with dew-drops, and the hazy golden mist, through which palms, tree-ferns, and curious leafage of all descriptions loomed out more and more plainly until we saw everything in the foreground quite distinctly. It was a transformation scene on a gigantic scale, and its loveliness was such as only Turner at his best could have portrayed. The delicate arching outline of the nebong palms was sharply defined against the sky overhead, and large masses of a wild musa fringed both banks with immense leaves and clusters of delicate rosy bracts.

How comes it that none of our good landscape-painters ever visit the tropics, where the beauty of form and

colour in the landscapes is more glorious than anywhere
else, and yet nearly all the tropical pictures one sees
remind one of the daubs of a bad scene-painter?   Here
and there clumps of bamboo reminded one of the early
summer freshness of the weeping willow beside the
silvery trout streams at home.   A gorgeous scarlet
flowered climbing bauhinia draped some of the low trees
which nestled down near the water.   We turned out for
a ramble with our guns while our people cooked breakfast.   I never saw birds so numerous in Borneo before.
The first shot brought down a little green tree-pigeon,
with a magenta stain on its white breast and on its head.
A Kadyan boy we had with us blazed away with an old
Tower musket to his heart's content, and surprised us by
bringing in a long-tailed rufous-brown species of pigeon,
which we had first secured in the Sulu Islands.   Two or
three other rare Bornean birds were obtained.   Breakfast over, we set about climbing.   Our path lay through
the tall forest, and in places the undergrowth was so
thick that our guides and men had to cut us a path with
their parongs.   For the first mile or two vegetation was
scanty, but as we ascended ferns and selaginellas became
more plentiful.   We stayed here and there to examine
fallen trees for epiphytal orchids, which however were far
from abundant.   About half way up the hill we came to
a gorge, down which a considerable body of water flows,
but it is screened from sight by huge boulders, which lie
near together, forming a sort of " giant's causeway,"
across which we picked our way.   We peered down the
chasms, but could not catch a glimpse of the stream,
although we could hear it quite plainly as it forced its
way among the stones far below.   In one wet spot
several species of aroids formed a little colony all to
themselves.   Of those collected in flower, one proved

distinct enough to be made the type of a new genus when submitted to the botanical authorities at Kew. It grew in tufts on wet mossy stones, forming rather compact plants a foot in height. The spathe is of a bright rose colour, borne on a scape nearly as long as the leaves. I was especially interested in this plant, as I had seen a species singularly like it beside the Haya Haya stream at the foot of Kina Balu. As we approached the summit, we were stopped at one place by a perpendicular wall of sandstone rock, and we had to make a wearisome detour in order to gain the crest. I had been led to explore this hill at all risks, having been told by natives that a golden large-flowered phalænopsis was here to be found, but after a hot and weary search on rock and tree alike, no trace of any species of this genus could be found; and as I afterwards offered my informants a month's wages if they would bring me a flower of it without any result, I am inclined to think the thing a myth, like its "bright scarlet" congener. The only thing which consoled me for my disappointment was a beautiful golden-blossomed dendrobium, which has always been rare in our gardens; and I was also enabled to collect a large number of *Vanda Hookeri*. This last is the "Golden Duck" orchid of the Brunei Malays, and exists in quantity in the marshes near the river, and always, so far as I saw it, epiphytal, on a slender-stemmed red-fruited pandan.

This hill is not above five or six hundred feet above the sea, and yet on its crest the air was quite fresh and cool. We obtained extensive views from the top over a well-wooded country. Neither pitcher plants nor rhododendrons were seen, although both exist abundantly on the Lawas hills, only a few miles away. In descending a wide detour was made through the forest in search of plants, but distinct forms were rare. On reaching the boat we bathed, and changed our clothes, which was necessary, as we were drenched to the skin, and covered with dirt from the half-rotten tree-trunks, over which we had scrambled. It was about three o'clock, of course very hot; and our boat formed quite an attraction to the bees, butterflies, and some lovely blue day-flying moths, which fluttered in the sunshine. The wild bees were indeed rather troublesome; and some of the men who were nervous at their proximity, and began to buffet them, were stung. As we ate our luncheon of boiled rice and jam, they frequently settled on our plates, but they did not attack us.

The journey down the river was an easy and pleasant one. The water, which had been so high and turbid the night before, had now regained its proper level, and except exactly amid stream the surface was as smooth as a mirror. The curving nipa leaves and other vegetation were most sharply reflected from the placid surface, so clearly indeed, that one could scarcely see where reality ended, and the shadow began. The presence of the nipa palm beside the banks of eastern rivers, is almost always evidence of deep water. In the shallow parts the pink-blossomed banana and bauhinia-draped trees were most beautiful, here and there varied by elegant groups of pandanus. We stayed at intervals to examine the vegetation more closely, and did not reach the Murut settlement before nightfall.

We paid off our guides, and stayed here an hour or two to rest our men. We slept in the boat, and found the mosquitoes very voracious. When the moon rose we continued our journey. In Bornean travel, near the coast, boats form the best conveyance. There are no horses, nor indeed roads suitable for them; so that all journeys inland must be performed on foot. Buffaloes

may in some places be obtained. If no heavy loads
have to be carried, however, one may travel quicker
without them, except where deep and rapid flowing
streams have to be forded, and there they are most
useful.

We stayed at one little sago station, where the natives
were preparing the raw product. The process is very
simple. The trees are cut down just as they attain
maturity, the time being known by the production of the
branched inflorescence. The leaves are removed, and
then the trunks, which are ten to fifteen feet long, and
as thick as a man's body, are split longitudinally into
two halves. A man then cuts out the pith, with which
the whole centre of the trunk is filled. This requires
some skill. The implement employed for the purpose
is an axe, formed of a bamboo-stem, fixed in a stout
wooden handle, and lashed with rattan. By repeated
strokes of this instrument the pith and fibres are scooped
out in thin layers, care being taken to cut it out as free
from lumps as possible. The pulped pith is then carried
in baskets to a washing apparatus. This consists of a
rudely-constructed vat, elevated on piles, beside a river
or brook, whence fresh and clean water is plentifully
obtainable.

From the vat a spout conducts the water into a trough
below. The bottom of the vat is covered with a mat or
bark-strainer. The pith is now placed in the vat, and
trodden, water being occasionally poured over it during
the progress, and the result is that the fine sago starch
is washed through, and settles in the bottom of the
trough below, the coarse particles and other impurities
being retained by the strainers, at the bottom of the
treading-vat. After the fine sago has been allowed time
to settle in the trough, the water is run off, and the

white putty-looking mass below is packed up in bags, and sold to the Chinamen, by whom it is again washed and dried, previous to its being shipped to the Singapore market. Two species of sago palm grow here, forming stout-stemmed trees, thirty or forty feet in height. They are readily distinguished by the one having smooth bases to the sheathing leaf-stalks, while the other has the leaf-sheaths set with stout black spines. The smooth variety is most abundant. The dried leaf-sheaths of this palm are utilised in the manufacture of neat baskets, being neatly sown together with strips of rattan, and fitted with lids. Rattans are much used in house building, the largest timbers being secured by their aid only.

It is singular that pegs or nails are never used by the Malays, except in boat-building; and the neatness and ingenuity with which rattan is used by these people is wonderful. In one of the Kadyan villages, on the Lawas, I saw a violin, the back, front, and sides of which were actually stitched together with slender strips of rattan. It had been copied from a European model, and had a much better tone than one would expect to find under the circumstances.

The musical instruments made and used by the Malays and aboriginal Borneans are inferior to those of Burmah and Siam, or even to those used by the Javanese. The pentatonic scale is employed, and the music is monotonous and plaintive in its character. This is especially true of the women's songs, which are mostly of a dirge-like kind. I remember a Kadyan girl used to sing sometimes during my first visit to the Lawas, and the effect at night more especially was extremely weird and melancholy. She had a rich mellow voice, rising and falling in minor cadences, and dying away sweetly tremulous as a silver bell. This poor girl's life, however, ended suddenly. She usually walked through the clearing every day into the forest beyond to fetch in fire-wood. One day she did not return as usual, and a search was made for her along the paths in the neighbourhood without success. Some men who were returning from gutta collecting, however, found her lying beneath a large tree, and beside her was a large branch, recently broken off. It was supposed that this branch had accidentally fallen, and struck her, so causing her death.

Modifications of the " cheng," or calabash pipes, are made both by the Kayans, on the Baram river, and also by the Dusun villagers, near Kina Balu. There are distinct differences between the instruments as made by each tribe. That from the Baram consists of seven pipes; six arranged in a circle around a long central one, all seven being furnished with a free reed at the base, where they are inserted in a calabash-gourd. Holes are cut in the six outer pipes for fingering; the central pipe is, however, an open or drone-pipe, the tone being intensified by fixing a loose cap of bamboo on the upper end. It is played by blowing air into the neck of the gourd, or by drawing the breath according to the effects desired. The Dusun pipes are formed of eight pipes, four short, and equal in length, and four long and unequal. Reeds are cut at the lower end in all the pipes, but the fingering is performed on the ends of the four equal short pipes, there being no holes cut in the pipes for this purpose, as in the Kayan instrument.

I brought home examples of both varieties; and these are now in the Veitchian Museum at Chelsea. Two or three varieties of flutes are made, also an instrument resembling the old wooden flageolet, so common in England before the advent of the tin whistle.

McNair, in his work on Perak, mentions a curiosity, in the shape of an aëolian flute, formed of a bamboo, in which holes are cut, so as to produce musical sounds when acted on by the wind. An instrument like the Jew's harp is made of a single strip of bamboo; and a curious stringed instrument is made of a joint of large yellow bamboo, the nine or ten open strings of which produce notes similar to those of a banjo, when twanged with the fingers. A specimen of this instrument may be seen in the Veitchian Museum at Chelsea, together with one of similar design but of much more complicated and finer make from Madagascar. Wooden drums, formed of hollow tree-trunks, and having goat or deer-skin tightly stretched over the ends, are common, and of various sizes. The old war-drums were made thus; but this instrument is now nearly obsolete, being to a great extent replaced by metal gongs, of native manufacture certainly; but doubtless the idea was copied from the Chinese.

Nearly every trading prahu or boat carries one of these gongs; and the Muruts are very fond of such music, and keep up an incessant din on these instruments at their festivals. Sets of eight or ten small such are often fixed in a rattan and bamboo frame, and beaten with two sticks, dulcimer fashion; and I have seen similar contrivances formed of iron bars; and even strips of dry hard bamboo wood in the Sulu isles, the scale in this case being similar to our own.

It is very uncommon to hear performers playing in concert, unless in the case of gong-beating; indeed, music is at a low ebb throughout the island. The songs of the boatman, on the other hand, are often pleasing and melodious. A good many of their songs are Mahomedan prayers, or chants; but occasionally the theme is on secular, and often very amusing subjects. It is common for one man to strike up a song, improvising his subject as he sings, and then all the crew laughingly join in the chorus. They keep time to the music in paddling; and I always encouraged my boatmen to sing, as it relieves the monotony of the bump, bump of the paddles against the side of the vessel, which becomes very tedious after the first hour or two. One always has to be prepared for squalls when on the sea. They are especially common at night, after very hot days. You see a black cloud lowering on the horizon. Then a cool breeze fans your cheek. You at once strike all sail. The breeze gets stronger and stronger, until you find yourself rocking about on a rough "choppy" sea, amid a hurricane of wind and rain.

Thunder and lightning are especially common during the wet monsoon. The mountains behind " Thunder and Lightning Bay," to the north of the capital, are often perfectly illuminated by lightning flashes; and at times the thunder is deafening to hear. As to the lightning latent flashes of electricity are visible most nights throughout the year; and it is not uncommon to see a continuous play of lightning on the horizon, especially after very sultry days. At times the sea is so highly phosphorescent, that the boat leaves a wake of bright light in the water, and the paddles look as though moving through a caldron of molten silver. This phenomenon is most commonly observable after calm sultry weather.

The sudden manner in which the rivers rise after heavy rain is wonderful; and the flat forests beside or near the rivers often become flooded. You may go to bed at night, and awake to find the native house in which you slept surrounded by acres of water a yard deep in the morning. This is especially true of flat tracts, through which streams flow near the great water-sheds inland. Considerable damage results to the cultivated patches on the hills from these sudden rains; and formidable land-slips not unfrequently take place on the steep hills near the rivers. Cultivation near the capital is, however, of a poor description, compared with the plains of Menkabong, Tawaran, and Tampassuk, or the hills further inland.

A lover of nature who sees a tropical country for the first time, cannot help but enjoy the bright light and heat, the vegetable glories of flower, fruit, and leaf, called forth by the rain and sunshine—of a clime where winter is unknown. And yet, with all the sunshine and showers, the tropical blossoms are in a way aristocratic and exclusive, and never mingle socially in bosky masses, as do our own wildings; and it is not possible to name half-a-dozen of them that could at all compare with the blue-bells, or heather, the buttercups, primroses, forget-me-nots, anemones, violets, and rosy lychnis of our own cool moist woods and pastures.

During a year's rambles in one of the richest and most fertile of tropical islands, I saw nothing really fresh and spring-like; nothing like the "green and gold" of daffodils, and the tender young grass of April, or the royal glory of a summer iris, or an autumnal crocus on its mossy bed. This much is ever lacking in the forest primæval; and even in gardens—Eastern gardens—beautiful as they undoubtedly are in many ways, the sameness, the cloying degree of permanency observable in the forests, becomes intensified, and so still more unsatisfying. The plants seem always to present the same aspect; and although most of them are at their best when revived by the rains, just after the dry season, yet the charm of freshness is destroyed by the number of evergreens everywhere, and the driblets of bloom kept up by them nearly all the year round.

Still the beauty of tropical gardens is lovely of its kind. You have, or may have, all the tropical treasures of Kew—palms, ferns, and orchids—around you in the open air; but all this is as the beauty of a lovely woman, jaded by over-enjoyment, the whirl of a whole season's gaieties! There is elegance of form, and charm of colour, all the refinement of cultured beauty, sure enough. Victoria water-lilies, and dainty nymphæas in open air pools, the flesh-tinted blooms, and umbrageous leafage of the sacred lotus also; the noble amherstia, with its pendants of crimson and gold,—groves of feathery-leaved palms—all this, and very much more, is common; but it is astonishing how soon one tires of this plethora of floral charms, and how eager becomes the longing to sniff the homely fragrance of pinks and wall-flowers; to stoop for a violet from a mossy hedge-bank, or a snow-drop even from a cotter's garden. Indeed, there is no gainsaying the fact, as has been pointed out by Wallace and others, that the most lovely and satisfying, the most sociable of all flowers, are those of temperate climates.

CHAPTER IX.

A VOYAGE TO SULU.

AFTER having spent some time on the north-west coast of Borneo, varied by collecting expeditions further in the interior of the Murut and Dusun countries, I took a passage on the small trading steamer *Far East*, bound for Sandakan and the Sulu Archipelago. An intelligent young Scotchman, Mr. W. C. Cowie, part owner and engineer, was on board, and enlivened the voyage with a fund of information relating to the habits, customs, and trade of the natives among whom we were going. We were accompanied by his brother, who was going to reside in Sulu for trading purposes, and several Chinese and Malay traders also had taken deck passages. We sailed about 7 A.M. on April 5th, and the weather being fine we obtained capital views of the Bornean coast as we steamed along.

This was the greatest season of drought which had been known here for some time, nearly five months without rain, and this under a tropical sun, and in several places we could see jungle fires raging along the coast.

The monsoon was dead against us, and we met numerous native boats flying down to Labuan before the wind. These were laden with pearl-shell, trepang, etc., and were mostly from the islands of Balabac and Palawan; some, however, had come round from the north-east coast of Borneo, and even from the Sulu isles. In about a fortnight the monsoon is expected to change, when they will find no difficulty in returning safely. At sunset, and again at sunrise, we saw " Kina Balu " towering up into the clouds, and apparently very near to the coast, but the distance is very deceptive. It was dark when we entered Sandakan Bay, and about three o'clock on the morning of the 8th, I was awakened by the rattling of the anchor-chains, and found we were at Sandakan itself. It is merely a small trading station consisting of about a dozen " ataps," or palm thatched houses built over the water, and a long " jimbatan," or jetty, also on piles, serves as a roadway and a landing stage for produce.

At the time of my visit the only European residents were Mr. W. B. Pryer, who acted as agent and resident for the company, who had just obtained cessions of territory from the Sultans of Brunei and Sulu respectively, and Mr. Martin, a trader. There was formerly a depôt here belonging to the " Labuan Trading Company," managed by a Mr. Sachze, who died rather suddenly, as is believed by poison administered by his wife, a beautiful native woman given to intrigue. We landed at daybreak, and Mr. Cowie and myself took our guns and went for a walk in the forest behind the little group of houses. We followed a path which had been recently cut, and which led us in a northerly direction for about half a mile until we came to a stream descending the steep hill side in a series of little falls. Pigeons were plentiful here, but the trees were too high to allow of our shooting them. We also disturbed a colony of large red monkeys, who were break-fasting on a tall fig-tree in fruit. We clambered up the hill-side and walked along the ridge for some distance. The surface vegetation was very meagre, only a few ferns being obtained, all of which I had seen before, with the exception of a bipinnate form of *Blechnum orientalis,* having fronds five feet in length.

We retraced our steps along the ridge and descended near the houses, following for some distance the little stream which supplies beautifully clear and cool water to the houses, and ships which call in here occasionally. This stream falls over the sandstone rocks about a hundred yards from the houses, to which it is conveyed by a large bamboo aqueduct. Quite near to the rocks a neat little bath house has been erected, and through the upper part of this structure the bamboo water-pipe is carried, and by blocking it up with a plug a delicious shower-bath is obtainable. We sent for our towels and clean clothes from the ship, and enjoyed our morning ablutions very much. The noble *Dipteris Horsfieldii* was luxuriant on the rocks here, and a fine scarlet ixora was a perfect mass of bloom. While searching for plants on the wet rocks near the bath-house, I was startled by a snake popping its head out of a bunch of herbage just level with my face! I struck at it with a stick I had in my hand, but it made its escape apparently unhurt, and perhaps more frightened than I was, although I entertain a horror of these crea-tures. Returning to the ship I shot a fine fish hawk as it flew overhead on its way to the forest. After breakfast we paid Mr. Pryer a visit, and enjoyed looking over splendid collections of Lepidoptera and Coleoptera which he had made here. Some of the butterflies and beetles were especially fine, and several were supposed to be new to science. He had also a small collection of bird skins made here, but I noted nothing among them different to those of the north-west coast.

When Mr. Pryer first came to live here the natives had annoyed him a good deal by coming below the house at night and stealing rice. This they did by making a hole through the bags with a spear, so that the rice ran through the interstices of the lath floor, and was caught in a vessel held below for that purpose. One day, however, a tolerably large and healthy alligator was brought in for sale, and with the eye of a naturalist, Mr. Pryer at once saw his chance. The ugly creature was purchased and confined beneath the house, and it is needless to add that the nocturnal pilfering in that direction was immediately discontinued. Alligators of enormous dimensions are said to be very common here, but we had to be satisfied with a glimpse of a shark in the bay. Elephants are said to come down to the banks of the Sagaliad river, and a young rhinoceros was actually shot there a few months only after the time of our visit. Having borrowed a boat and obtained a native crew we landed on two of the islands in the bay, and found them equally barren. The only plants of interest we noticed were one or two species of palms, which I had not seen elsewhere, and of one of these I obtained a large quantity of seeds. We saw plenty of curlew, and large flocks of milk white cranes or " padi birds," rested on the trees near the shore. It was nearly dusk when we returned to the ship, and being wet and dirty, as one almost invariably is on exploring tours in the forest and jungle, we were glad to visit the little bath-house once more, and change our clothes before dinner on the cool upper deck of the little steamer.

At daybreak I was awoke by the rattling of the chains as the anchor was weighed, and in a few minutes afterwards Sandakan was behind us as we steamed away to the Sulu Archipelago. We reached Meimbong on the evening of the 10th, and anchored just off the traders' houses, which, as is usual here, are built on piles far enough out from the shore for vessels to anchor at the little jetty before the doors. Sulu is about thirty-six hours steaming from Sandakan, but in this case we were longer. We reached the islands at the entrance to the harbour of Meimbong just at sundown, and were much impressed by the indications of cultivation and fertility which they presented. We could also see the culti-vated patches and the fruit groves on the Sulu hills quite plainly, while the cool fresh evening air was deli-ciously perfumed, with what we afterwards found to be a mint-like plant (*Hyptis suaveolens*), very common throughout the island, especially in waste places and cornfields.

After dinner we went ashore to see an old Chinaman named " Peah," one of the principal traders in the place. His house was half house and half warehouse, consisting of a large front room the entire length of the house with some private apartments behind, the kitchen, as is usual, being a separate structure at the end of the dwelling. Half the large front room consisted of a raised platform about four feet in height, carpeted with finely-worked pandan mats, and covered with a fancy chintz canopy, fringed in front. Cushions were piled up on the parti-coloured mats, and between these and the partition be-hind fancy coloured boxes were piled ostentatiously, each secured by a brass lock of Chinese manufacture. On entering we found " Peah " sitting on the platform talking to some Sulu traders, his wife, a neat little Chinese woman, and about a dozen slaves and attendants, mostly Sulu girls. The room was but dimly illuminated with cocoa nut oil lamps, but a couple of composite candles were brought on our arrival, and installed in two fancy glass holders. The girls ran away to the kitchen to prepare chocolate, which, together with biscuits, was soon handed round, after which one of the dusky belles brought us nipa leaf cigarettes very deftly made.

A long " bichara," or talk on trading and other topics now took place, gin and water being handed round at intervals. We afterwards had some music on a kind of harmonica, formed of about a dozen small gongs of graded sizes, arranged in a bamboo frame, these being beaten dulcimer-like by two sticks to an accompaniment of five or six larger gongs and of some Malay drums. The whole made a deafening noise as I thought, but at a distance some very pleasant effects are produced, the smaller gongs sounding quite sweet and bell-like in tone.

It is not an uncommon practice for Sulu parents to sell their children, or for them to be taken into slavery, as payment for some debt previously contracted by their parents or guardians. It is a kind of slavery, however, like that in Borneo, which is not so objectionable as it sounds, since they enjoy pretty much liberty, and are often far better off in the way of food and clothing than if they were free ; nor are they torn from their home and friends as in the case of the poor African of years ago. As I have said they are well treated and are rarely chastised, but we had one instance of this being done during the time we lay in harbour here. A well-known Chinese trader from Labuan " Cheng Ting" had brought with him a young Chinese servant, or " boy" about twenty years of age, and for a Chinaman remarkably handsome, with a jet black pig-tail hanging nearly as low as his heels. This " boy" was a great favourite with " Peah's" Sulu girls, especially with one whom we, not knowing by name,

had christened the "gipsy," a remarkably well made girl
with expressive eyes, high cheek-bones, and luxuriant
hair, all of which was, doubtless, altogether too much for
the tender susceptibilities of a young oriental. We lay
close along side the pile wharf, and one night were awoke
by a woman's piercing shrieks, and the loud voices of
several men, and on our going to see the cause we found
the youthful oriental in the hands of a couple of "Peah's"
coolies, who stripped this celestial Adonis, and tying him
to a post by his queue, they gave him a dozen or so with
a rattan, at which he did bawl most lustily, much to the
amusement of his captors. And she, the dusky Venus,
was handed over to Mrs. "Peah," who corrected her
privately in the women's apartment, and afterwards
chained the erring damsel in a space below her own bed,
so as to prevent her stealing out to midnight meetings
again during our stay. I do not think either of the cul-
prits were hurt much, and despite the yells of the "boy,"
the rascal was jolly enough and full of bravado when he
came on board in the morning.

The first morning after our arrival I and Mr. Cowie
took a boat at sunrise and pulled down to the market
place. Leaving our boat at the Orang Kayu's house we
walked through the narrow gateway, and crossing the
place where the market is held, just outside the barricade,
we followed the course of the river for some distance, and
obtained capital shooting at the large blue pigeons, evidently the same species as that so common in Borneo.
We should have had much better sport, only that about
a dozen of the "lads of the village" followed like curs
at our heels, and they ran riot as soon as ever they
saw a bird fall, and in their eagerness to clutch it they
did a good deal of damage to a long-tailed rufous brown
pigeon which I shot here for the first time and wished

to preserve. Their frantic leaping, splashing and yelling in the little stream and on its banks also frightened away many birds before we could get within range, while anything like remonstrance was so much labour thrown away. White and green paroquets flew screaming overhead as they left the tall trees near the coast, where they had evidently roosted for the night, and were now most probably on their way to their feeding grounds, the fruit trees in the forest further inland. We crossed several cultivated patches, and growing in clumps near the native houses we saw quantities of *Musa textilis* cultivated here, and also in the Philippines, the fibre being used for cordage, and it is also largely imported into this country under the name of "manilla hemp." On waste places beside the river, *Quisqualis indica* was very abundant, forming bushes about four feet in height, its slender branches being literally borne down to the ground by the weight of its flowers, which hung in immense clusters from the points of its branches.

On our return we made a detour to the right and came upon several graves, a few of which were fenced in with bushes and had rude headstones, or a post to mark the spot. Other graves were neglected and overgrown with weeds. Here a variety of the "Frangipane" (*Plumieria acuminata*), was very lovely, bearing immense clusters of its waxy flowers which exhale a most delicious odour. These flowers are white with a yellow centre, and are flushed with purple behind. This plant, or, as seen here in Sulu, small tree, is common throughout the Malay region, and is by the natives esteemed as a suitable decoration for the graves of their friends. Its Malay name of "Bunga orang sudah mati," meaning literally, "Dead man's flower." We returned to the river near the

market-place and obtained a nice cool bath previous to
returning for breakfast on board. About two o'clock we
all returned, and leaving the boat in a creek a little
beyond the headman's house, we bore across the plain to
the right through an orchard-like grove of teak-trees. I
had stopped to load my gun before starting, and when I
hastened on to rejoin my friends, I found them at the
foot of a dead teak-tree, where they had kindly awaited
my coming to point out a pretty pink-flowered orchid
which was clinging to the naked branches right in the
blazing sunshine, and flowering most profusely.

We at last came to an undulating plain of coarse
"lallang" grass four feet in height, while the soil at our
feet was thickly paved with vitrified slag or scoriæ, the
product of the island during its volcanic epoch. It was
very hot, and the walking over the sharp stones, hidden
as they were in the tall grass, was, to say the least of it,
very troublesome. We had expected to find deer or wild
pig in the patches of thick jungle which occur here and
there, but the dogs were too wild and did not hunt the
ground well. Along the edge of a bit of old forest we
obtained an occasional shot at a bird or two, and amongst
others we secured a golden oriole with black wing, tips
and tail, a small hawk, and a large greenish paroquet,
together with several pigeons. The black and white and
large blue pigeons were extremely plentiful here, as also
were white paroquets, but these last were too wary to
allow us within range.

I made several dips into the patches of old forest in
search of plants, but nothing of interest was seen. Orchids appeared to be very rare, and with the exception
of a dingy yellow-flowered cleisostoma which grew rather
plentifully on the teak trees, nothing more was seen.
We had had a long and wearying walk, and it was about

half-an-hour before sundown when we returned to the boat and pulled to the ship for dinner. I was very tired, but altogether pleased at having secured at least one new species of orchid as well as two or three birds that I had never seen before. After dinner I occupied myself in sketching my new pink orchid and in helping my "boy" skin the birds I wished to preserve.

I was happy in the labour, and no description could possibly convey any idea of that delight which fills one when new and beautiful objects of natural history are discovered for the first time.

CHAPTER X.

A ROYAL PIG-HUNT.

Soon after dinner one of the Sultan's "ministers" came
on board to tell us that a grand pig-hunt was to be held
on the morrow, at which the Sultan and suite were to be
present, and as royal boar-hunts are not every-day affairs,
we all made up our minds to get ponies and go to see the
sport. These pig-hunting forays are as popular in Sulu as
a royal stag-hunt at home, only that the Sulus have perhaps a better reason to hunt their wild pigs, since they do
a deal of damage to the growing crops. About 9 o'clock
in the morning we went down to the headman's house
at Meimbong and got our ponies saddled, and after a ride
of about half-an-hour through long grass and bushes we
came upon the beaters and dogs in a strip of low jungle
at the foot of a little hill. The men were yelling and
shouting so as to frighten the pigs from their covert out
into the grassy plain, where horsemen, each armed with
a long slender-shafted hunting-spear, were waiting in

readiness to give chase and dispatch them. We, too,
waited here a little while, but finding no signs of sport we
rode on to a clump of low trees on the hill side where we
were told the Sultan and his people were waiting. We
found His Highness had dismounted, and was sitting on
the trunk of a fallen tree, smoking and watching for signs
of sport. He looked pleased to see us, and after he had
shaken hands with Mr. Cowie, whom he had long known,
I was introduced to him. Mr. Cowie told him I had come
to explore the island for natural history purposes, and
that I particularly wished to ascend the two highest mountains. He seemed rather amused to hear of a traveller
looking for flowers and birds, but graciously replied that
I could go where I liked and he would tell his people to
help me, adding, that the best way of reaching the highest
mountain would be to come to his Istana and sleep there,
after which the mountain could be ascended in a day from
that place. I had previously been recommended to his
good offices by the government at Labuan through their
consular agent, Inche Mahomed, of Brunei, who had
landed here in Sulu a day or two previously in H.M.
gunboat " Fly," Capt. McNeil. As I saw His Highness
here seated on a fallen tree I could not help noticing
how emblematical the position was, since at the best his
position here as Sultan is but nominal, so fallen are the
fortunes of his house. Only two months after my visit,
i.e., in July, 1878, the Spaniards, after nibbling like timid
mice at the Sulu cheese for centuries took formal possession of the whole island by hoisting their flag in the
Sultan's capital of Meimbong.

Behind him the Sultana and the ladies of her Court
were mounted on ponies, one or two scarlet and gold
coloured umbrellas being held over them. Altogether
there were ten or twelve mounted ladies and several

female attendants, betel-box carriers, &c., on foot. The Sultan himself had forty or fifty followers standing around in a broken circle. He is about thirty-five years of age, and has a bright and intelligent countenance. His dress consisted of an embroidered silk kerchief tied turban fashion on his head, a dark close-fitting jacket of semi-transparent material, embroidered with red and yellow flowers, and having tight sleeves. Under this he wore a white merino vest. Like most of his followers he wore breeches which fit very tight below the knee, and are wide and baggy in the seat. These were black and beautifully embroidered with flowers just below the knee. White socks and elastic-sided boots of European manufacture completed what my sailor friends called "his queer rig." His eldest son, an "awful young sweep," of about twenty years of age, was much more gaily attired in a white striped blue vest and trowsers, and a bright buff head-dress, while, like his father, he wore the short heavy Sulu sword or "barong." The Sultana and her suite kept in the background, of course, but were evidently much interested at our visit. I noted that she wore full Turkish trowsers of blue silk richly embroidered, and a blue vest fitting very tight and ornamented with gold buttons, lace in front, using the universal sarong as a covering for her shoulders; around her head a clear buff kerchief was tied turban fashion; white cotton stockings and a pair of Chinese slippers completed her outward visibilities. Nearly all the Sulu women wear a deal of yellow, which contrasts vividly with their luxuriant black hair, and like the men they ride well and also in the same style,—exactly, fair reader,—*à la fourchette!*

We also had dismounted, of course, and had stood talking and looking on the particoloured scene and swarthy faces around us, when suddenly a cry from the jungle below, a regular chorus of men and dogs, told us that the bristly boar had at last been driven into the open grass to run for his life. Everybody, Sultan and all, scrambled to their ponies and away we all went, a gay cavalcade truly, down the hill-side. Presently the pig came in sight, followed by one or two miserable-looking curs and half-a-dozen men and boys on horseback, each armed with the long light-shafted spear. We now saw of what sterling metal the Sulu ponies are made. On they came with dilated nostrils and widely-spread forefeet, scarcely requiring a touch of the reins to guide them as they avoided a jutting rock here or a half-hidden "snag" there, and all the time turned and wheeled as quickly as the hunted pig itself. No European horse would have kept its legs ten minutes on this uneven ground, paved as it was with immense blocks of volcanic scoriæ. These intelligent little beasts seemed actually to understand and enjoy the sport. One young fellow, mounted on a shapely little grey, at length came up alongside the pig. Throwing his hempen bridle on the pony's neck, and deftly handling his long spear, he wounded the boar in the side, at which it turned and rushed at the horse, its long white curved tusks gleaming beside its open jaws. Quick as thought the pony avoided him, and ere the pig could stay its impetuous rush the rider's spear was struck right through its body at a thrust, the gleaming blade having entered the soil to a depth of several inches. It was killed on the spot. The rider unfastened a length of slender manilla rope from his saddle and threw it to a man on foot, who slipped a noose over the body of the pig and afterwards tied the other end of the rope to the horse's tail, and thus it was dragged away to the heap of slain porkers some distance off. Seeing a couple of horsemen galloping in another direction we concluded they had a

pig in chase, and so it proved. We headed the game and
they soon came up to it, and a thrust or two with the
deadly spear and all was over with poor piggie. This
was a small black fellow about half the size of an English
boar. Not entertaining the prejudices of our Mahomedan friends we begged the body of this last pig, and
when the captors asked for what purpose we required it,
we discreetly replied that we wanted it for our dogs.
This was satisfactory, and one of the men volunteered to
drag it down to the boat at his pony's tail.

I shall not forget the Royal Pig Hunt in Sulu for
some time. There we were among the tall grass and
jungle, and the ever changing position of the numerous
gaily attired horsemen was a beautiful sight to see. A
group of fox-hunters at home by a covert side is a pleasing sight, but here in the region of perpetual sunshine
and palm-leaves—in this " beautiful isle of the sea "—the
sight was not only pleasing but quite a novelty to us—a
thing seen for the first time, and perchance an experience
never to be enjoyed again. Down below us we could see
long files of horsemen wending their way to another piece
of covert which the men on foot and dogs were now beating, while, on the little rounded hill above, the Sultana
and her ladies formed a bright and picturesque group on
horseback, their large vividly-coloured umbrellas standing
out clear and sharp against the cloudless sky.

We saw the Sultan again towards the close of the day,
and had a further chat with him, in which he much regretted that the English would not help him to resist the
agressions of his neighbours, the Spaniards, whom the
Sultan detests, and perhaps not without reason. He sent
a man to see how many pigs had been killed, and on
being told seventeen, he observed, that they had sometimes killed as many as fifty in one day's hunting.

Thanking him for his invitation to us to visit him at
the Istana, which he had again repeated, we bade him
him adieu, and returned towards Meimbong, well pleased
with our day's adventures. The Sultan and his suite
rode towards the Istana, but his son, before alluded to,
accompanied us with a *posse* of his young followers.
When we reached the arable plain near the market-place,
we came upon another group of hunters, and nothing
would please the young rascal but that I and Mr. Cowie
should try some of his father's horses. They are beautiful creatures of the Sulu breed, but with a little of the
Arab blood added. They are never shod, and in picking
their way among rocks or fallen trunks of trees they are
as sure-footed as a goat. We had some capital racing.
The Sulu saddles are of wood, very small, with high
wooden pommels, resembling those of a cavalry saddle.
The stirrups are represented by a woven hemp riband four
feet long and about an inch wide, with a loop at each end,
through which the big toe of the rider is inserted. This
riband passes through an opening over the top of the
saddle, and is not fixed, but slides backwards and forwards according to the pressure brought to bear on it by
the rider. Of course, I could not ride on one of these
little saddles with sliding stirrups, so I had them taken
off and returned to my boyish practice of bare-backed
riding. These ponies had been out hunting all day and
yet showed no traces of fatigue, indeed they flew over
the dry clods at full speed and evidently were quite
used to racing—appearing to enjoy it as much as we did
ourselves.

After this sport was concluded we returned on board
to dinner, after having stopped for a few minutes at the
ford near the market to get a bath in the stream, which is
here as clear and sparkling as a Derbyshire brook. This

day's public amusement taking place as it did so soon after my arrival was a most fortunate thing for me, since I thus obtained an introduction to the Sultan and most of his people, and wherever I wandered in the island afterwards I was always well received, which was lucky, since the Sulus are not noted for their civility to strangers. Even the small cotters who cultivate their little farms and fruit groves up on the hills had heard of me, and were very hospitable when, as happened soon afterwards, I found my way up amongst them. The Sulu hills are especially beautiful.

Nearly every day, morning and evening, we used to go down to the little Meimbong river near the Orang Kayu's house to bathe; and in the evening especially the tops of the highest hills were lovely, glowing with warmth in the golden light; now clear, now hazy, the last tremulous kisses of the lingering sun. I used to walk a mile or two up the left bank of the winding river nearly every evening before I had my bath, and I nearly always took my gun, as the birds here were tolerably plentiful, and in some cases very beautiful or interesting. There are at least a dozen kinds of pigeons and doves; and three of the species I shot, I had never seen before. Paroquets are common, and fly shrieking overhead morning and evening. I shot four kinds in all, two large green ones, a white one, and a small green one having a blue head, and a pair of long-shafted, racquet-shaped feathers in its tail.

One of the most conspicuous of the birds here is the gold and black oriole before mentioned, and a blackbird having a grey back and immense flesh-coloured orbits is not uncommon on trees beside the river. Two species of kingfisher were seen; one the common blue kind, with a white ring around its neck, and a discordant,

laughing note : white padi birds, curlew, sandpipers, and
a crow, are also quite common; eagles, ospreys, and
hawks also abound; and I especially noticed an eagle or
harrier circling over the grassy plains, regularly hunting
the ground, and occasionally stooping as if to secure its
prey. This bird is pure white, with black wing tips and
tail. A water-rail was seen beside the river near the
town, and night-flying birds of the owl tribe were also
observed; but the familiar " chuck-chuck " note of the
" night-jar," so common on moonlight nights in Labuan,
we never once heard here. I saw one large owl dead,
and much regret that I did not skin and preserve it, badly
as the thing was mutilated. It resembled our native
" barn owl " in general appearance and colour, but was
much larger, the spread of its soft fledged wings being
over four feet. I saw one species of hornbill on the hills
and a pheasant, which, from the momentary glimpse I
caught of it, I took to belong to the " fireback " species,
so common in some parts of Borneo.

Deer are said to be plentiful; but we did not catch a
glimpse of them, although when riding in the interior I
have often disturbed the wild pigs among the long-matted
grass near the river. An enormous species of day-flying
bat was quite common here near the Sultan's palace, and
most weird and supernatural did they appear on dull
days, solemnly flying from one tree to another, their great
wings distended against the leaden sky overhead. As
far as I could see they were feeding on the durian trees
which surround the Istana, and probably sipping the
nectar from the large white flowers. I shot one which
measured four feet six inches across its outspread wings,
and its head was as large as that of a little terrier dog,
and of a similar shape, being of a dark foxey brown
colour. Its eyes were of a sickly pale brown tint, with a

small black pupil, and its entire body in the warm limp-
ness of death exhaled such a repulsive musky odour, far
worse than any downright stink I ever experienced, and
so penetrating and adhesive, that my hands smelt of it for
days, in spite of carbolic soap and repeated washings.   I
had no means of ascertaining whether this is really a
distinct species, or whether it is conspecific with the
large nocturnal fruit-bat of Borneo, immense flocks of
which may be seen passing overhead at dusk to their
feeding-grounds, the fruit orchards.

Of all the smaller forms of animal life in temperate
countries the butterflies are the most absolutely beautiful.   In the tropics they are especially so, being there
found of the largest size and most lovely hues.   In the
rice fields and by the open pathways, lively little golden-
winged kinds flutter in the sunshine.   Some are quite
wholly golden, others amber, with black fringes to their
wings; many varieties enliven the river margins, and
others sail aloft around the tops of the great forest trees.
The nearly dry bed of a forest stream is an attractive
spot to many of the finest tropical butterflies, especially
if it be chequered with shade and sunshine.   In such a
place they may be seen by the hundred, flitting, flutter-
ing, skimming or wobbling to and fro, enlivening the
cool greenery with their colour, beauty, and variety of
motion.   Here you see them at home and happy.   Their
colours defy description, so variable do they appear as
seen in the sunlight; sulphur and black, amber and blue,
velvety bands, purple shot with bronze, wings of blue,
inclining to green, and of green inclining to blue, and
of velvety blackness banded with pea or apple-green, are
only a few of their combinations.   Their beauty of
presence is so satisfying, that we almost forget their life
history, the egg so dainty in form, and often so beautiful

in sculpture, the caterpillar, attractive in its way, and chiefly remarkable for its leaf-eating powers; then the long sleep in a silken hammock, and finally a sunny awakening into life and beauty as a daintily painted butterfly. There must be something in the climate or vegetation of the Sulu islands especially favourable to insect life, and nowhere else did I see butterflies so plentiful as here, not only in the forest and by the river, but around the houses of Meimbong itself.

The site of the market being littered with fragments of fruit and other *débris*, was especially attractive to them; on being disturbed they fluttered away in crowds, only to return almost immediately to feast on the wasted sweets, and to open and close their gorgeous wings in the sunshine.

We were fortunate in obtaining plenty of fresh fish while lying in harbour here, and there were many kinds, some being strikingly beautiful in colour. Herrings and mackerel—or fish which so closely resemble them in size, colour, and flavour, that we did not distinguish the difference, were often brought on board. A singular white "ink fish," having large dark eyes and long tentacles, is eaten both by natives and Chinese. A large fish of a vermilion colour, in shape like a large carp, is plentiful and nice eating, as also is a similarly shaped species of an ashy grey colour, its sides delicately banded with blue and yellow. In the river are freshwater fish a couple of pounds or more in weight, and good angling is obtainable. Captain McNeil caught a nice basketful or two with rod and line by whipping down stream in the true Devonshire style. One of the fish he captured would weigh nearly two pounds, and had a sharp spined dorsal fin like an English perch. Mr. Cowie maintains that he has seen real spotted trout taken out

of this water; but I think some other kind must be
meant, although the water is quite pure enough for that
gentlemanly little fish.

From what I have written it will be seen that although
Sulu cannot now afford elephant or tiger hunting like
Malacca, India, or Ceylon, there is plenty of sport obtainable here nevertheless; indeed there are few countries
eastward where better hunting, shooting, and rod-fishing
can be obtained.   Sulu as seen from a distance on board
a ship out at sea, appears to be nearly all under cultivation ; but on riding into the interior a good deal of
uncultivated land and jungle is seen.   The jungle portion
has mostly been under cultivation in former years, and is
now lying fallow previous to its vegetation being again
cleared off by fire ready for the rude plough-culture here
adopted.   As approached from the westward the island
is really very picturesque, two or three of its peaks
rising from two to three thousand feet above sea level ;
these are separated from the coast by gentle undulating
hills or flattish plains.   One or two of the high hills are
quite denuded of the old forest, and cultivation extends
to their summits.   The two highest peaks, however, are
still clothed with the forest primeval, and it was these
two that I so much wished to explore.   The highest is
Bu'at Timantangis, or "Hill of Tears."

I was curious to know why such a poetic title had been
applied to the highest of the Sulu peaks, and so I made
inquiries.   In all cases the natives agreed as to the
"reason why," which is this.   When the Sulu boats sail
away towards the horizon on their trading excursions,
this peak is the last bit of their native land which is
visible; it is the "white cliffs of old England" to them ;
and the wanderers being accustomed to remember their
peaceful sunlit homes and their friends, drop a tear as

the last glimpse of their native earth fades from sight, perhaps for months, or even years; hence the name Bu'at Timantangis, or the "Hill of Tears." Bu'at Dahau is, however, but little less in altitude; and it is doubtless at its apex that the last crater in the island existed, although of course it has long been extinct; yet the course of the *débris* thrown out can be seen down its sides, which are scarred or furrowed by volcanic action in a very marked manner. Sugh, the ancient capital,—or Banawa as the place is now called—is in the hands of the Spaniards, and pretty regular communication is kept up from thence to Manilla and the Philippine group. One of the Chinese traders who came with us visited the place and brought back several jars of excellent biscuits and a few boxes of fine Manilla cigars. There are two market places in Meimbong, and there are three markets during the week; and as very few places afford a better epitome of the thrift of a people or the produce of a country than a market, I will briefly allude to what I saw of these held here.

We went to bathe early one morning, and saw the market-people coming in from all directions and bringing produce of the most varied character. Most of them— both men and women — were mounted on ponies or buffaloes; some indeed ride their cows to market as being preferable to walking, their produce being slung across the saddle before or behind. Every man carried a spear, and a couple of hours later the space beneath the clumps of bamboo just to the left of the market gate, was crowded with people, the women trading, and the men standing talking in groups, all the business of the day being done amid a forest of spears. The country people from the hills were very much interested in us as we moved about amongst them and their goods. Sweet potatoes, mangoes, bananas, yams and corn cobs, were offered for sale in neatly woven baskets made of cocoa-nut leaves. The leaves of piper betel made up into little packets, and lime beautifully fine and white (made by burning coral limestone and shells) were offered to betel-chewers ; nor was a good supply of the betel nuts them-selves wanting. We especially noticed a very large fruited variety of *Areca catechu* here, which I had never before seen, the individual fruits being as large as a hen's egg, and of a clear bright yellow colour. The typical form so common in Singapore and Labuan, has fruits the size of a pigeon's egg only, and of a clear orange-red colour.

Tobacco leaves of native growth and manufacture were exposed for sale in bundles, and some of it is made up into balls as large as a man's head, and several pounds in weight. Although tobacco can be easily grown here, it is but little valued, owing to faulty preparation ; and the inferior Chinese tobacco is preferred by the Sulus to their own produce, and is a regular kind of currency in which almost all small payments may be made. Thus, the hire of a pony for a day is about two bundles ; a day's wage for a man about the same. The wholesale price in Singapore is about sixpence a bundle, or even less. At the time of our visit rice was very scarce and dear in Sulu ; indeed as much as ten dollars per picul was paid, while horses and cattle were relatively very cheap. Thus good buffaloes could be bought for eight or ten dollars each; cattle at six to fifteen dollars a head, and ponies at ten to twenty dollars ; indeed many of the people were well nigh starving owing to the last war and the dry season combined; and in many cases they were glad to sell their cattle for rice, or the means of obtaining it. Among the few articles of native manufacture offered for sale, I noticed embroidered kerchiefs and sarongs, also rope of good quality. Fish, eggs, cocoa-nuts, jack-fruit, and cucumbers, were exceedingly plentiful.

It is not uncommon to see some few of the Sulus from the hills wearing tunics of chain armour, having brass plates on the breast and down the back, all the rest being fine chain-work. At the time of our visit Mr. Cowie bought one of these tunics for about two pounds, which he paid in rice. The Sulus themselves say that these were formerly made in the island, but I think this is extremely doubtful; and it is far more probable that this armour formerly belonged to their old enemies the Spaniards, from whom they have obtained it during the numerous wars between them. The most singular thing is that the comparatively few Sulus who possess these tunics should continue to wear them, as they most assuredly do.

There are a good few Chinese settlers here in Meim-bong who have stalls on which to expose their goods in the markets. They supply needles, thread, betel-nut knives, cheap calico and print goods, handkerchiefs, and occasionally blades of the choppers generally used in Sulu, and other common cutlery, looking-glasses, boxes, &c. The currency here is now the Chinese brass "cash," the rate of exchange at the time of my visit being 900 to the dollar. Payments of small amounts however, say up to twenty dollars, can always be made in white or "grey shirting." The packets of Chinese tobacco before alluded to, serve for small change.

CHAPTER XI.

THE SULTAN'S ISTANA AND THE "HILL OF TEARS."

A moonlight ride—A fragrant weed—The Istana—Modern armament—
"Gelah"—Royal hospitality—A social servant—The Sultan—State
sword or "Barong"—A Sulu dinner—A long audience—Curiosity
of the ladies—Departure to the mountain—A newly-made grave—
Orchids at home—A treat for our cattle—Rough climbing—Ferns
and mosses—The summit—Good views—Old traditions of the mountain—A picnic under cocoa-nut palms—"Gelah" *v.* Hennessy—
Return to the Istana—Further audience of the Sultan—Former
civilisation—Carved wood-work—Old manufactures—Old enemies—
Physique of the Sulus—A pearl among the swine—Market-people—
Slavery—Language—Land culture—Native food products—Domestic animals—Sea fruit.

ONE evening about sundown, immediately after an
early dinner on board, we set off to the Sultan's Istana,
which is situated just at the foot of Bu'at Timantangis,
the highest mountain in the island. The distance from
the harbour at Meimbong is seven or eight miles, a
pleasant ride indeed across an undulating and tolerably
well cultivated plain. We had ordered our ponies to be
in readiness at the Orang Kayu's house, and the boatmen who accompanied us from the ship soon saddled
them for us and made all ready. Mr. Anson Cowie
accompanied me. We had three ponies, two for ourselves, and one for a Sulu lad who had charge of our
stores, guns, &c., and who came to attend to the ponies
and accompany us up the mountain, to ascend which was
the main object of our journey. All the little details

requisite at starting attended to, it was nearly seven
o'clock as we rode through the market gate, just opposite
the headman's house—a veritable needle's eye—there
being barely room for a slim Sulu pony and its rider to
squeeze through. The moon was in the full, and rose as
we started over the plain. We had a delightful gallop,
and had no need of a guide, as the horses knew the
way perfectly well. It had been a remarkably hot day,
but it was now deliciously cool, the soft air being grate-
fully redolent with the odour of a mint-like plant (*Hyptis*)
before mentioned. We laughed and sang to our heart's
content, and doubtless much to the surprise of the few
Sulus we met hurrying homewards.

It seems strange that these beautiful and well cultivated islands should be still the last great stronghold of
piracy in the eastern seas. This has been the great blot
on the Sulu character for centuries ; and they are also
credited with having poisoned many of the traders who
formerly visited the island, and to whom they had become largely indebted for goods. We reached the Istana
soon after eight o'clock, and tying our ponies to the
verandah we ascended to the audience-chamber above.
Here, in this chamber, we noticed two small Armstrong
guns mounted on low carriages, and a Gatling gun or
mitrailleuse was also conspicuous. The presence of the
modern armament here would have been rather puzzling
had we not known that the Sultan had obtained these
guns from the steam-ship *America*, as the first instal-
ment of the rental or payment which has to be made
annually to the Sultan on account of his having ceded
Sandakan and his territory in North Borneo to Baron
Overbeck's Company.

Velvet-lined armchairs were immediately placed for us
at a round table below the raised platform, and refresh-

ments consisting of excellent chocolate and sweet biscuits were brought in. The Sultan's own servant or "boy," "Gelah," a most amusing fellow, saw that we were properly attended to, and told us that His Highness would soon be in to welcome us. After the chocolate, brandy and excellent Manilla cigars appeared under the direction of "Gelah," who seemed to know the habits of Englishmen tolerably well. He spoke Malay better than most of the others, and this language formed the only means of communication we had. The attendants not having brought a corkscrew, he sent off to fetch one, and then poured us out a glass each. It was Three Star Hennessey, and very good. After helping us, the imp took up one of the chocolate cups, poured a little water into it to rinse it, and then slung it out at the open door. He then very coolly nearly filled the cup with brandy and tossed it off neat without wincing; he also helped himself to the cigars as though to the manner born. As soon as we entered several boys, superintended by an old woman, had brought in a lot of cushions and arranged them on the platform near us. A lamp, and fancy betel and cigarette boxes were next brought and arranged. The Sultan himself appeared on the platform soon after we had finished eating, and shook hands with us very affably before he reclined on the cushions which had been placed for him. He came in with a dignified step and reclined very gracefully; but as conversation warmed up he sat upright on the edge of the platform with his legs dangling down in front, apparently as free and easy as a schoolboy on a rail fence. A good many Sulus came in during the evening, so that at ten o'clock the space between the platform and the door was pretty well filled. Some of his people had evidently told him of my propensity for sketching, and he asked to see my sketch-

P

book. Amongst other things therein was a rough sketch of a "barong" or sword, and its carved sheath belonging to the old Orang Kayu at Meimbong, which His Highness at once recognised, and he sent off "Gelah" to fetch a valuable one of his own, which was, as he told me, of Sulu manufacture. The blade was beautifully finished, having an inlaid representation of a scorpion on one side and a centipede on the other, together with some Arabic dates of important events. The handle was of ivory, carved and mounted in chased gold and pearls. I made a sketch of this weapon, at which he was greatly pleased, and he watched every line and touch with great interest.

We had dined previous to our leaving the ship, and I had congratulated myself earlier in the evening at having been lucky enough to escape eating more than a biscuit with my cup of chocolate; but even after ten o'clock our table was loaded with more edibles. There were dishes of snowy rice, biscuits, excellent fish, curried fowl, eggs boiled, and some bananas and other fruit. The whole was daintily cooked and well served. With a graceful wave of the hand he requested us to satisfy the hunger which, as he said, he felt sure had been occasioned by the long ride we had been so good as to undergo in order to visit him. Of course there was nothing for it but to fall to; and I must say that we both enjoyed the fresh fish and rice, and the well-made curry very much. Clean water and glasses were placed on the table, and chocolate was again brought in. After this meal more brandy and water and cigars were introduced to our notice by "Gelah," and we kept up a conversation with His Highness until after twelve o'clock, when he withdrew after having had a peep to see that our sleeping apartment was in good order. As soon as his back was turned towards us—

almost before, " Gelah " pocketed all the surplus cigars and took another cup of neat brandy,—his example being followed by one or two of the other attendants.

We retired to our room for the night ; and then the Sultan's son, Datu Mahomed, and " Bottelah," the Sultan's secretary, together with two or three others, including " Gelah," came in for a chat, so that we did not get a chance of sleeping a wink until after two o'clock. Even when we were alone in our sleeping apartment, and had reclined just as we were in our clothes on the cushions and finely worked mats spread out for us, I somehow felt conscious that we were watched ; and once I caught a glimpse of a dark figure gliding past a square opening in the wall above. Our room communicated with the audience chamber which we had just left, by a window-like opening about two feet square. The lights in the large chamber had been extinguished, while we, as is customary in the East, had a glimmering oil lamp in our room, so that any one in the audience chamber could see us plainly, without being themselves seen. We had no fear of treachery, and yet could not help feeling a creeping sensation of uneasiness as shadow after shadow passed the opening to the right of which we lay. At length a shadow lingering longer than usual, I sprang to my feet and put my head through the opening. A little suppressed scream, and the patter of bare feet on the platform on the other side, followed by muffled titters and whispering, told the tale.

The ladies of the court, debarred by etiquette from seeing us publicly, had taken advantage of the darkness to obtain a peep at us. Barefooted, they had moved more silently than mice on the platform in the next room, and had satisfied their curiosity by stealing to the opening one after another, and looking down on us to

their hearts' content. After this we got an hour or two
of rest, and awoke at daybreak, when everybody was
astir. We found our breakfast ready, and our ponies
were saddled and at the door.

The men whom the Sultan had promised us as guides,
and a buffalo to carry down plants, were also waiting,
and " Gelah " was eager to accompany us by order of his
royal master. Breakfast over, we started off in excellent
spirits up a gently rising path leading past a burial
ground, and beneath some of the finest Durian trees in
the island. A newly made grave ornamented with flowers
and the young flower-stems of the betel-nut palm, was
pointed out to us as being that of a man who had been
shot at the Istana in a squabble about one of the ladies
of the court. It appears that the man's wife having died
he wanted to carry off a relation of his who now belonged
to the Sultana's suite, and in the row which followed he
met with his death.

Our ride was a very pleasant one, and led us up through
several cultivated patches with here and there a belt of
jungle. Soon after leaving the Istana an aerides was
seen flowering very freely on the trees, also the ubiquitous *Dendrobium crumenatum*, with pseudo bulbs four feet
in length, the flowers much larger than usual. *Cymbidium aloifolium* was everywhere plentiful, clustering in
large masses on the boles of large trees in the clearings.
At an elevation of about 1000 feet we came to a village
and fruit grove, and here we stayed to rest awhile as the
sun was now very hot overhead, and a drink of cocoa-nut
milk proved very grateful. On the trees here I obtained
a greenish yellow flowered dendrobium, which proved
to be a new species very similar to the *D. d'Albertisii* of
New Guinea. At about 1500 feet we reached the skirt
of the old forest, and had to dismount and do the rest

of the ascent on foot. We had brought ropes with us, and removing the saddles and other gear we tethered the horses and buffalo to bushes in a little natural meadow where they could make a good meal off the fresh mountain grass. This was a great treat to them, as the coarse herbage of the plains was at this season very dry, and the horses in Meimbong were being fed on cocoa-nut leaves owing to the dearth of other fodder. We descended a gully, and crossing a little stream com-menced the ascent on foot, leaving a Sulu lad in charge of our goods and animals. We had at first a rough climb over tree roots and loose stones. In one place the ascent was nearly vertical, and the boulders being easily detached from the dry soil, it was dangerous for our followers below. An areca palm bearing large clusters of small scarlet fruit below a spreading crown of dark green leaves was very handsome, and both ferns and selaginellas were luxuriant in the shade. I collected specimens of all I saw for scientific purposes. Pigeons and paroquets and other birds were seen here on the trees overhead, but although we shot at several and saw them fall, the branches overhead were so dense that they lodged there, and we could not induce any of our fol-lowers to climb for them on account of the deadly tree snakes, which are said to infest the place.

Our guides did not like the ascent, and tried to make us believe that the point of the ridge was the top of the mountain, but we insisted in pushing further up the ridge and at length were rewarded by reaching the summit. The air was very fresh and cool here, and by climbing a low-branched tree we obtained splendid views of the sur-rounding plains and hill tops and of the sea. We rested here for some time. A strong-growing species of penta-phragma, bearing pure white flowers in the axils of its oblong fleshy leaves grew here plentifully, and an aucuba-like shrub bore clusters of red berries as large as peas. Tree ferns also grew up to the top, and their stems were draped with long green moss, which looked very fresh and pretty. Two or three species of anæctochilus also grew here, their rich velvety leaves being illuminated with gold and silvery veins. From one spot in the descent we could see the coast and the outlying islets very plainly, also more newly-formed coral islets inlaid with lagoons. We saw abundant evidence of wild pigs and deer up this mountain, but the wild cattle which formerly existed plentifully are now quite extinct.

During our conversation about this mountain last night the Sultan told us some wonderful stories of birds' nest caves, and of a cavity or hole at the top lined with mother of pearl (tepoy) large enough for several men to bathe in at the same time, also of the wild men who lived in the forest, making their habitations in the trees, and of other wonderful things, all of which he discreetly added we should not be able to see without we had supernatural assistance. The gods truly were unpropitious, for we saw none of the mysteries of the mountain to which he had referred. Wild men may formerly have inhabited the trees of the forest here, as the "jakuns" still do in Jahore, and what he told us may have been a well-worn old tradition handed down for many generations. It is not improbable that his reference to the crater at the top was the remains of an old tradition of the volcanoes which once, without a doubt, did exist here in the island.

We descended to the village, leaving the men to bring on the horses and gear, and here "Gelah" procured us some hot water, and we sat down under the shady trees and enjoyed our lunch of chocolate and biscuit. "Gelah" told us he did not care for chocolate and asked for some brandy. I gave him half a tumblerful, which he drank and became very communicative. He lighted one of the cigars he had appropriated last night — indeed he had been smoking them all the morning— and then he told us that many of the Sulus were bad men and great thieves, adding that he was a good man himself, and that was why the Sultan liked him. He then helped himself to more brandy, tossing it off undiluted as before. He then launched out into a long story of a pirate fleet having left Tawi-Tawi about a year before, and remarked that they had but just returned with a good deal of plunder. Wallace mentions* that these Sulu pirates sometimes visit the Aru islands near New Guinea and Ceram on their predatory expeditions. They only attack small trading prahus now, but in former times even large sailing vessels were not safe from their attacks.

We now mounted our ponies and retraced our steps to the Istana, which we reached at dusk pretty well tired. We rested some time and gave the Sultan an account of our ascent. He pressed us to remain all night, but this we did not care to do, and thanking him for his hospitality and assistance, we mounted our ponies once more and rode back to Meimbong in the moonlight. Arriving at the Orang Kayu's house we found the boat there to meet us and take us on board, but it was then low water in the river, and we had to wait some hours, so we went into the headman's house, and lying down, slept until near midnight, when our men awoke us and rowed us up the river and across to the ship. It is a common opinion, and in the main I believe a correct one, that the Sulus are great thieves. I never lost anything among them,

* "Malay Archipelago," vol. ii. p. 212.

and a small bag I left accidentally at the headman's house containing two or three dollars, a knife, ammunition, and other trifles, was handed on board in the morning untouched. From what I saw of Sulu and the inhabitants it appeared to me very evident that civilisation had formerly been much higher than it is at present. This is especially to be seen in their old buildings and manufactures. Thus the oldest of the dwellings had beautifully carved woodwork over the windows and doors, and had been erected of wood and with much more care-

ful taste and labour than is now devoted to the same kind of work.

Nowhere else in the East did I see more evidence of tasteful purpose in design than here in Sulu. Here is a little sketch I made of a carved wood heading to the door of the Sultan's Istana. Motive two conventional alligators holding a disc on which is written a Malay inscription in Arabic characters, the whole surrounded by open work. Some old knives were also most beautifully decorated, the blades being of splendid finish, and the hilts and sheaths of hard wood, carved very artistically. In Brunei city I had noted a few lattice windows in the

older pile dwellings rather pretty in design, but not at all
equal to the free and vigorous carving of the Sulus.

The older manufactures again, such as krisses, barongs,
spear-heads, betel-boxes, indeed metal work generally,
and particularly the artistic element, were formerly much
finer than is now the case. The Sulus themselves, a
well-built and originally a brave race, have deteriorated,
and after resisting the incursion of their old enemies, the
Spaniards, for generations, indeed centuries, are now
utterly dispirited. Some of their chiefs indeed have in-
trigued with their old foes, and the result is that their
country, and probably the last of her Sultans, is virtually
under Spanish rule. The Sultan himself is a bright
and intelligent man, but given to opium smoking, and
some of his headmen and Datus composing the "ruma
bichara," a council chamber by which the Sulu has long
been governed, taking advantage of his ease-loving nature
have beguiled him with flattery, and advised him to sign
one treaty after another until the entire Sulu Archipelago
may now be considered as virtually belonging to the
Philippine government.

As a race the Sulus are well developed, taller, and
paler in colour than the Malays generally. The women
are often very pleasing, with luxuriant hair and bright
expressive eyes. Some of them, notably the wives and
daughters of the chief men, are very pale, white almost in
comparison with the women of the island, who are more
often exposed to the effects of climate and labour.
Several ladies of the court were pale in colour, with
regular Italian-like features, and one of the wives of Datu
Haroun—a sweet gentle creature—might readily have
been mistaken for a European. She was essentially
lady-like in voice and manner, and deserved a far better
fate than that of nominal wife, but virtually slave of a

crafty and cruel traitor to his country.　Upon the women
here, as throughout Borneo, devolves a large share of the
everyday labour, and nearly all the trading in the markets
is conducted by them, while their lords and masters stand
listlessly by spear in hand, or gather in little groups to
talk.　Everywhere we saw them at work making mats or
baskets, or met them in dug-out canoes and outriggers
going to or coming from market, or from the place where
the fresh water is daily obtained, below the Orang Kayu's
house.　The women of the better class spend much of
their time in embroidery and in cooking, indeed we were
assured that the food set before us at the Istana had been
prepared under the Sultana's personal supervision, which
I can well believe, and I do not think English ladies
could have prepared such a repast as it was in a better
way; indeed the snowy bowl of rice would, I think, prove
inimitable to most of our lady cooks at home.　Riding is
fashionable in Sulu, and none but the very poorest walk
far.　Anything seems acceptable as a steed, and if the
aristocratic grey pony with somewhat of Arab fleetness and
gentleness is not obtainable, buffaloes, and even the cows,
are taken as substitutes.

It is really a very pretty sight to see the market people
coming to market from the hills, men and women alike,
mounted on ponies or cattle with their baskets, bags, and
bundles of produce flung across the saddle before and
behind.　The men, especially, mounted on their high
wooden saddles, armed with the national spear, and clad
in chain armour tunic, forcibly reminded one of the illustrations of Don Quixote, a resemblance considerably
heightened by the gaunt leanness of their steeds.　A
plurality of wives is general with the Datus, and others
who have means to keep up an establishment, and these
women are for the most part purchased from their

parents, although formerly they were not unfrequently captured during piratical excursions. St. John * mentions an instance where a pirate chief from Tawi-Tawi captured a Spanish schooner in 1859, and finding the captain's daughter on board, he made her his principal wife and treated her with every attention; she subsequently bore him a child, the Spanish authorities having failed in their attempts to recover her.

As I have before intimated slavery is still common in Sulu, although there is no regular great slave mart such as existed only a few years ago at Sugh, the former capital. It is no uncommon occurrence for parents to sell their daughters, and visitors to Sulu are solicited even now to purchase wives at prices varying from fifty to two hundred dollars. I knew of one instance in which a trading captain presented his native wife, a Sulu girl, to the captain of another steamer, and the officers of Dutch vessels trading here in the Malay Archipelago nearly always keep native wives on board, and as a rule I believe these women are kindly treated. Throughout Malasia woman's position is unfortunately a very low one. If possessed of personal attractions she is directly or indirectly sold to the highest bidder, and while her youthful charms last she may be spared actual toil, while her less attractive sister labours daily in house or field, but eventually a younger, fairer wife supplants her, and during her declining years she is—

> " In daily labours of the loom employed,
>   Or doom'd to deck the bed she once enjoyed."

All this is, of course, a very unsatisfactory state of things here as in other nations eastward, nor is it likely

* " Life in the Forests of the Far East," 2d. ed., vol. i. p. 404.

to be much improved under Spanish rule. And yet we must never forget that it is a time-honoured institution, and is not, to say the least, more objectionable than polyandry as practised among the tribes who live on the banks of the Upper Jumna and Upper Ganges. Polygamy is sanctioned by custom, and " custom is religion in the East." Each Mahomedan is permitted to have four wives. Before we blame a religion so wide spread and powerful, however, we must not forget that it is a religion which practically preserves its millions of followers from other forms of intemperance, and notably from the use of intoxicating liquors, that great bane of many Englishmen everywhere, and especially of many of those who live in the Eastern tropics.

The language spoken in Sulu, notwithstanding that it contains many Malay words and others of Arabic origin, is yet practically very distinct, approaching much more nearly that spoken by the inland tribes of Northern Borneo. In physique and bold fearless bearing there is also a striking resemblance between the north Borneans and the Sulus, while both races display the same acuteness, mingled with suspicion, in all matters of trade. So striking is the resemblance in physique, language, and conduct, as to suggest the possibility of their having originally descended from one common stock, and I am inclined to think that the same language was used by them before the advent of the now dominant Malays, who had Arabic blood in their veins, and to whom is doubtless due the introduction of the Arabic character and Islamism, and whose language is now the *lingua franca* of Malasia. The government of the island, although in a great measure in the hands of the Sultan, can scarcely be called despotic, since the people are represented in the council chamber, or "ruma bichari," by their Datus or headmen, and but few if any important matters were decided by the Sultan personally, without the opinion of the native chiefs. During our visit to the Istana His Highness regretted very much that he had not power to drive out the Spaniards.

The cultural capabilities of the island are considerable, and in the hands of the Spaniards they are likely to be still better developed. The principal cultivated crops are rice, maize, coffee, manilla hemp, cocoa (*Theobroma Cacao*), tobacco, and tapioca. During the rides I took in the island I had good opportunities of seeing the arable land, and I was much impressed with the produce obtainable from the soil at a slight expenditure of labour. The deep soil is loosened by a rude plough, drawn by a single buffalo. This is done in the dry season, and seed sowing and planting commence with the rainy weather. I saw coffee bushes growing apparently wild around the little farm-houses on the cool hill-sides, especially on Bu'at Dahau, which I ascended a few days after our return from Bu'at Timantangis, and every leaf was fresh and green without a trace of the leaf fungus which of late years has proved so hurtful in Ceylon. The cocoa-yielding Theobroma does equally well and fruits freely, forming indeed what may be called the national beverage in Sulu. Excellent tobacco is grown here, and this, if skilfully prepared, would furnish cigars equal to those of Manilla. Cotton would do well, and the highest red land on the mountains, rich as it is with ages of forest debris, might be advantageously planted with coffee or other crops. Rice, tapioca, tobacco, and sugar cane would do best on the plains. An immense quantity of fruit is produced in the island, especially mangoes and bananas. The fragrant durian is also plentiful, together with langsat, and several other kinds. I noticed two distinct varieties of cocoa-nut cultivated here, one bearing small oblong fruits of a bright orange yellow colour, the milk of which was delicious in flavour, and another, the outer husk of which could be eaten in its young state, it being white as ivory, and very sweet and tender.

I have already alluded to a breed of ponies as being peculiar to the island. These are larger and in every way better than the Deli breed, imported to Singapore from Sumatra. They are never shod, nor is emasculation ever resorted to. Goats and poultry are very abundant. Of the former, a dark brown race resembling deer in gracefulness and activity, are kept by the hill people. The fowls of Sulu are distinct from those of Borneo, and are believed not to be many degrees removed from their wild prototypes. Of the other natural produce of the island the frutto del mare deserves notice, being especially valuable, worth, indeed, many thousands of dollars yearly. Pearls of all colours in quantity and of excellent quality, are obtained here yearly by the divers, most of whom are of the ubiquitous Badjow or Sea gipsy race. Tons of pearl shell (tepoy) and sea slug or beche de mer (*Holothuria*), of different kinds, are also exported annually.

This last repulsive-looking product is picked off the coral reefs at low water, and after being dried is esteemed a great delicacy by the Chinese, to whom it is sold. The pearl-shell obtained here is of fine quality, each valve being frequently as large as an ordinary dinner-plate, and an inch in thickness. At least a dozen kinds of salt-water fish are obtainable, and I frequently saw the fishing-boats off the town at night, each with a light gleaming over the water, and I noticed that they all seemed to have secured a fair supply of fish when they came alongside in the morning.

CHAPTER XII.

A ROYAL VISIT.

WHEN we started from Labuan it was expected that the whole voyage to and from Sulu would be made in fifteen days. On our arrival here, however, the expected cargo was not ready, and it was found that another fortnight must elapse ere we could leave. This extra time I spent in riding over the island in every direction, and I was rewarded by specimens of plants and birds which had never reached Europe before. One night on my return to the ship for dinner, I was delighted to hear that the Sultan had arranged to pay a State visit to Meimbong, and that he had signified his intention of coming on board, this being indeed one of the principal reasons of his visit. It had been arranged that he and his suite would remain in the harbour for one night, sleeping in "Peah's" house, the largest and most comfortable in the place. Mr. Cowie at once resolved to decorate the ship, and also to fire a salute from the guns on board, as he had an Armstrong amidships and two iron muzzle-loaders forward. The visit was to be made in two days' time, and so there was plenty of time for preparations, and the little wharf assumed an appearance of bustle and activity I had never seen there before. A fine young bullock was slaughtered by " Peah," and his slave girls were as busy as bees in the little kitchen on the end of the pile jetty, preparing food and sweetmeats for the visitors. Edible swallows' nests, and the finest and fattest of sea-slugs were placed in bowls of water to soak, while rice was cleaned in large quantities, and freshly-caught fish were brought in alive and retained in tubs of sea-water until required. Enormous brass betel-boxes were cleaned and replenished with fresh lime and nuts, and the mountaineers brought down the largest and freshest of pepper or sirri leaves and fruits on the morning of the visit. Inside the private apartments finely-worked mats and embroidered cushions were placed for the royal guests. Business seemed entirely suspended for the time, and both Chinese and Sulus were evidently looking forward to a general holiday. On board, the sailors had made the little *Far East* nice and tidy, the bunting of all colours and signal halyards were got into order, and the mate sacrificed his old flannel shirts to make bags for the powder with which the salute was to be fired.

About eight o'clock on the appointed day a shot was fired from the Armstrong, and we were all surprised at the long rolling echo and reverberation it made among the hills. About ten the Sultan and Sultana with their entire suite and numbers of Sulus who formed a sort of irregular guard of honour, arrived at Meimbong a gay cavalcade, the brightly-embroidered jackets of the nobles, and the crimson, blue, and yellow petticoats of the ladies being very effective in the bright sunshine, the whole

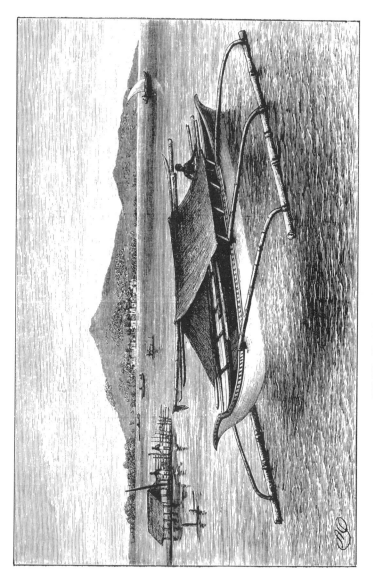

DAPANG, OR OUTRIGGED BOAT, SULU ISLANDS

effect being again heightened by the flashing of numerous
spears. Filing through the narrow gate in the stockade,
they waited for some minutes ere the boats were quite
ready, and then embarked, a movement which occupied
nearly half an hour. Knowing that the boats would
block up the river when they eventually started, we returned to the ship, from which an excellent view of the
procession of boats was obtained as they crossed the harbour to reach the houses on the wharf. The sight was
extremely bright and pretty as the boats, with their gaily
attired occupants, emerged from the mouth of the river
and came across the bay. The Sultan's boat was first,
and the fat old Commander-in-Chief of the forces sat on
the prow, paddle in hand, to steer clear of all impedi-
ments. Next came the Sultana and her chief ladies in
a larger boat, two or three richly embroidered umbrellas
being held aloft, while her infant son and nurse came
along in a third boat with numerous attendants, and
overshadowed by a splendid yellow silk three storied
umbrella, decorated with streamers to steady it, each of
these last being in the hands of a dusky slave. The
following boats, of which there were about a dozen, carried
the attendant nobles, headmen, minor ladies of the harem,
and the necessary attendants or slaves. Besides these
there was, of course, quite a crowd of natives in outrigged
boats and canoes of all sizes.

His Highness landed on the " jimbatan," and stood to
watch the landing of the Sultana and her suite. He was
surrounded by his people, all being, as is usual here
always, armed. One man carried a heavy Lanun sword,
while two others carried loaded revolvers in a very
awkward manner. His son, Datu Mahomed, came on
board as soon as he landed, and asked Mr. Cowie not to
fire the salute until the ladies had retired indoors. He

Q

had several young followers with him all smartly dressed
in embroidered jackets and breeches, with gaudy kerchiefs wound around their heads. He stayed on board
while the salute was being fired, and although it shook
the little vessel a good deal, and did some damage to
the skylights and crockery, he did not seem to mind it
much. The guns were fired with great regularity, and
the reverberation among the hills was grand. After
the firing was concluded His Highness came on board
and went over the whole ship. He was particularly
interested in the little Armstrong breech-loading gun,
and examined its mechanism very closely, he also ventured down into the engine-room, and was evidently
astonished at the machinery therein. After looking
round the vessel he sat under the awning on the saloon-
deck smoking and talking until we had finished dinner,
and was very much interested in our European style
of eating. He has repeatedly been invited on board
English gun-boats which call in here occasionally, but
this was the first time he had ever ventured to set his
foot on board a foreign vessel. Mr. Cowie was very
anxious that all should pass off well, as it was very evident that His Highness was very nervous, and foreseeing
this possibility, the vessel had been laid alongside the
"jimbatan," or wharf, so that he could step on board and
leave without any trouble.

He left just at sundown, appearing very pleased with
his visit, and he expressed his intention of again coming
on board in the morning, bringing the Sultana with him.
The houses on the wharf were crowded towards night
with Sulus from all the neighbouring islets, and when the
lamps were alight presented a very animated sight to a
stranger. The common Sulus are rather intrusive, and
the native boatswain would have had much trouble to

have kept the ship clear of them had it not been for the dogs on board, four splendid creatures. They were a retriever, two small terriers, and a formidable bull-dog, which Mr. Cowie told me was the best safeguard from the pilfering of natives he had ever invested in during some years of Eastern cruising and coast trade. This hint may be of some service to future explorers—a good bull-dog or a terrier or two would, indeed, be the best of guards to have at one's camping ground, since it is next to impossible for anyone to approach without their giving due loud-voiced warning.

We went ashore after dinner and found "Peah's" house filled to overflowing with guests. Room, however, was made for us, and chocolate, biscuits, cigarettes, and gin offered in turn. Incessant talking, varied by gong music, and now and then a melancholy song by one of the court ladies, together with food and drink to all comers, seemed to be the programme. The singing, to our ears, sounded like a dirge—the pentatonic scale being used by these people as by the Malays and Chinese. One young girl after singing part of a ballad relating how a beautiful princess was stolen by pirates and eventually became a Sultan's bride, " her skin being pale as the jasmine flower, her breath sweet as the areca bloom," eventually went off in a fainting fit, and had to be carried out into the fresh air. Her place and legend was immediately taken up by another girl, and I was told that the thread of it was so long that several days would be occupied by anyone who should attempt to sing the whole story. Our interpreter, for the nonce, was Datu Mahomed, who is very fond of Europeans. He introduced us to several people of note in the island, and gave us much information which otherwise we could not have obtained. Men and women here met pretty much on a common ground, and were apparently un-trammelled by that strict and exclusive etiquette so characteristic of the Bornean Malays. Some of the ladies were very comely and richly dressed, notably the court ladies and the pretty wife of Datu Haroun, the former Sulu governor of Sandakan. This lady spoke Malay well, an accomplishment which few of the Sulu women possess, and we spent a very pleasant quarter of an hour in her company.

The dress of the Sulu women consists of a pair of loose trowsers of white cloth generally, but for holiday times often red, yellow, magenta, or blue silk, and a loose jacket ("baju") also of silk, often braided down the front, and ornamented with large gold or silver buttons. Over these a long sarong, or petticoat, is worn as a sash, cloak, skirt, or petticoat and belt combined, according to the fancy of its wearer at the time, for to the Sulus and Malays the sarong supplies the place of the dress and bonnet of civilised society here at home. Most of the "sarongs" worn by the ladies I saw to-day were of silk, very richly embroidered with flowers, butterflies, or com-plicated designs of a foliated pattern, the same on both sides the material, and really producing a beautiful effect. The colours were mainly gaudy and barbaric in splendour, but here and there real taste was evident. One lady wore a buff sarong of very rich texture, with a neatly-worked border in black, while another, in a green and black check or tartan, was especially noticeable. Rings of gold and silver, often richly set with stones and pearls, are worn on the left hand as a rule, but ladies of the highest class have both hands studded with jewelry. Ear orna-ments are not so much affected as by the Malays, and although most of the girls have apertures slit in their pretty little ears, these are rarely used for earrings, being, indeed, as often made receptacles for cigarettes as any-thing else. Ornate cloth or silk kerchiefs and head-dresses of black, yellow, or red, set off their raven tresses to advantage on high days and holidays, and among an assemblage of fully two hundred women, such as we saw here to-day, not two were dressed alike. Yellow is the colour which predominates most, and the amount of chrome which would render a European lady most conspicuous and vulgar, seems only to enhance the dusky charms, bright eyes, and luxuriant hair of these Sulu belles. Only the Sultana and one or two others wore stockings, and slippers were only used by the elite, and to these they seemed a superfluity, since they mostly carried them in their hands. The abundance of hair possessed by these women is a noticeable feature, and they do not dress it so neatly as the Malays, but merely comb it out straight, after which it is loosely knotted up so as to form a mass on the top or one side of the head.

From the opportunities I had of seeing the Sulu women generally, I should say that they are far superior to the men, and evidently have, as has been before noticed, great influence with their husbands. A present to the Sultana and one or two of the Datu's wives, would be amply sufficient to ensure the safety and popularity of a traveller here, a secret well known to the rich Chinese traders, who make visits hither occasionally during the year. Wishing to pay our respects to the Sultan ere leaving for the night, we sought His Highness in vain for some time, but at last found him with one of our Chinese friends, smoking opium in a gloomy little com-partment, from the close, penetrating odour of which we were glad to escape as quickly as possible. We went on board, but did not sleep much, owing to the talking and gong-beating, which continued almost all night. We awoke at sunrise to find nearly every one astir on the wharf, the Sultana and her suite having thus early seated themselves outside the houses to take the air.

Much amusement was caused by a large retriever dog, "Neptune," which Mr. Cowie had on board, and which delighted to plunge after any trifle flung into the water. In about half-an-hour the boats were brought, and Her Highness and about fifty ladies went off to a sandy shoal in the bay to bathe. We could see them quite plainly from the ship flopping over the sides of the boats into the sea, and floundering about like fat seals. They evidently enjoyed themselves; and after a quarter-of-an-hour's racing and splashing, they returned to the boats, and then proceeded about a mile out to sea, where some Badjows amused them by diving for pearl-shells and coral.

Returning to the wharf, the Sultan and Sultana came on board; and after Her Highness, who was only attended by two of her ladies, had looked over the ship, he bade us adieu. The boats were then brought alongside the wharf; the ladies embarked first, then the Sultan and his suite. Splash went the polished paddles; a wave of the hand from His Highness, a dip of the flag at the mast-head of the little steamer, and the first royal visit paid by a Sultan of Sulu on board a steam-ship was over. Both before and after this visit we saw a good deal of the Sulus; not only the traders, but the nobles and officers themselves often came on board on business, or to take a cup of tea and have a chat. One or two of them had a weakness for gin "cocktails," but their general beverage was tea or lemonade. All were armed with straight knives; but most had the short heavy Sulu knife or sword stuck in a silk sash or waist-cloth. Much of the conversation was on the subject of market prices for pearl shell, trepang, and birds' nests, varied by inquiries as to the object and operations of the new Borneo Company, to whom their Sultan had quite recently ceded Sandakan, and the east and north part of Borneo which belonged to him.

During all the time we had lain in harbour here, the weather had been dry, not a drop of rain having fallen for nearly four months. The plains were very dry and parched, and jungle fires were not unfrequent as the dry grass caught fire and sprang into a blaze very quickly. It is owing to these fires in jungle and forest that teak of large size is now so rare ; since at one time the island must have been one immense forest of this valuable wood.

After the ascent of Bu'at Timantangis I had often longed to explore Bu'at Dahau, the next highest of the two peaks of Sulu, both of which are visible for a long way out at sea. We could see the mountain quite clearly at sunrise every morning, from our anchorage at Meimbong; and one fine morning I set off, accompanied by Mr. Anson Cowie, who proved himself to be a most intelligent and genial companion. As guide, I had been so fortunate as to obtain the services of one of the Sultan's officers who lived at a village half way up the mountain side, and at whose house we were to leave our ponies and undertake the climbing on foot. We bore to the right on leaving Meimbong, and had a pleasant ride of seven or eight miles across the fragrant mint and grass-covered plains ; but by reason of my dismounting here and there to gather a curious orchid or fern, or perchance to get a shot at a beautiful bird, it was nearly noon ere we drew rein at the door of our guide's house. Our way at first had lain through the undulating plain ; then the Meimbong river was crossed under some fine-spreading trees, on which white, blue, and green pigeons fluttered in

plenty. Then we rode up a narrow path fringed with
tall overhanging jungle on either side, leaving only bare
space for our ponies to pass in Indian file. Then came
a rounded hill-side, and numerous cultivated patches—
little farms with palm-thatched houses sheltered in groves
of durian, cocoa-nut, mango, and other fruit trees. Here
coffee and cocoa-trees were noticed in vigorous health
and fruitfulness; and along the edges of the arable
patches a very pretty species of curcuma was blooming
freely among the grass and verdure. The leaves had a
purple stain along the mid-rib. The flowers were white,
with a blotch of lemon-yellow on the lip, the inflorescence being white, suffused with bright amethyst, purple
at its apex. We noticed tame paroquets hanging outside
several of the dwellings we passed on our way.

At one point near the foot of the mountain, we came
upon a party of thirty or forty men accompanied by
dogs, and armed with long spears; they were going to
hunt some wild pigs which had done damage to a plantation of sweet potatoes and yams the night previous.
Our way now lay up the clearings on the mountain side.
I dismounted and led my pony; and on my shooting
at a pigeon, it became restive, and broke away. It
was luckily met and caught by a Sulu man who had
followed us, in the hope of earning a little tobacco.
Arriving at last at the mountain village, we entered our
guide's house, after having tethered our horses and given
them some cut grass on which to feed. The sun was
now very hot, and we were glad to rest; we were hungry,
too, and thoroughly enjoyed some fish and rice, which,
together with some chocolate, was soon set before us by
these hospitable people. Pigeons, paroquets, and large
hornbills, were here plentiful, and came to feed on some
large trees which were in fruit near the village.

After our luncheon I started with our guides to ascend the mountain, leaving Mr. Cowie, who had a lame foot, to shoot around the village until my return. We reached the summit in about an hour, but were much disappointed, as the vegetation was not nearly so luxuriant as that on Timantangis. Orchids were scarce, and ferns wanting in variety and beauty, although several were new to science. Near the summit I heard a little song-bird singing very sweetly; and although I did not see it, I am convinced it was the same species I had previously heard with so much pleasure on "Kina Balu," at a much higher altitude. This mountain is well wooded at the top, but not so densely as is Timantangis; nor is the undergrowth so rich in variety. The views from the top are simply lovely—a panorama of fertile farm-dotted hills and golden plains, stretching away to the blue sea, where the main island is fringed by coral islets. A native pointed out the harbour to us, and the peak of Pulo Siassi was plainly visible. In the descent I made a detour from the little spring or watering-place near the village, and passing through clumps of coffee-bushes, with here and there ripe fruit in plenty, we came beneath a grove of large durian trees which were in bloom, the ground beneath being covered with their fallen blossoms. Here I shot several pigeons and paroquets; and in returning to the village we repeatedly saw a large amorphophallus bearing fœtid flowers as large as a sugar basin, and of a dark maroon colour. On cutting open a flower I found its basin half full of ants of two kinds and numerous small black coleoptera were running about in the spathe. I may say that I have rarely ever examined tubular flowers here in the tropics without finding insects of some kind engaged within, and in the case of aroids particularly, their spathes are generally full of such tiny guests, whether "unbidden" or not I cannot say, but it is probable certain kinds are attracted by fœtid odours as others are by sweet ones, while in many cases nectar or pollen supply the little visitors with food. The bright scarlet flowers of the erythrina trees in Labuan sheltered myriads of tiny flies and beetles which, in their turn, afforded food to large flocks of starlings and other birds which were always attracted to these trees when they were in bloom. Quite accidentally I came across the evidence of a celebrated traveller in South America, Waterton, who at p. 98 of his *Wanderings*, says "almost every flower of the tropical climates contains insects of one kind or other," thus bearing out what I have observed to be universally the case in the eastern jungles and gardens.

On returning to the house I found Mr. Cowie had shot a beautiful paroquet and two pigeons I had never seen before, and he had directed his men to bring all the ferns and plants he had met with on his way around the jungle patches near the houses. Our birds and flowers securely packed, we walked around the village and paid a visit to a hospitable old hadji who lived here, apparently prosperous and happy. He told us that many of the women had been much frightened on hearing that a white man was coming to their village, adding that he had had great difficulty in assuring them that we were not Spaniards. He had erected a neat little musjid, and his son, a tall well-favoured youth, who had accompanied his sire to Mecca, had just been married to a very comely Sulu girl. This hadji had a tradition that the aboriginals of the island had been driven out by the Chinese emigrants many years ago, even before the Arab Sultans and Datus became the dominant party here. He may be right, since it is a well known fact that the Chinese had extensive settlements in the northern portion of Borneo, as in part attested by the native names of the places in which their settlements were made, as Kina Balu (Chinese widow mountain), Kina Batangan (Chinese river), Kina Tanah, Kina Taki, and others. There is one tribe of Dusun who wear pigtails, and although they use the Dusun vernacular, yet they converse in very fair Chinese after a little practice, having never quite lost the tongue of their Chinese ancestors, of whom these are the lineal descendants by Bornean women. This peculiar tribe inhabit the Bundu country, but St. John mentions Muruts from the Limbang, who spoke Hokien Chinese on their being confronted with Chinese in Brunei, the capital, although they failed to express themselves in the Malay language of the coast!

Just as the sun was sinking behind the trees we mounted our ponies and started for Meimbong. The air was now cool and fresh, and a pleasant ride of two hours brought us to Meimbong. This was my last ride in the island. All the cargo had been stowed below, the hatches closed, and early in the morning we were to leave. We were awoke at daybreak by the steam-whistle, and just as the sun tinted the peaks of Timantangis and Dahau we steamed slowly out of the harbour for the Island of Siassi, one of the Tapal group, where more cargo awaited us. We arrived at Siassi about noon, but the cargo could not be put on board until the next morning. We stayed at Siassi all the following day, and I took the opportunity of riding inland, and to the peak, which I found capped with old forest; but owing to the extreme drought, everything here was parched and dry, and but few plants of interest were seen. As most of this island is entirely denuded of old forest, of course birds are scarce; indeed, I saw enough of it to convince me that

it was a bad collecting ground generally. The only steed
I could obtain was a large black bull, which I hired for a
bundle of tobacco. He was all right when I had fairly
mounted, but whenever I got off to shoot at a bird, or
gather plants, he became exceedingly restive, and the
only way to mount him again was to put the rope (by
which I steered him, and which was fastened to a twisted
ring of rattan cane in his nose) round the trunk or branch
of a tree, and then to pull his nose up to it by sheer
force, holding it firmly with one hand while I sprang on
his back. The few country people I met appeared
rather surprised, but I expect the bull was well known,
and so that served as a passport to me. Near the houses
on the shore a bushy euphorbia, with candelabra-like
branches, and a clump of yuccas were seen, both doubtless introductions. I returned about three o'clock. After
dinner I and Captain Cowie visited one or two of the
traders' houses, which resemble those of Sulu in internal
arrangement, large beds or platforms occupying the principal apartment, covered with fine mats and pillows, the
valuables in boxes being piled up behind. In the morning we bore away for Sandakan, which we reached ere
daybreak the next day. The steam-ship *America* was in
the bay, having Baron de Overbeck on board. We
stayed here one day for cargo of trepang, rattan, pearl-
shell, and birds'-nests. These edible swallows'-nests are
highly valued by the rich Chinese, and it is from a cave
on the face of the sandstone rock on Pulo Bahalatolois,
at the mouth of this bay, that the finest white nests are
obtained. These rocks rise nearly perpendicularly from
the sea, and to reach the entrance to the cave a man has
to descend a distance of a hundred or more feet with the
aid of a rattan rope tied to a tree on the slope above. It
is dangerous work, as the least slip, and the man would

be dashed to pieces on the rock-strewn shore below. The nests thus obtained fetch as much as eighteen dollars per catty, a weight equalling 1⅓ lb. English. The finest birds'-nests are clean and white, as if made of isinglass; the worst resemble dirty glue, to which feathers and other impurities are attached, and between these extremes there are all sorts of intermediate qualities. These nests are obtained in rocky caves throughout Borneo, Java, and Sumatra, but nowhere are they obtainable finer in quality than here, at Sandakan Head. Large quantities of small or seed pearls are obtained here, also Bornean camphor, the produce of *Dryobalanops camphora*, a large tree often one hundred to a hundred and fifty feet in height. As a product, it is quite distinct from the common camphor of commerce, which is obtained from *Laurus camphora* by the Chinese of Hong Kong, who send nearly all of it to our markets, while they, in their turn, highly esteem the Bornean produce, and pay high prices for it. It is obtained in the form of tears and crystallised lumps from the trunk of the tree, and in general appearance is so like the finer kinds of " dammar " gum, that this latter is often used by the collectors as an adulterant. The Chinese traders, however, are rarely imposed upon. The camphor, in its pure state, resembles solidified spirit, and being extremely volatile, it burns with a clear light flame. To detect adulteration, the Chinese are said to spread a little on a white cloth and set it on fire; the pure camphor burns cleanly, and does not soil the cloth, whereas the dammar, if such is mixed with it, melts and sets the cloth on fire. The people from the Teutong river, and the Kayans on the Baram, collect large quantities of camphor and caoutchouc, and prahus with a cargo of these products, worth from one to two thousand dollars, visit Labuan,

Sarawak, and other ports during the season. On our leaving Sandakan, on our return voyage to Labuan, we obtained a capital view of Pulo Bahalatolois, and on our rounding the point, the rattan rope dangling down the rocks to the dark entrance to the swallows' cave was plainly visible. This island has a very commanding position, and a battery here would sweep the entrance to this fine bay. We were four days in reaching Labuan, there being a thick fog along the north-west coast, and we were aground twice, although fortunately we got off again without injury.

CHAPTER XIII.

KINA BALU, *viâ* TAMPASSUK.

IT was now the end of July, and I had been waiting
four or five days, expecting the arrival of the steam-
ship *Far East*, in which I had hoped to have again
taken a passage, with my friend, Captain W. C. Cowie;
but as his vessel was now overdue, and my own time was
limited, I resolved to leave in a native boat at all hazards.
I soon chartered a prahu, large enough to carry twenty
men, and our stores; and on July 31st I was ready to
start. I had given my Chinese "boy," Kimjeck, and
the men orders to have all in readiness; but when I
reached the little jetty, at two P.M., I found only half the
men there, the remainder being as busy as bees on shore,
running in and out of the Chinese shops, buying betel-

nut, salt, dried fish, onions, and other private stores for the voyage. As soon as they saw me, however, they came running down, and we all went on board. Altogether our craft was heavily laden; but as these native boats are generally carefully built, we saw nothing to fear.

At 3.30 we bade our friends, who had kindly come down to see us start, "good-bye;" and, amid the cries of "Salaamat jelan!" from the men's friends on shore, we hove anchor, and sheered off with a tolerably good wind. We soon got our large mat-sail hauled up, and with the Union Jack astern (we carried the "mails" for Tampassuk by the way), glided out of the harbour, and, rounding the old flagstaff-point, steered nearly due north. We did this, intending to stand out, and make "Pulo Tiga," an island lying about forty miles northward of Labuan, by the morning. In this, however, we were doomed to disappointment; for after an hour or two of indifferent sailing, a bit of a squall arose, and the wind having changed, we hove in shore, towards Lumbedan, intending to anchor under the shelter of a little islet of the same name for the night, and start away in the early morning.

This was now the only judicious course left us, since we were close in-shore, on a dangerous coast, and the squall of wind and rain was coming down on us like a hurricane. Our men pulled in around the island, and were approaching the shore, to enable us to land, when the boat rose a little on the surf, and the next moment her bows came down on a rock, and this knocked a large hole in her bottom. We subsequently found out that all her lower timbers were rotten. Happily we were not far from the land, and could make ashore, or the consequences might have been serious. As it was we suffered enough, being drenched with rain and surf; and as the boat rolled about, and filled rapidly, most of our things got drenched likewise. As is usual with Malays on such occasions, there was a great deal of excitement, and everybody shouted orders or instructions to his neighbour.

However, Smith, an excellent fellow Mr. Boosie had allowed to accompany me, and one or two natives, handed out our clothes and personal effects, which others carried ashore, after which we got out the bags of rice, and other stores all safely, and having emptied the craft of all her loose gear, we hauled her up on the smooth sandy beach, and then, as it was getting dusk, set about preparing ourselves a habitation for the night. Some of the men were sent to cut firewood, others to cut timbers for our hut; others went to search for water, while my "boy," hastily securing a few dry sticks, lighted a fire, and began preparing our evening meal.

We had with us plenty of the common "kajang' mats, which may be purchased in Labuan for a few pence each, and serve admirably for roofing boats, or the little jungle-houses, for which a Malay will cut and fix timbers in a few minutes. We had also a good oil-cloth, twelve feet square; and in less than an hour after our shipwreck we had a roomy tent erected in which to eat and sleep. We soon got on some dry clothes, and then had our bedding placed at one end, with our baggage piled up behind, and at the other end our rice and dried fish, goods for barter with the natives, and other stores, were arranged. The guns, rifle, and the tower-muskets, carried by the men, together with our revolvers, &c., were cleaned, and oiled, and suspended overhead; and the lamp being lighted, and hung in the centre, we began to look quite cheerful.

We had our dinner about seven o'clock, and then a

smoke and a chat over our misadventure.   Several men
came over from the opposite coast of Lumbedan, where
there are a few native houses, to look at us ; and I asked
them to bring over a boat in the morning, which they
very civilly promised to do.   About nine o'clock we
sought our blankets, and turned in for the night, and
slept well, notwithstanding our recent mishap.

August 1st.—We were all astir by daybreak this morning ; and, after having had our customary cup of coffee
and dry toast, we set our followers to work to spread
out the wet rice on mats in the sun, and to rearrange
all our stores.   Some of the men were sent to cut down
"nebong" palms, the young tops of which form a
delicious vegetable when boiled, and others were employed in cleaning our arms, cutting fire-wood, and other
necessary work.   While this was going on, I took my
gun, and went out on a stroll around our little island.
The vegetation I found was rather dense, and the whole
surface rocky.   I noticed several species of palms, and an
epiphytal fern or two, and plants of the white-flowered *Dendrobium crumenatum* hung here and there on the trees.

I shot two of the beautiful white island pigeon (*Carpophaga bicolor*), called "Pragam pulo" by the natives,
and a larger species, of an ash colour (*C. ænea*), the
wings and neck being shot with purple and bronze tints.
This is a very large and handsome bird, common in
Borneo, and when cooked, is very good eating.   On my
return to the tent I found the man from the coast had
brought over his boat, as promised, and I at once sent
it off, with eleven of my men, with a letter to Mr. A.
Boosie, the manager of the coal mines in Labuan, asking
him to lend me one of his boats, in which to continue
my journey.

It is a lovely day to-day, and our rice and clothes are

getting dry again. "Kimjeck," after he had done his work this morning, started off on a collecting excursion, and has just returned, with a couple of broad-tailed, dusky-coloured rock-snakes, one a very fine specimen. Beetles and butterflies, he tells me, are alike unobtainable, and he can find no flowers, so that we can do no collecting on the island. Knowing that it will be night at the earliest ere our own men can possibly return with the boat, I and Smith went over to Lumbedan with some natives, who had come in a boat to look at us, and had a walk in the tall forest, which forms a back-ground to the houses near the shore. Here we found the "nebong" palm attaining to a large size ; and some woodcutters promised to cut us a few young tops by the time of our return.

This forest, although originally rich in plants, like that of Labuan, has suffered severely during recent years from the now ever recurring jungle-fires of the dry monsoon. We could find nothing of interest. A large-leaved crinum grows in the sand by the shore ; and a scarlet-flowered ixora with narrow foliage, was blooming here and there in patches. We shot a long-tailed paroquet, and a blue kingfisher, the only birds we saw, and retraced our steps to the village just before sunset. We were thoroughly tired, and rested here some time, watching the young Kadyans playing at foot-ball on the beach. The players stand in a circle, three or four yards in diameter, and the ball is kicked in the air by the player to whom it falls nearest. To do this properly requires great dexterity, as the ball is struck with the sole of the foot; and a party of good players will thus keep a ball in the air for several minutes by each kicking it upwards just as it is about to fall. The ball itself is a light hollow one, of rattan open-work, about the size of an ordinary cricket-ball; and the game closely resembles shuttlecock, as played in China.

Having obtained our palm-tops, we purchased some eggs, cucumbers, and fine ripe water-melons from the woodcutters, whom we had passed in the forest in the morning, and then waded across to our quarters on the island, which we could now do, as it was low water. It was becoming dusk, and we were glad to throw ourselves down on our rugs, and rest a little before we ate our frugal repast. During our absence my " boy " has " tidied up " the tent, and it now looks quite cosy and comfortable, being dry and sheltered, although on two sides the sea washes up to within a few feet of us at high water. The soft yellow mats are pleasantly enlivened with our rugs and scarlet blankets, the rifle-barrels glisten above our heads, and the smoke curls gracefully upwards from our cooking-fires on the beach. Just as it was dark we heard our men shouting ; and soon after six of them came in with the borrowed prahu, and told us that their companions were following them in the large boat, which Mr. Boosie had kindly lent to us. This was good news ; and we ate our dinner in high spirits. In about an hour's time the men came in with the boat, and we hauled her up high and dry on the sandy shore before retiring for the night. With the boat I was cheered by letters from several of my friends in Labuan, all of whom were sorry to hear of our disaster.

August 2nd.—A lovely morning. We were up before daybreak, and soon had our boat launched, and all our goods and stores safely stowed away, ready for starting. About seven o'clock we got away, with a good breeze behind us, and then we took our breakfast in a little deck-cabin, which our men had cleverly rigged up for us with a few crooked sticks, tied firmly with rattans, and covered with kajang mats, thus forming a capital shelter from sun and rain. Not feeling very well, I lay

down, and fell asleep, but was soon awakened by a con-
sternation among the men, and much shouting. A
refractory fish was the cause of all the noise, the steersman having hooked him ; but the fish was large, and
objected to come on board. After much trouble they
hauled in their capture, and a fine fellow it was, fully
thirty pounds weight.

We were very comfortable in our new craft, which
sailed well ; and although the wind slackened considerably about noon, we reached Pulo Tiga before sunset,
and went ashore to cook our dinner and lay in a fresh
stock of firewood and water. Half-a-dozen fires were
soon alight, and we took our guns, and went for a walk,
but failed to get a shot. We caught sight of some large
hornbills ; they were, however, too wary to allow us
within range.

This island is a large one, without any inhabitants,
except now and then a few Chinese woodcutters, or native
fishermen. Native boats from Sulu or Palawan frequently call for wood and water ; and the remains of
numerous fires occur among the drift wood along the
beach. Wild pigs are very plentiful, and turtle are
also found here. From a distance the island is seen to
consist of three rounded hills, covered with forest ; hence
its native name " tiga," or " teega," signifying three in
the Malay language. We returned to dinner with hearty
appetites, and thoroughly enjoyed a portion of the fish
we had captured in the morning. My " boy," who acted
as cook, had forgotten to inquire how he should prepare
it ; and so, to make sure, he had divided our share,
boiling one-half, and the other he cleverly roasted over
the clean embers of a wood-fire.

Hungry as we were, salmon from an Irish stream,
cooked fresh over a fire of strawberry-tree wood (*Arbutus*),

could not have tasted more delicious. The wind had
now completely died away, and the current setting in
strong against us, we anchored in a sheltered bay until
the morning.

August 3rd.—Awoke about three A.M., and finding a
fresh breeze springing up, we aroused our men, and got
up sail. In about an hour, however, the wind dropped,
and the men had to take to their paddles. We had a
nice view of the coast just after sunrise, and we also saw
Kina Balu very distinctly. We had changeable winds all
day, but managed to reach Gaya Bay about five o'clock;
and, as wind and current were now against us, and the
men were tired with paddling most of the day, we went
ashore on one of the islands to cook, and resolved to
remain here all night, or until a favourable breeze sprang
up, which we might expect at any time after sunset.
Here, as at Pulo Tiga, the beach is sandy, and is fringed
with tall casuarina trees, through which the winds sigh
as mournfully as they do through the leaves of a pine
forest here at home.

The broad-leaved pandan (*Pandanus dubius*) is common
here, having a tall, cylindrical trunk, like a cocoa-nut
palm, and bearing a branched crown of dark-green leaves.
Here also we could obtain plenty of nebong tops; and
on waste patches, near the shore, *Tacca pinnatifida* grew
abundantly This plant is interesting, as affording a
kind of starch, much used as food by the South Sea
Islanders, but not valued here, where rice is plentiful.
Here we found plenty of the large blue pigeon; and
although they were very wild, we managed to shoot two
or three; and these, with the fresh palm-tops, were a
great gain to our culinary department.

August 4th.—Again a beautiful sunrise. We pulled
from under the lee of the island about six o'clock, and

stood out on our course, with a slight breeze. Off the mouth of the Menkabong river we came upon a tiny fleet of native boats, the owners of which were fishing with hook and line. We found out that they were some of Pangeran Rau's people, a chief who holds the country around Qualla Menkabong, and at whose house I had stayed on a former journey into the interior. We were glad to purchase some freshly-caught fish from these people, which we afterwards enjoyed for breakfast. Fried ·in a little pure oil, and sprinkled with a little oatmeal, they were very nice. Palm-tops boiled formed a delicate vegetable accompaniment to them.

We are five days out to-day; and as our bread, which we of course brought with us, is beginning to turn mouldy, my " boy " has dipped each of the remaining little loaves in water, and is busy baking it afresh on a tin plate over the embers. Treated in this way, our old bread is really very nice; indeed, not a bad substitute for hot rolls.

One of our men had a line out astern all the morning as usual, but never perceived a nibble until about 1.30 P.M., when there was a sudden commotion, owing to his being nearly jerked out of the boat by a large fish, which had taken his bait. The fish was fairly hooked, but the men had a good deal of trouble to haul him in. He was a splendid capture, fully fifty pounds or more in weight; and it took two men all their time to lift him into the boat, even after a spear had been driven through him. We all admired him very much as he lay on deck; indeed, half a hundred weight of good fresh fish would be welcome anywhere. It was of a variety, called " Linko " by the Malays, and in general appearance reminded one of a fine salmon.

A little later in the day another kind, about half the

size of the last, was caught, this being called " Tingerie."
We reached the mouth of the Abai about 5.30 P.M., and
tried hard to make the mouth of the Tampassuk ere dark,
in which we failed ; and after being tossed about for an
hour in vainly endeavouring to get over the bar, our men
were glad to pull back to a little island, near Qualla
Abai, where we could land to cook, and anchor for the
night. It was a lovely, moonlight night, and very quiet
in our snug little anchorage. We dined and slept on
board, and so escaped the myriads of mosquitoes on the
grassy shore.

August 5th.—Awoke at sunrise, the air being deliciously fresh and cool, and the sky clear. We were glad
to get a very good view of Kina Balu this morning, the
long rocky ridge standing out first purple, and then blue,
against the sky, while fleecy masses of silvery clouds
were ever changing their position on its rugged sides.

After a delicious bath in a little fresh-water pool
near the shore, and breakfast, we pulled to the Qualla
Tampassuk, and found a strong current coming over the
bar. Our men pulled over, however, all right ; and then
came a good five hours' pull up the river before we
reached the old quarters of Rajah Muda, now occupied by Mr. Pretyman, who had come to live here a
month or two ago, and for whom we had brought on the
mails from Labuan. The whole distance from the bar
is only about five miles ; but the river winds much : and,
as it was the wet season, a deal of water coming from
the ranges inland had swelled the river beyond its usual
limits, and the men had to pull against a heavy stream.

The vegetation of the banks is luxuriant; and after
pulling a mile or two, native dwellings, and cultivated
patches of bananas, cocoa-nut trees, tapioca, maize, and
other products appear. We reached Mr. Pretyman's

residence about 1.30 P.M., and found him and his people
tolerably well in health and spirits. He was surprised
and pleased at our unexpected visit, and promptly
ordered his men to kill a fine young bullock for ourselves and men. After luncheon we crossed the river
and walked to the top of the adjacent coast-hills, from
whence a good view of the winding stream and surrounding country is obtainable. These bare grassy hills rise
out of the plain, which serves as pasturage for a few
buffaloes, and here and there patches are irrigated for
rice culture. I made a small collection of the herbaceous
plants, annuals, and grasses of the hill we ascended;
and on the top we found a round-headed tree, which
bore edible fruits, remarkably like walnuts in form and
flavour.

In descending, we came across plants of a very lovely
gardenia, forming bushes, varying from a foot to two
feet in height, and bearing large white flowers in the
axils of its glossy leaves. A gentle spring-like shower
was falling in the last rays of sunlight, and the perfume
of this dainty flower was most balmy and delicious, quite
unlike the odour of any other plant I ever saw. On my
return from the mountain I was careful to secure plants
of this species, and they reached London quite safely
three months afterwards. As it was now dusk we returned to dinner, and spent a very pleasant evening,
talking over home news, and our plans for reaching Kina
Balu.

August 6th.—We were up at sunrise and set to work
in packing our stores into suitable parcels for each man
to carry, and we hired two buffaloes so as to be able to
carry an extra supply of rice. These details took time,
and it was fully noon ere we bade our host farewell and
were fairly started on our journey. Our guide and buffalo

driver was an intelligent Malay, named Abdul Rathman, who knew the country well. Our first stopping place was to have been Ghinambaur, but as we were late in starting we failed to reach that village before dark, and had to stay at some Dusun huts by the way. At first our way lay through the plain, and here the roads, or rather tracks, through the tall coarse grass were frequently knee deep in mud and water; then we crossed some low hills of red sandstone which were nearly destitute of herbage, owing to the earth being washed off the rock by heavy rains. In places the tracks over these hills were more like drains than anything, and during a heavy shower the water rushes down these water-worn runnels carrying every atom of soil or pulverised rock into the plains below, so that these last consist of a rich alluvial deposit, well adapted for rice and tapioca culture.

On the second range of these low hills is a Badjow village, most of the houses being much exposed, without a tree or any kind of shelter. The rain came down in torrents as we passed this place, and some of our Labuan men took shelter from the cold rain and wind which was indeed very piercing. We had to cross some rice fields, in one of which a man was ploughing. The plough was of wood, shaped something like an old English plough in the beam, but with only one handle, and no coulter, wheel, or share-board. This was drawn by a solitary water buffalo, and rooted up the greasy black earth to a depth of five or six inches. At one side of the field we saw a rude harrow formed of bamboo stems lashed together, the side shoots being cut at about six inches from the stem, and these act as prongs to scarify the soil. The whole system of land culture here is very rude, and yet it is far in advance of that practised by natives anywhere else in Borneo, if we except the plain near the

FORDING TAMPASSUK RIVER ON BUFFALOES.

To face page 250.

banks of the Tawaran river, a few miles further to the south. Passing the last group of Badjow houses we came to the river again and found it running rather high, the water being much discoloured by the earthy matter washed down from the hills during rains. This was the beginning of difficulties, for we had to unload the buffaloes in order to prevent our rice from being wetted, and then we rode them across, while the men carried the packages on their heads, and held on by the saddle-gear or tails of the animals. After piloting across one detachment in this way we returned for the others, and so managed to get all the men over safely, and keep the goods dry. Our road got worse and worse, now through tall coarse grasses which, arching overhead, nearly excluded daylight, then through bits of forest where one's face was in danger from overhanging boughs and creepers, crossing dirty streamlets, and clambering over roots and stones, while in places the path suddenly dropped downwards into a sort of slimy trough or drain, the sides of which were as high as the saddle, and down which one's buffalo slided rather than walked. Of course we were drenched to the skin, and our clothes, which were nice and white at starting, were covered with mud, but there was nothing for it but to keep on, which we did until nightfall, when, finding it impossible to reach the village of Ghinambaur, we " put up " at some field huts, and in the absence of mosquitoes, passed a comfortable night on the floor of one of the huts warmed by a cheerful wood fire.

August 7th.—Arose at 5 A.M. and took breakfast. We had simmered a piece of beef in a pot over the fire all night with onions, two or three chilies, a bit of fresh ginger, and just a handful of rice for thickening, and the result was a very palatable soup; boiled beef and biscuit

completed our meal. We "squared up" with our landlord by paying a fathom of grey shirting and two black
Chinese looking-glasses for our house (which we had all
to ourselves), firewood, and a nice young fowl for our
dinner. About six o'clock I mounted my steed, and a
ride of about two hours brought us to the luxuriant fruit
groves which surround Ghinambaur. We found a scattered village close beside the river, each house having its
own clump of cocoanut and other fruit trees. A mottled-
leaved alpinia was common beside our route, and a pretty
climbing plant with opposite leaves, each bearing a
thunbergia-like white flower, was not unfrequently observed among the grass and low shrubs. A rynchosper-
mum and two species of mussænda were very conspicuous.
One of the last-named was a bushy plant two to four feet
in height, bearing bright orange-scarlet flowers among its
dark glossy foliage, each flower being set off by a pure
white bract nearly as large as one's hand. As seen among
the grass this plant was very distinct and effective. Its
congener is a climbing species not nearly so showy.

We rested in a Dusun house for an hour awaiting our
stragglers, two of whom were sick. Whilst waiting we spread
out our rice to dry, as it had become damp, doubtless
owing to the drenching rain of yesterday. Our hostess
was a rather attractive Dusun girl, whose husband was
away on a hunting excursion. She was very obliging, and
seemed quite pleased at our visit. The house was small
but very neat and clean, having, moreover, an air of comfort about it not often seen in Dusun dwellings. Among
other goods we noticed netting needles of wood, similar
in principle to our own, together with excellent fishing
nets, weaving instruments, by means of which a strong
and durable cloth is made from the macerated fibre of a
species of curculigo called "lamba" by the natives.

This is afterwards dyed with native grown indigo. Water bottles of bamboo, sieves and fans of different kinds used in cleaning rice, well made baskets of rattan-cane, knives and choppers were also represented, and we especially noted an excellent adze lashed to its shaft by neat rattan work. This implement is used in cutting and trimming planks from the large forest trees, saws being unknown here. I noticed a small basket of true cotton of excellent staple, but it is not much used, "lamba" fibre being obtainable in any quantity from the jungle without any trouble, and its fibre is more readily worked with the help of rude implements. For sewing thread we found our hostess using the fibre of pine-apple leaves (*Ananassa sativa*), which serves the purpose well. This plant must have been introduced to Borneo many years ago, for it has become thoroughly naturalised, apparently wild, indeed, and not even jungle fires seem able to destroy it. In the Philippine Islands the plant is common, although the dainty manufactures of "pina" fibre formerly made there are now to a great extent discontinued. As examples of skilful handweaving, these "pina" fabrics are even superior to the celebrated hats of Panama, and a dress made in the best manner would cost from a hundred to three hundred guineas.

The villagers who accompanied the "Orang Kaya," or headman, on his visit to us a short time after our arrival, were very much interested in our firearms, and begged of me to "shoot something." To please them, I took a chance shot with a Snider rifle belonging to Smith, and brought down a couple of cocoa-nuts which hung on a tree about one hundred yards off. There was a general rush to pick up the fallen nuts, and the blackened place where the ball had struck was examined with much astonishment.

We now marshalled our followers and again made a

start on our way. We found the roads awfully wet and slippery, and in about half an hour's time it rained in torrents, and the river being now so swollen and turbulent that there was no hope of our being able to cross it to-day we had to pull up at a little village called Buramhangan. The house where we stayed was about one hundred feet above the river, which we could hear rushing and roaring all night. We were soon surrounded by the villagers, most of them young people, and remarkably handsome. The men, especially, had very regular features, dark expressive eyes, and their jet black hair when free from the loose coil in which it is generally worn hung down as low as the waist in lustrous masses which a woman might envy. They appeared to be very thrifty, and had abundance of poultry, swine, and buffaloes. Their manufactures seem to be cloth, baskets, hats, and mats of various kinds, together with fishing nets (made in exactly the same manner as our own), and household utensils of bamboo and cocoanut shells.

August 8th.—We awoke just before sunrise. A lovely morning, and the river has fallen much during the night. We tried to hire another buffalo from these people, but as they would not come to terms quickly we had to push on without it, having fully made up our minds to reach the village of Sineroup ere nightfall. Our path lay up the hill for about half a mile, and then we bore down hill to the left. The path was like a drain, and awfully dirty. Smith's buffalo made a bit of a start, and its girths being loose he and the baggage toppled over into the long grass and brushwood beside the path. A little further on I had the same luck, although fortunately for the rice and sleeping-gear which my beast carried it happened in a dry place. The roads were very bad, and also the fords, but we plodded steadily onwards, and by four o'clock P.M. we climbed the hill and were safe at Sineroup. The last ford but one was rather turbulent, and our men being a long way behind we did not wait for them, and they did not get in until night-fall. We stayed here in the headman's house, and found him a jolly fellow with a striking Chinese physiognomy and vivacious manner. He and his family gave us a hearty welcome, spread mats for us on a little raised platform near the window, and gave us a fowl and some rice, so that we had satisfied our hunger before our men arrived.

We were now fairly into the country of the "Dusun," or "Piasau Id'an," the meaning of this last literally being "Cocoanut Villagers." Generally they are a clean-skinned and handsome race, far superior to their neighbours the "Muruts," who live farther south, and whose land-culture is but indifferent. So far as I could learn, polygamy is not practised by these aboriginals, and they always appear contented and happy. The dwellings which, near the coast, are generally of "atap," or thatch made from the leaves of the "nipa" palm (*Nipa fruticans*), are here nearly entirely of bamboo, the roof being thatched with "atap" of cocoanut or the sago palm. Here at Sineroup the headman has a very clean and convenient bamboo-house, and a good deal of wealth in the shape of brass gongs, large ornamental water-jars, cooking pots of brass and earthenware, finely worked mats, &c., while half a dozen sturdy buffaloes are contentedly grazing on the green below the house. Of pigs, poultry, and domesticated bees, he has plenty. I had placed my dirty boots outside the house on a little veran-dah, and during the night they were either knocked down by visitors or else fell through below the house. When I asked my boy for them in the morning, we found that the pigs had eaten up all but the soles. Luckily I had

others, or the loss would have been one of the worst that
could have befallen me, since in all long foot journeys,
and especially in mountain climbing, good boots are of
the first importance.

In the tarippe trees (*Artocarpus Blumei*) here, we noticed very ingenious traps of bamboo, set to catch the
" basing," a sort of squirrel or tree-climbing rodent, which
plays havoc with this delicious fruit just as it approaches
maturity. At this village our guide thus far, Abdul Rathman, is to return, so we have engaged the headman here,
" Gantang," to accompany us on our next two days' journey as far as Kiau, which is the last village on the way
to the mountain. The scarcity of birds and animals is
very marked as we proceed inland. One reason for this
may possibly be the absence of virgin forest, nearly all
the country bordering on the Tampassuk river having
been by some means—possibly former cultivation, aided
by jungle fires—stripped of all its primæval forest.

August 9th.—We were up at daybreak, and at once ate
our breakfast. As usual, we had to await the coming of
our guides, and it was fully nine o'clock ere we got fairly
started. I notice that many of the natives here wear
semi-circular betel-boxes tied around them, and charms
are very commonly worn. These last are seemingly of
the most varied description, anything seems to do for a
charm—shells, teeth, and bones of animals, seeds, stones,
and bits of rock, tiny bells, and especially a kind of fossil
wood called "kayu lagundi," or, "tree of youth."
These are enclosed in the folds of an old kerchief and are
tied around the body. Great confidence is felt by the
wearers of certain good charms, and they are very popular
among the Sulu pirates, who will fight like demons,
believing themselves to be invulnerable. All the villagers
had come down to see us start, and they followed us down

to the river, which is not far from the houses. Rain during the night had caused the current to run strong and high, and none of our men dare venture across. We had a rope for such emergencies, and my interpreter, a lusty Badjow, named Suong, swam across and tied it fast to a tree. It was now easy for our men to cross, and we all got over safely. A little higher up we had to recross again, but the current here was stronger, and all the goods had to be carried across by our Dusun followers, who had accompanied "Gantang," the headman of Sineroup. Fortunately nobody was drowned, but the time occupied in crossing was so long and we were all so tired with our exertions that we were glad to stay at a wayside village instead of going on to Kambatuan as we had desired. We saw a good many attractive plants to-day, but unfortunately the dangerous difficulties of our journey left us but little time for collecting. And yet, although hungry and fatigued to a degree which no one can imagine who has not travelled in a tropical land without roads or bridges, one could but feel enthusiasm as ferns of filmy beauty, orchids of curious structure and vivid colours, graceful glumales, flowering shrubs and palms, met our eager eyes for the first time.

One of my first " finds " this morning was a singular bolbophyllum, which grew on the branch of a tree over a stream, and which, as I had from the first suspected, has turned out to be " quite new." It has been named, in gratitude to the Hon. P. Leys, M.B., Colonial Surgeon of Labuan, *B. Leysianum*, Rchb. f. Its structure is so very extraordinary that nothing but an engraving could give any adequate idea of its characteristics. A creamy flowered dendrobium (*D. cerinum*, Rchb. f.), grew on trees here and there, bearing its flowers in clusters, and a dwarf cymbidium (*C. Spinksianum*, Rchb. f.), was also met with

in bloom, as also was a white-blossomed ixora, bearing
pendulous compound clusters of fragrant blossoms. A
curious strong-growing vanilla draped trees in most
places, and on some wet mossy rocks beside a rushing
torrent, a glossy-leaved phalænopsis (*P. luteola*) dis-
played its golden blossoms, each sepal and petal mottled
with cinnabar. Cœlogynes were everywhere abundant
on trees and rocks alike, and on the latter overhanging
the streams hung masses of a waxy-leaved æschynanthus, bearing axillary clusters of crimson, black-striped
flowers, each standing erect from a gracefully modelled
purple chalice. Ferns and mosses hung on the dripping
river rocks in glorious profusion. Numerous, indeed, were
fair Flora's temptations to lingering dalliance on our
way, but we had an ulterior object in this journey which
nothing must interfere with. Our mission was to push
onward, letting nothing hinder our march—difficulties
and inclinations must alike be conquered if we would
that our journey be crowned with success!

Kambatuan reached, wet and fagged, we were glad of
a change of clothing, preceded by a brisk rub with a dry
towel, ere we thought of food. Our guides had selected
a roomy house, and we soon had a cheerful wood fire
ablaze on the hearth, which, as is usual here, was in the
centre of the large public apartment occupied by ourselves and our retainers. A fowl and some eggs were
soon purchased, and our whilom host was very hospitable, having spread some nicely-worked mats near the
fire, and instructed his daughters to make cigarettes for
us, which, with the kindness which clings to their sex all
the world over, they, seeing that we were strangers,
wet and tired, were nothing loth to do. These cigarettes, under the native name of "rokos," were always
forthcoming, and are made of tobacco (segope), both

grown and manufactured by these inland people. It is cut very neatly, and is made up for sale into ropes or rolls a yard or more in length, these being folded so as to make convenient bundles about nine inches long. Although not given to trickery, it is customary for these people to make the rope " core " of refuse tobacco, or of the leaves of kaladi, or other plants, and over this the really good manufactured tobacco is wound. The result of this is that the useable produce is not above one-fourth of the apparent bulk, and although all are well aware of the subterfuge, and carefully examine every roll of this tobacco before they purchase it, yet the practice continues year after year. For smoking, this dark shaggy tobacco is carefully unwound from the " core " (or " prot," literally stomach), and enfolded in a neat wrapper formed of the young leaf of the nipa palm, or occasionally in the thin husk of the maize cobs, both of which serve the purpose of cigarette paper by burning slowly but freely, producing neither flame nor flavour. There is scarcely a more national trait observable among Borneans than the smoking of the "roko." It is the one luxury common to all. From the Sultan to his meanest subject—male or female—everyone indulges in smoking them; indeed I have repeatedly seen unweaned infants partaking of the solace of the breast and of their tiny "rokos" alternately, both the gift of indulgent Bornean mammas.

August 10th.—All night we could hear the rain pouring down in torrents, but it cleared up towards morning, and at sunrise all was beautifully clear and bright. This is the view we obtained of the mountain as seen this morning at 7 a.m., all the lower part being obscured by the trees in the foreground. By 7.30 we had breakfasted, and were on our way. Yesterday had been a most unfortunate day so far as real progress towards the moun-

tain was concerned, and although all our guides were loud
in their protests that it would be impossible to cross the
streams after the late heavy rain, we were doggedly
determined to go on. We crossed the river twice, and
now, at 8.30, all further progress seems impossible, since
we have to cross again, and this at a place where the
river is a boiling torrent nearly five feet deep. The
Dusun themselves seem to have no great difficulty in
crossing, but our Labuan men are afraid. The great
difficulty is to keep one's legs under one in the strong
current, and to facilitate this being done the Dusun often
take up a heavy stone and carry it on one shoulder. Our
men bathed here whilst waiting, and most of them took
up a stone and cast it into the water ere they flung themselves in. This they do to propitiate the "antu," or
river god, who they tell me might otherwise be offended,
and afflict them with sickness. As we sit beside this
rushing river, the most gorgeous butterflies flit here in
the chequered shade afforded by overhanging branches.
Yellow, white, and brown species vie with each other in
activity. Now and then the most splendid ornithoptera
are seen, their strong and swift flight resembling that of
a bird. One lovely fellow, fully six inches across the
wings, settled on my boot as I remained motionless
watching it. It was of a velvety blackness, with a bold
band of pea-green across the wings. Another species
rather smaller has a band of metallic blue. These delicate insects are generally most numerous by rivers, or in
sunny places by the dry beds of streams, and, singularly
enough, are most abundant during the cool wet monsoon.

August 11*th*.—A lovely morning, and at sunrise we
obtained charming views of "Kina Balu." The rugged
top crags were especially well defined, as also the sloping
plateau, which seemingly forms the watershed for one of

the highest falls. Apparently we are quite near to the mountain, and the waterfall is distinctly audible, which does much to increase the delusion. As the sun's power increased, however, the view lost its distinctness, and in half an hour's time heavy white mist clouds had swept around its summit, and all its beauty of tint and shadow was lost to view. We ate a hurried breakfast, and started for Koung, a large and prosperous village situated a little to the south-east of Saduc-Saduc, the mountain ascended by Mr. Thomas Lobb in 1856. Our way lay diagonally down a hillside drain until we came to the river, which we forded, and then bore to the left across level rice-fields and patches of luxuriant kaladi (*Caladium esculentum*) and Indian corn, both of which evidently succeed best on these rich low lying alluvial plains. We crossed the river four or five times ere we at last found ourselves on the splendid village green of Koung. This green is a mile or more in length, lying at the foot of a range of sandstone hills which shelter it from the north, while the river skirts its southern side, and another hill rises from the river banks still further southward. It is, in fact, a well watered grassy plain between two sheltering parallel hill ranges, and affords the best pasturage for cattle that I have seen anywhere in the East. Of this the villagers take every advantage, for nowhere have I seen finer kine and buffaloes than here. We reached the headman's house at Koung about four o'clock in a drenching downpour of rain. Some trees beside the stream were draped with a glorious climber, having scarlet flowers (*Bauhinia Kochiana*), and a glaucous climbing plant, having lilac flowers, had completely overrun some of the forest trees on the opposite bank. We took up our quarters in the house of the headman, "Lapayang," to whom Mr. Veitch and myself had given a

Tower musket on the last journey I made in this direction. I notice that such of my men as speak the Brunei language can converse with the Dusun very readily after a few days' residence amongst them. This fact was noted by Mr. St. John, and from what I know of the language myself after a year's residence, and aided by vocabularies carefully collected, I believe the language of these people is intermediate between that spoken in the capital, Brunei, and that of the Sulus. Bees-wax and caoutchouc or rubber are frequently offered for barter as we pass through the villages. "Lapayang" welcomed us in his own way by firing a salute, and a gong was beaten to announce our arrival. I was sorry to find that his father had died since my last visit, when he had received us with many expressions of good-will, and told us of Mr. Low's first visit to the mountain, which he remembered well. As we had arrived before our supplies, "Lapayang" brought us some rice and a fowl as a present, and one of his sisters gave us some eggs and a fine cluster of bananas. I felt thankful when we arrived at Koung, since I knew the way from this place to the mountain quite well, and had not to trust to lazy guides, who have not the slightest idea of time or its value to the traveller. My buffalo also had reason to be glad, for here the plucky little beast had the luxury of good herbage on which to feed, a much better thing for him than the miscellaneous browsing afforded by our former halting places. The river runs about fifty yards from our quarters, and is very much swollen, having in many places overflowed its banks. Capital shooting may be had here at the large blue pigeons which roost in the trees beside the river, quite close to the houses.

August 12th.—Again a lovely morning as we crossed the ford just at the end of the village and pushed on for

Kiau.   The road lies by the sides of the river most of the
way until the turn to the left is taken up the open rice-
fields, which lie below the last-named village.   We crossed
this river thirteen times to-day, and some of the crossings
were deep and rapid.   Met troops of natives—male and
female—mostly laden with large baskets of tobacco, which
they were taking down to the villages nearer the coast to
barter for cloth, knives, and other goods, as no traders
appear to venture further inland than the first Dusun
villages.   Most of the men were armed with a long slender-
shafted spear, which is especially useful to them in fording the streams.   In addition they had the "parang," a
sort of scimetar-shaped sword, having a good keen edge.
This is slung to a broad belt worn sash-wise over one
shoulder, the part which crosses the breast being ornamented with cowrie shells sewn on very thickly.   I was
very glad when we reached the little farms of the Kiau
villagers, and could see their dwellings and palm-trees in
the distance.   In some of the clearings the crimson-
leaved dracæna (*D. terminalis*) was conspicuous.   It has
here slender stems five or six feet in height, each terminated by a tuft of bright coloured leaves.   Going up the
hill slowly, I made a little collection of the weeds found
among the rice and kaladi crops.   Among these were two
pretty little plants of the daisy family (*Compositæ*), the
one with purple and the other with yellow florets.   A
tiny species of torenia formed spreading tufts of purplish
leaves and stems, and bore rather pretty purple and white
flowers.   A woolly-leaved gnaphalium attaining a foot in
height, and bearing dense clusters of yellow immortelle-
like flowers, was especially noticeable.   There are numerous springs of cool water, clear as crystal, in this hillside,
and these are brought down to the path in tiny troughs or
aqueducts of bamboo, so that one has only to stoop very

slightly to drink, and water-vessels are readily replenished. The whole hillside is dotted with flat-roofed field-huts of clean yellow bamboo. These afford shelter during the mid-day siesta enjoyed by the workers in the field, who are for the most part women and children. Tiny streamlets are met with now and then, and in favourable spots the most graceful tree-ferns of the primæval jungle still linger, although fully exposed to the hot sun. The lower parts of their black trunks, however, are shaded by coarse herbage, and their roots revel among the earth, *débris*, and wet stones below. In some places the wet earth and stones beside these streams were carpeted with lovely mosses, and of these several rare kinds in good condition were obtained. We met one of my old guides, " Kurow" (see p. 97), this morning as we came along. He came up to me laughing and vociferating loudly. " Soung," who interprets Dusun for me, says that he wants me to understand that he, " Kurow," is glad to see me again, and that he will do all he can to help me. We reached the village about three o'clock in a dense white mist, and it commenced raining heavily a few minutes after our arrival. Among the plants we saw to-day was a splendid large bolbophyllum (*B. Petreianum*). A vanda grew on the trees overhanging the river, but was not in bloom. The deliciously-perfumed snow-white flowers of *Dendrobium crumenatum*, which were especially beautiful on the immense boulders of granite on the green at Koung, was also often met with to-day, and at one of the fords a large-growing cœlogyne (*C. racemosa*) bore drooping spikes of yellow and white flowers, the entire inflorescence being nearly a yard in length. While my boy was cooking dinner I made sketches of the most peculiar plants of botanical interest met with *en route*, much to the surprise—I might almost say awe—of the natives, who

DUSUN BORNEANS AT A STREAM.

To face page 264

crowded around me and watched every line—and especially the colouring—with great interest. I was surprised at the small number of women who came to see us in comparison with those who flocked into the house when we were last here. I found, however, that this was owing to their being away engaged in rice planting and other field labour. The headman of this village, named "Lemoung," had died since my last visit, and we saw his grave on the little hill just as we entered the village. A little hut had been erected over it, and this was decorated with eight little streamers of white cloth. His son, "Boloung," now "reigns in his stead." When we took our evening meal most of the women had returned from work, and the house was crowded, and the greatest curiosity was evinced as our plates, knives, forks, and glasses were spread out glitteringly in the lamplight. These people are very different from the Malays of the coast, and never tired of laughing and talking about ourselves and our goods. The women are not in the least secluded, and are far better proportioned, as well as more amiable and industrious, than are their Malayan sisters. Their clothes consist of a " sarong," or short petticoat, fastened around the waist, and reaching to the knees, and a strip of black cloth is bound over the breast. Their ornaments consist of brass wristlets and anklets. Necklets of beads or brass wire are also worn, and over the breasts, as also around the waist, coils of rattan cane dyed black or red are worn. Ferrule-like pieces of tin are often strung on these rattan coils, and strings of beads are also worn around the waist. Ear ornaments are generally of wood, and as large as a wine-cork. Both men and women have holes pierced in their ears, but these are not unfrequently utilised as cigarette-holders, much in the same way as the Zulu Kaffirs at the Cape

carry snuff-boxes in their ears. Everywhere here inland
we find the native cloth is made from the "lamba"
fibre dyed a deep blue-black with native indigo. I procured specimens of this fibre-weaving apparatus, and
prepared cloth, and these may now be seen in the large
Economic Museum at Kew. After dinner "Kurow," our
old guide, and "Boloung," the headman of this village,
came in with the avowed purpose of having a chat.
They were particularly anxious to hear about the white
man who had come to live on the Tampassuk river (Mr.
Pretyman), who they had been told intended to make
them all pay tribute, which was evidently unpleasant
news to them. They also wanted to know where I had
been since I left their village, and were very much interested in all I told them about the Sultan of Sulu. The
house was full of people of all ages, who had come to see
us, and among them were a party from a village three
days' journey inland. These were on their way to the
coast villages to trade. The produce they had with them
was tobacco, bees-wax, india-rubber, and a little "lamba"
cloth and raw cotton. These people had never seen a
white man before, and seemed rather interested in all
we did; and in the accounts their Dusun neighbours
gave them of us and our doings, the gist of which was
that we came from a large prahu, or ship, to dig up grass
and shoot birds, that we ate and drank all sorts of curious
things, but singularly enough, as they thought, would not
eat rats or tiger-cats, these being esteemed great delicacies
here by the native trappers. Here, at Kiau, as at all the
Dusun villages along our way, we noticed large quantities
of tame or domesticated bees. These are kept in cylindrical hives formed of a hollow tree trunk, and are placed
on a shelf fixed under the overhanging eaves of the
houses. In several instances the hives were on shelves

inside the houses, a hole being made through the " ataps " corresponding with the hole in the hive, so as to allow of egress and ingress, a plan similar to that adopted by the bee-keeping natives of Kashmir.

August 13*th.*—I and Smith have been busy all morning, overhauling our stores and goods, and getting ready for our going up the mountain to-morrow. Our rice had suffered from damp, but as we find we can buy some here, it does not matter so much. Several fowls were also brought in for sale this morning, so that we are not likely to starve. Having put all our gear into order after our seven days' march, we took our guns and a couple of men, and took the path leading eastward, which led us across one or two rice and vegetable plots, in which tobacco plants were growing freely, and at last we crossed a recent clearing and reached the forest, which crests the spur or hill range on which the village of Kiau stands. We turned northwards and climbed the hillside, which was stiff work, being in places nearly perpendicular. Here I found a pretty foliage plant, having strap-shaped leaves six inches in length, glossy green, boldly variegated with silver-white above, while the underside of the leaves was of a deep blood colour. Of this I gathered as much as I desired, and a wild plantain or banana growing near, I cut one down, and packing my plants close together in damp moss and earth, I enveloped them in the cool moist sheathing layers of the banana stem. Thus packed, they occupy but little space, and are easily carried without risk of damage by drought or friction. Saw several cœlogynes in flower on the surrounding trees, but other orchids seemed scarce. I made a collection of ferns, mosses, &c., for drying, but nothing striking from a horticultural point of view was seen. We gained the crest of the ridge after an hour's hard work, and followed it eastward for two or three miles, but without any change in the vegetation. On returning, we did not descend the way we came, but followed the crest in a westward direction, and from one point we got a capital view of one of the waterfalls on the mountain. It was now becoming misty, however, and we returned to the village, which we reached just in time to avoid a drenching, for the rain came down in torrents. I sent one of my men to fetch " Kurow," and when he came I told him I wanted to bargain with him to take me to the mountain in the morning. He at first said he couldn't bargain, because " Boloung," the headman, was out. He had scarcely spoken, however, before " Boloung" himself entered from the other end of the house. Finding this loophole closed, he said he could not bargain to-day, because it was an unlucky day to him. He had visited all his traps and snares this morning, he said, and there was nothing caught, adding that he knew it before he started; this was his bad day. " Boloung " said they would come in and bargain in the morning. Fortunately I was not entirely dependent on them, and could have found the way myself, intricate as it is. Anyone who had not travelled here before, however, is entirely dependent on these people as guides, and their utter disregard of the value of time is perplexing enough to a stranger with limited supplies of food for himself and followers. It was these people who turned back Mr. Thomas Lobb when he attempted to ascend Kina Balu from this village in 1856, and the moral force of a well-armed and rather imposing party is still necessary in order to keep their avarice within moderate bounds, and to obtain from them the little assistance necessary. When Mr. Low ascended the mountain in 1851, he gave many presents to these people, and even now the wealth the village obtained through his visit is much talked of among the hill villagers. When Mr. Lobb was there, five years later, he had but a small party of followers, and not being prepared to pay in cloth and other goods so liberally as Mr. Low had done, they refused to help him, and he was compelled to leave without ascending the mountain, as he had desired to do. Even in 1858 Mr. Low and Mr. S. St. John had to " guard carefully against pilferers," and had a little hostility to contend with as well. On their second expedition, in the same year, however, they experienced a better reception. Some years later, I believe in 1866, an Italian expedition came here for natural history purposes, and the Dusun account is that they ascended 6,000 feet.   This expedition, according to native accounts, paid twice as much as was necessary, a precedent which gives these hill villagers an excuse for extortion. When I and Mr. Peter Veitch came here, eight months ago, we had a well-armed force at our backs, and we taught the Kiau people how to moderate their desires by paying a just price for all they gave or sold to us, and for all services performed, but we gave no presents. Livingstone * deprecates the system of giving presents in his first work on travel, and he is not the only traveller who has had reason to complain of a mode of procedure which invariably causes inconvenience to others. These people were always well-disposed towards us, and this time I find our plan was a good one, for there is no misunderstanding ; fowls, rice, and other provisions are far more easily procurable now, since the natives know that all will be fairly paid for, whereas under the old system their object was to give a small present in the hope of receiving something far more valuable.

* " Missionary Travels and Researches in South Africa."   John Murray. 1857.

August 14*th*.—" Kurow " came in this morning, and commenced to " bargain " cautiously by asking to see the goods we were willing to pay for guides. " Suong," our interpreter, who was an adept at trading, spread out some cloth and other things to the value of a few shillings, and after a deal of talking an agreement was arrived at by " Kurow " and " Boloung " consenting to accompany us in return for these things and an old coat of mine, upon which " Kurow " had cast longing eyes ever since my arrival. Among the goods was an entire length— twenty-six yards—of grey shirting, and this was brought back for me to divide into two halves, each of these dusky chiefs seeming firmly convinced that the other would " best " him if possible. Having, after some slight trouble, divided the cloth to their liking, and handed them the other goods in pre-payment, another difficulty arose, both declaring that they could not start to the mountain to-day, as they had no rice, and must needs go to the next village to obtain some. By this time all my men were ready to start, and as I had said I should set out to-day, I was determined to do so at all risks. I explained to them that they had plenty of rice in their village, but that if they really wanted more " Kurow " had better accompany us, and " Boloung " could obtain supplies and come on after us on the morrow, adding that we should start at once, and if their agreement was not kept we should of course take back the goods we had pre-paid them. It must be distinctly understood that in Borneo pre-payment for goods or services to be rendered is the national custom, just as it is in South America. In the latter country the natives who collect the india- rubber or caoutchouc in Brazil may serve as an illustra- tion of the fact. I left my " boy," who was rather unwell, and the only old man in our party, to " abide by the stuff" in the house, and shouldered my gun and left our guides to think matters over. We had not proceeded above a mile, however, before "Kurow" overtook us, and went on ahead as cheerful as possible. After an hour or two of rough walking on shelving forest-paths, varied here and there by slippery logs, we came to a mountain-stream, probably one of the tributaries of the Haya-Haya. Here, in a large stone trap, the worthy "Kurow" was fortunate enough to find a large wild cat. I had not spoken to him since he overtook us, but I could not resist the opportunity of reminding him that this was one of his lucky days! We crossed here, the water being deliciously fresh and cool, and another hour's stiff walking brought us over the base of the next spur, and to our old quarters, the "Sleeping Rock," where we were to rest for the night. This is a gigantic overhanging boulder near a foaming torrent. A pretty little maidenhair fern, before alluded to, grew here in great plenty, and attained the greatest luxuriance among the *débris* of former camp fires. Overhead a colony of mason bees had established themselves, forming multitudes of little rounded mud nests on the face of the rock, and when we lighted our fires the smoke disturbed them much. A still greater nuisance, however, was our guide, "Kurow," who made a fire and commenced to cook his wild cat by roasting it, hair, skin and all, without the slightest preparation. When Mr. Veitch and myself slept here during my first visit, he had two rats—rather high they were too—which he roasted entire, and ate with great satisfaction! The soil near the bottom of these immense spurs is very rich, as attested by the luxuriance of bamboo and species of ginger which are comparatively puny on poor land. Beside the mountain torrents a pink-spathed aroid (*Gamogyne Burbidgei*, N. E. Br.) is common, and rather

pretty. A species of dwarf palm (*Areca*, *sp.*), bearing clusters of small scarlet fruits, is noticeable, and a
trailing plant, allied to the jasmines, bore axillary clusters
of white waxy flowers, each having a brown eye-like spot
in its centre. The perfume emitted by its blossoms was
delicious, and resembled that of spring hyacinths. A
red-fruited raspberry (*Rubus rosæfolius*), and several
species of ferns and selaginellas carpeted the low shady
forest along our route. The only bird we saw was a
lyre-tailed shrike of a dark ash colour. Our dinner
consisted of a fowl cut up and boiled with a little rice,
and when it was nearly done we added a small tin of
Julienne soup to it, thus securing some substantial potage,
and we were hungry enough to appreciate it at its full
value. A cup of coffee and a cigar made us forget all our
bruises, and knowing the stiff day's work we had for the
morrow, we retired to our blankets early.

August 15th. — We awoke about 5 A.M. and aroused
our followers. A Malay named "Jeludin," acted as
cook in the absence of my regular "boy," and he prepared a very palatable breakfast of the remains of our
dinner, supplemented by nicely boiled rice and dried fish.
"Kurow" breakfasted off wild cat roasted *à la* Dusun,
and a little rice which we gave him. After breakfast he
sat smoking, and "Suong" came and told me that he
would not go up the mountain. On my asking him his
reason for resolving thus, he replied that he could not
go because he had no trowsers, nor coat, nor head-cloth.
I had given him a warm tweed coat previous to starting,
but this he had left in his house. I at once told him
through "Suong," that if he did not go as I had paid
him to do, I should tell all the headmen as we returned
to the coast, that he broke his bargains, and was afraid
to go up the mountain. This threat had the desired

effect on him; for after reflecting on it several minutes, he arose and prepared to start, saying with charming *naïveté*, that " I was a good man, and that he liked me." About seven o'clock "Boloung" and five or six of his followers rejoined us, as they had promised, and we set off on our way up the spur.

Our path at first lay up the bed of the torrent, but we left this in a few minutes, bearing up the spur to the right, past a bamboo fence in which rat-traps were placed at intervals of a few feet. Here and there, too, we noticed the dangerous spring pig-spearing apparatus, so commonly met with in the forests of the Murut and Kayan tribes who live further south. The deposit of forest *débris* at the base of this south spur is very rich in ferns and herbaceous plants. A melastomad here and there bore clusters of pretty pink flowers. Of this plant, which grew in the moss beside the path, there are green and purple-leaved varieties. A glossy-leaved ardisia, having clusters of red berries, the foliage being claret-coloured beneath, was conspicuous; and the stems of a shrub four feet high were covered with clusters of ver-milion-tinted berries the size of small peas; another shrub, a yard high, having lance-shaped serrate leaves, bore clusters of pure white, gesnera-like flowers. As we climbed higher up the mountain side, rhododendra, bearing white, scarlet, yellow, or magenta-coloured blos-soms, began to appear, and epiphytal and terrestrial orchids also became more plentiful. The curious pitcher-plants also increased in profusion, some being of a wondrous size and of the most singular form, colour and texture. At one place in a secluded mossy nook, where Mr. Veitch and I had obtained plants during our last ascent, I found that some cuttings we had accidentally left on the ground had thrown out numerous fresh roots into

T

the wet moss on which they lay! The delicately perfumed
little orchid, *Dendrochilum glumaceum*, was flowering
freely, its elegantly drooping inflorescence resembling

RHODODENDRON STENOPHYLLUM.

the most dainty filagree work. Golden and white-
flowered cœlogynes nestled here and there beside our
path. In one place, the curious little *Rhododendron
ericifolium* was in bloom; and another species, growing
on mossy trunks, bore waxy, bell-shaped flowers of a
clear orange-scarlet colour. The dark glossy green

foliage of this last reminded one of that of a sciadopitys in form, being linear, and arranged in whorls. It has been named (*Rhododendron stenophyllum*, Hook. f.).

As we ascended the temperature fell faster and faster, and at intervals we were completely enveloped in dense clouds of mist, while at other times they were dispersed, and the sun brightened up the mountain side. One place we passed this morning is rather dangerous, almost like walking on the ridge of a high building, the descent on one side however being a sheer precipice of 1,500 feet, and the other side is steep ; but there are a few bushes near, which give one confidence. At 8,000 feet we again enter a dripping cloud, or rather it sweeps down to meet us, and the trees here are of low stature and gnarled, the branches being so low that in places one has to crawl through them. Casuarina trees are commonly met with. The ground and lower bushes are covered with wet mosses, and white hair-like masses of usnea sway to and fro in the higher branches. The cold increased, and my Labuan men felt it very much. I looked at my thermometer at three o'clock during a heavy shower, and at an altitude of 9,000 feet, and it registered 56°. In England one would consider this a delicious temperature ; but when we started this morning we had a temperature thirty degrees higher.

It was curious to notice the effect the depression of heat and the rain had on my men, who had never in their lives known the thermometer below 70°. They appeared perfectly paralysed ; and the Dusun themselves were but little better. We reached our former camping-place, the cave, about 3.30, wet, cold, tired, and hungry. Five of the fellows were so far chilled and exhausted that they gave up when within ten minutes of the cave, and huddled themselves close together under some dry rocks. I sent twice for them to come on to us, but they would not move, and passed the night without fire or food, rather than bestir themselves to prepare either. We managed to start a fire after some difficulty, and then pulled off our cold wet garments. I got one of my Malays to rub me briskly all over with a coarse towel, and then put on two flannel shirts, trowsers, and jacket, after which I felt comparatively comfortable. One of the Dusun fetched us some water from a stream half a mile off; and it was so icy cold as to make one's teeth chatter to drink it—rather a novelty in the tropics.

"Jeludin," although shivering, set about cooking our dinner; and "Suong," who was the most useful man I had, chopped up enough wood to last us all the night. The men who came on with us sat shivering under the rocks for over an hour, before I could induce them to set about lighting themselves a fire. It was, indeed, really painful to see the poor fellows so utterly paralysed. "Boloung," the chief of the Kiau Dusun, who had accompanied us, had carried up a fowl under his arm the whole way; and when he reached the cave, I was agreeably surprised when he presented it to me, and I took it as a great compliment, for it is extremely rare for a Dusun to put himself to so much trouble even for a friend, much less for a stranger like myself. This fowl, although lively enough in the morning, had become so wet and cold during the ascent, that it appeared to be dead; indeed, I thought it was dead for some time, but on holding it near the fire, it revived a little. Our Dusun followers made their encampment under a dry, overhanging rock, a quarter of a mile ahead of us. We had a view of the great waterfall on the bare granite rocks of the mountain opposite, and could hear the dash of its current into the stream below very plainly.

After dinner we made up a good fire; and never did I fancy a cup of hot coffee so delicious as this seemed to be; while the primest of fragrant Havannahs have been far less comforting than was the modest cigarette of native grown tobacco, which one of my followers made and presented to me on the spot. Our fire blazed up brightly, and diffused both warmth and fragrance in our rocky dwelling; and, wrapping our rugs and blankets around us, we were soon asleep, surrounded by our Labuan men, who crowded around the fire, and kept it replenished with fuel throughout the night.

CHAPTER XIV.

August 16th.—We were up by daybreak; and while "Jeludin" was preparing breakfast, I went out with the men collecting such plants as I wanted, and packing them in the native sago-sheath baskets (granjombs) with which we had provided ourselves. I was anxious to begin thus early, as I wanted to start most of the men back to Kiau to-day. After three or four hours' hard work, we loaded twelve men and started them off on the downward journey; and as we intended staying two days longer up the mountain, they had orders to collect other plants which I had pointed out to them near Kiau. After start-ing them off, I was glad to take breakfast before explor-ing further for other things which I much wished to procure. After our repast I started off over the ridge of the spur, progress, however, being very slow, as nearly all the way one had to climb through branches, roots, or low shrubs. A glossy-leaved begonia, with large white flowers, was common beside the streams, and three species of cœlogyne were met with growing among the rocks and

bushes. A great many small-flowered orchids of various
genera were seen, but few were in bloom. Dacrydium,
phyllocladus, and a peculiar casuarina of drooping habit
were seen, and several herbaceous plants, among which I
noted a drosera and a species of dianella, much resembling
those of Australia. Among ferns were at least two species
of trichomanes, two or three gleichenias, a peculiar form
of dipteris resembling *D. Horsfieldii*, but dwarfer and
quite glaucous, nearly white indeed below, and a strong-
growing blechnum. Several mosses in fruit were gathered,
and most of them were either absolutely new, or had not
been discovered in Borneo before. Here and there I came
across patches of an acre or two in extent of rocky
mountain side without any tree-growth. These rocky
patches were carpeted with coarse sedges, among which
the great *Nepenthes Rajah* grew luxuriantly, an enormous
crimson-tinted pitcher depending from each of its large
lower leaves. These gigantic urns were for the most
part filled with rain-water, among which were the remains
of ants, beetles, and other insect-life. Nearly all the
pitchers were found resting on the surface of the earth,
and in most cases they were hidden by the overhanging
leaves, sedges, and *débris* among which the plants grow.
It was, in the case of the younger specimens—plants a
foot high or so—that the pitchers were most evident and
luxuriant. Seedlings of this size were even more ornamental than their big jug-bearing brethren. Here and
there were specimens of *N. Rajah*, great clumps having
stems five or six feet in height, with very broad massive
leaves, and pitchers capable of holding two or three pints
of water. It is these large plants which flower most
freely, some of the stems bearing three or four spikes of
their rich maroon-tinted blossoms, around which two or
three kinds of flies or gnats were playing in the sunshine.

The female plants were not nearly so plentiful as were the males, and I am inclined to think that these tiny flies aid fertilisation, for some of the female plants were a long way distant from any males, and yet they appeared to have been fertilised. *N. villosa* is often found in these open patches with the larger kind just alluded to, but more frequently it affects the margins of the open patches, and luxuriates among the low bushes, by which its weaker and more elongated stems are supported. *N. Lowii* and the beautiful *N. Edwardsiana* appear never to reach so high an altitude as those just named. I cannot describe the elated emotions I felt in traversing this mountain side, and gazing on forms of vegetable life the most remarkable of any to be found in the whole world! Hunger, bruises, and the repeated drenchings we had received during our journey hither, these and all other of our troubles seemed to vanish as I gazed around me on the wonders of creation and inhaled the cool invigorating mountain air. We returned to our cave-dwelling about four o'clock. As I write up my diary, a tiny bird is flitting about quite close to me, and does not appear in the least afraid. It is but little larger than a wren, its body being of a dark brown colour; the head and shoulders are mottled with yellowish brown. From its lively and erratic flight, I suspect it is of the flycatcher group. It flits backwards and forwards from bough to bough, and frequently leaves a branch as though flying right off, and quite surprises you by suddenly and adroitly twisting itself round and dropping back into the place from which it started. Another occasional visitor is a blackbird, having a golden bill and a reddish-brown breast. It strongly resembles our own blackbird indeed, but is perhaps a trifle fuller in the body. Again, we heard the little songster alluded to in the account of my first visit

here. I know of no bird whose melody possesess the
ravishing sweetness and variety of melody of this one, its
song in the early morning being especially delightful.
Were it possible to introduce it, this little stranger would
be a most welcome addition to our domesticated song-birds
here at home. Space is limited here in this cave, and
one has to sit pretty close to the fire. Just after dinner
to-night, as I sat making notes in my pocket-book,
Smith, in lifting our extemporised kettle off the fire, let
it fall, and the boiling water fell over my feet. My boots
were off, and the pain was rather hard to bear. " Suong,"
who is equal to all emergencies, recommends me to put
some wet salt on the scalded portions of my feet, which,
to please him, I did, and the pain soon after abated. I
was very sorry for this accident, being afraid it would
prevent my extending my excursions up the mountain
side to-morrow, as I had arranged to do. It is raining
very heavily, and Smith reminds me that we have only
had two wholly fine days since leaving Labuan.

August 17*th.*—Our cave had become drier, owing to
the fire we had constantly kept burning, and we slept
well last night. One of our men, on going to his basket
this morning, found a rat in it, which he at once secured
and killed. It had doubtless been tempted by the warmth
and his little store of food. It resembled very nearly the
long-tailed grey Norway species, now so common in
England, and was quite distinct from the short-tailed,
long-snouted kind, of which " Kurow " had trapped two
specimens during our first visit here. When our Dusun
guides came in, one of them quickly appropriated it as a
desirable addition to his edible stores. Our own breakfast this morning was of oatmeal porridge (a nice change
from constantly eating rice) and tea and biscuit. I had
some difficulty in putting my boots on, owing to the

scalding my feet received last night. My feet were very painful at first, but getting warm with walking, they did not inconvenience me so much as I had expected. We had a long walk up the mountain side to-day searching for seeds and plants. The highest height we reached was 10,700 feet, but it must be pointed out that our object was to collect all the plants and seeds we could in the richest vegetable zone on the mountain, and not to reach the summit. Had our object been to ascend to the top nothing would have prevented our doing so; indeed, the real difficulties of climbing "Kina Balu" are very few, and not worth mentioning; indeed, we found our journey to its base from the coast far more exacting to our strength and temper. We were fortunate in our search to-day, having, after a long and disappointing search yesterday, failed to obtain the particular plants and seeds I was anxious to obtain. To-day, however, I was rewarded by finding a few in good condition. We returned to our cave at about four o'clock, and found our Dusun followers, who had been in another direction, had also brought me in a nice lot of seeds, plants, and flowers. They had complained of the cold nights on the mountain, and threatened to leave us this morning (as indeed they did last journey), but I promised them some rice for their evening meal, and eventually they had consented to stay another night. Before dinner we packed up our plants and seeds carefully, and arranged everything ready for our descent in the morning. I wished to start early, so as to have plenty of time for collecting on our way, as at one spot I much wished to make a *détour* to collect seeds. Our bird visitors came around us to-day again, and fearlessly came quite close to pick up the crumbs of rice we threw towards them. We have had rain more or less for two whole days, and it was bitterly cold towards eight

o'clock, when we wrapped our rugs around us to retire
for the night. My thermometer stood at 45° just outside
the cave, and during the night it had descended to 38°.
I awoke during the night quite stiff with cold, although I
lay close to a good fire. My rugs had slipped from my
shoulders, and I was glad to fold them tightly around me,
and to put more fuel on the fire. It was a lovely moonlight night, the light being so strong on the branches
opposite our cave as to make them look as if covered
with snow. Mr. St. John mentions having seen a sort of
hoar-frost here during one of his journeys. The great
fall looked like a silver streak down the rocky mountain
side opposite, and the rush of its waters into the chasm
below comes quite clearly through the night air.

August 18*th*.—While Jeludin boiled the water for our
coffee this morning, I carved my initials on the soft red
sandstone wall of our cave, and then clambered up a tree
just opposite to try and get a better view. All is mist
and cloud below us except seaward, where a strip of the
coast line and the rivers towards Menkabong and Gaya
are visible. I can see the great fall very plainly coming
down the face of the rock opposite, just where it dis-
appears into the wooded gully, below there is a magnificent grove of tree ferns, and as I am fully a thousand
feet above them, I can look down on their expanded
clusters of fresh green fronds, and the effect in the morning sunlight is past all description. About 7·30 a.m. we
started on our downward journey, at first climbing the
ridge through roots and branches which were notched
here and there for foothold. On reaching the path
above, a few minutes' walk brings us to a series of
great steps and an open space or two covered with
jutting rocks and boulders, sedges, low bushes, and the
great pitcher-plants. Here we made a short stay collect-

ing, much to the disgust of our Dusun guides, who pointed to the dark clouds and told us we should have rain, and much wished us to push onwards. Lower down still we came across plants of the beautiful *Nepenthes Edwardsiana*, scrambling up bushes and casuarina trees to a height of twenty or thirty feet. Both this species, and also the curious *N. Lowii*, are frequently perfectly epiphytal, all the old stems and roots originally in the ground being dead, but the top growth has rooted into the wet moss and *débris* which rests on the trees and bushes everywhere around. Of the first-named there are two distinct varieties, differing in the length and form of their pitchers. *N. Lowii* is first seen at about 5,000 feet, and is one of the most singular of the whole group, its urns being flagon-shaped, and of a hard leather-like consistence. Growing quite plentifully beside the path were tiny plants bearing tripetalous flowers of a white or pink tint, and very pretty. In some places it was quite bushy in habit and a foot in height, being literally covered with blossoms. Some large mosses, one of them having stems a foot in height, were also gathered, and a few inconspicuous orchids, epiphytal and otherwise, were observed in bloom. A plumose filmy fern (*Trichomanes, sp. ?*) depended here and there from the half rotten casuarina branches overhead.

Owing to the rain yesterday our descent was far from pleasant, and falls were not infrequent, in fact on both occasions I have found descending this mountain very troublesome and dangerous owing to the wretched paths one has to follow. I carried a sago sheath basket behind me, fitted with bark straps for the shoulders, and it was lucky I did so, for I had one or two nasty falls backward, and it saved my head more than once from contact with the slippery stones. Our guides have at

last gone on a-head quite disgusted at my stopping here
and there to take up a plant or gather seeds, which I
can never resist doing. My boots had given way like
brown paper owing to their being constantly wet, and
I had to tie them on my feet with strips of bark. My
feet had chafed where scalded, and were now very painful, while the constant strain on the legs during the
slippery descent was very exhausting. However after
many falls backwards and forwards we reached Kiau
about four o'clock p.m. thoroughly tired and hungry. I
felt thankful when I regained the hill above the village
where all the hard work is over. I had tired out the
patience first of our guides, then of my Labuan men,
and even Smith had at last left me lingering collecting roots and specimens, and so I was the last man of
our party to reach the village. As I descended the hill
three of my men met me and took my load of plants, for
I had both arms full besides the basket at my back.
Tired and wet as I was I could not resist the impulse to
look at the plants my men had brought down two days
before, and I was glad to find that they were fresh and
healthy. A mist swept around us soon after I got inside
the house, and the steady rain we had experienced all the
afternoon changed to a regular downpour. I was glad
to put on my dry clothes after a thorough good wash and
rub down with a towel warmed at the fire. I found that
the skin was off my feet in great patches, and they swelled
very much after removing my boots. Smith had a large
sore on his heel, and he agreed with me that our ascent
was child's play compared with the descent.

My " boy " had cooked us some rice and had bought us
some fine ripe tarippe fruit to eat with it. We afterwards
had a cup of nice warm chocolate each, and lighting our
cigarettes, our fatigue and bruised shins were soon for-

gotten, as we nestled cosily in our warm rugs in the glow
of a sweet wood fire. After our return crowds of people
flocked in to see us, and the house resembled a market
place, fowls, rice, sweet potatoes, maize cobs, rattan hats,
tobacco, wax, caoutchouc, and Dusun gourd-organs of
bamboo being among the produce and manufactures
offered. The men squat down in groups, and there is
a great deal of talking about the mountain and " Tuan
Hillow " (Mr. Low), and " Tuan Bunga," the name by
which I am known to these people as well as to the
Malays of the coast. It is quite a gala night, and the
young girls are full of questions about the mountain.
My men " Suong " and " Jeludin " told me that the cave
on the mountain was a good place to sleep in, as there
were no spirits there, adding that on the island at Gaya,
and also at Pulo-Tiga they had been afraid to sleep, as
the spirits were so many there ! By the first stream we
crossed to-day in descending the mountain, a pretty pink-
flowered impatiens was flowering freely, and on the wet
rocks we noticed a tuft of red-berried nertera. On a
dripping wet rock here also a very fine trichomanes
luxuriates, forming large mat-like masses of black roots,
and long finely-cut filmy fronds. Two boys brought in a
quantity of anæctochili to-night soon after our arrival,
and asked for needles in exchange, which we gladly gave
them. The talking and laughter of the natives, who
seemed quite pleased at our safe return, lasted until I fell
asleep about eight o'clock, how much later I do not know.
Previous to this I called " Suong," and bade him tell all
the villagers assembled that I intended leaving in the
morning, so as to give time for my men to prepare their
things, and that the natives, knowing our intentions, might
bring in any fowls or rice they wished to sell early ere our
departure.

August 19*th.*—First thing this morning I heard that our buffalo, which had been turned loose to graze on the green here, is missing. All the men went to seek it while we ate our breakfast. "Kurow" had so often tried to induce me to exchange this animal—a female—for a male of his own that I was for a time suspicious of his having stolen it during the night. We had intended to start for Koung to-day, but the loss of our buffalo will detain us, as we cannot well leave without it, partly on account of its use to me now that my feet are raw and tender, and partly because it will not do to allow a theft to pass unpunished. A Dusun woman brought in a basket of fresh ginger roots this morning, which I find is cultivated by these people. Several fowls and some rice were also brought in, and these my "boy" bought in exchange for our old biscuit tins and glass bottles. During our forced delay I walked out to take a last look at the village, and to make a few sketches and notes. In the little flat-topped hut, which served as a head-house, I found a pile of about fifty skulls in one corner, some being in a basket suspended on the wall. These, the villagers tell me, are the skulls of their old enemies, and their individuality seemed well known to one old man, who pointed out several to me as having once rested on the shoulders of some of the Chinese settlers, who, some few years ago, disappeared from this Dusun country altogether, although their peculiar physiognomy still lingers among the Dusun tribes into which they married, so that it is just possible that they became absorbed into the native tribes. Others were pointed out as the heads of their old foes the Lanun, whom the Dusun people detest, say that they formerly came up to the hills with the ostensible purpose of trading, but adding, that they really wanted to steal their children as slaves. I offered "Boloung" a good Tower musket for a couple of these heads, but so highly are they still valued by these people that he refused to part with them, even for so high a price. This custom of head-hunting may be said to have died out amongst the Dusun, since they failed to subsist by hunting, and have taken to the less exciting employment of land culture. One place was pointed out to me where thirty men and their chief had been slaughtered together and their heads taken, only a few years ago. This was at a ford near Sineroup, and a rude circle of stones still marks the spot where the bodies were interred; all the stones are single except that which represents the chief, which has a smaller stone on its apex. I find the custom of marking burial places with erect stones very common among these people. On returning to the house I find that "Kurus," one of my men, a shock-haired Bruneian, has brought in my buffalo, having tracked it through the soft mud to a bit of jungle at some distance from the village, and there he found him tied to a tree!

The large house in which we stayed is big enough to accommodate five or six families, and the large common room, which extends from end to end, will hold twenty or thirty men and their baggage quite comfortably, having three or four hearth-stones for fires at intervals. It stands on a grassy knoll just at the entrance to the village, and the group of pinang and cocoa-nut palms on the lower side give to it quite a picturesque appearance. All over this district tree-ferns are very beautiful, especially so in the valleys and glades which exist up among these cool hills. Every now and then the traveller comes upon whole groves of them, and solitary groups exist even in the cultivated ground. So sweetly fresh and green are they, and quite distinct in form and tint from all sur-rounding vegetation, indeed, these feathery tree-ferns, and the tall clustering wands of bamboo, form the most distinctive features of the landscape. We at length bade our friends good-bye, and the whole village came to the knoll above the stream to see us start, and the girls were especially interested and begged of us to come again and bring them some needles, looking-glasses, and cloth.

Coming down the hillside cornfields from Kiau I saw here and there patches of cotton (*Gossypium barbadense*), and a delicate pink-flowered variety of tobacco was in bloom, and being supported by stakes, were perhaps left for seed. On the steep side of the opposite hill are numerous little farms, and on each you see a tiny flat-topped bamboo-hut which is used for shelter and rest during field labour. The soil is a reddish friable loam, thickly sprinkled with large sandstone boulders and stones; while in the lower plains and valleys is a deep black deposit which under irrigation yields splendid crops of rice. Under European protection and management, aided by systematic Chinese coolie labour, the virgin tracts on these hill ranges might be worked with advantage in the production of coffee and cinchona. Once fairly started, and with improved roads, this district would possess many attractions, not the least being a comparatively cool and salubrious climate. At elevations of 3,000 to 5,000 feet a cool bracing air is readily obtainable, indeed, as suggested by Mr. Low, the Marie Parie spur would form a capital site for a sanatorium of the utmost value to Europeans. At higher elevations a really cool climate, almost European, in fact, is obtainable. To bring this fertile district into cultivation and to form anything like good roads, however, would be a task Herculean, and one only to be accomplished by an immense expenditure of labour and capital. The system employed by the natives in clearing their new farms is to fell the

trees and then to burn them during the dry season. The
old stumps are left, and to prevent the rich earth and
forest *débris* from being washed away by heavy rains,
logs are laid against these horizontally all down the steep
shoulders of the spurs. Land newly cleared yields
splendid crops of hill or dry rice, maize, kaladi, tobacco,
sweet potato, and other crops. There is very little primitive forest on these lower hill ranges and spurs, nearly
all the land not now actually under culture being fallow,
in the shape of low jungle. The only really virgin
forest is the tops of the hills beyond Kiau and the
spurs of Kina Balu itself on the south and east sides.
On our way to Koung to-day we had a lot of trouble
owing to the swollen and rapid state of the river, which
we crossed no less than thirteen times. All along our
way we saw little torrents of muddy water pouring into
the river from the hill-sides. The two last times we had
to cross the stream previous to our reaching the regular
ford at the entrance to Koung village were really very
dangerous, and I shudder when I think of the surging
torrents we crossed, and of the large treacherous boulders,
water-worn and as smooth as ice, which lay hidden in
their beds.

I rode my buffalo : Smith walked and clung to the
ropes which held the saddle. The banks of the stream
were overflowed so that we could not tell exactly the
proper place to cross. My buffalo was a brave and careful animal, and must have been possessed of immense
power, seeing how she carried me and dragged poor Smith
over safely. I shall never forget our last crossing. We
had missed the proper place to ford without our knowing
it. The place we had chosen to cross was, as we afterwards found, a succession of smooth boulders and deep
holes. The buffalo had to feel its way, and when in

mid-stream, unluckily, set its feet on a boulder. Splash
we went, all over together, into a deep hole. Ugh! how
I did shiver as I sank to my neck with the buffalo submerged beneath me. As we rose again I glanced around
and thought for a moment poor Smith had gone. In a
moment, however, he rose to the surface of the stream,
where he lay extended grasping the ropes of the saddle
with one hand at arm's-length, and gasping for breath.
All the time we were being carried down stream, and
bravely as the plucky buffalo struggled her feet continually slipped on the loose pebbles below. "Hold on,
Smith!" I gasped, as splash we all went over another
gigantic boulder, and the water surged up to my ears
although on the back of the beast. I clung like a sailor
in a gale. Fortunately for us the buffalo regained her
footing, and clearing the current by a great effort she carried me and dragged poor old Smith up the bank Koung-
wards. "That's a narrow squeak, old boy," I said, but
Smith was too exhausted to answer as he tottered and
staggered to a seat on a stone lying near. I also was
glad to rest, and although thankful for our merciful escape,
I could scarcely look sober as I glanced at Smith, who
was as white as a ghost, and staggered like a drunken
man.

"Well," said he, when he had recovered his breath,
"it's all very well laughing, but you don't catch me crossing in that way again."

And in justice to his veracity I must own that I never
did, for he avoided me and the beast at crossings ever
afterwards. Arriving at the ford at Koung a young
Dusun came and assisted Smith over, the water being
very high and rising every minute. He then recrossed
and led over my buffalo, who a few minutes afterwards
once more regained her liberty on the green, while we, as

usual, took up our quarters with "Lapayang" in his bamboo-house. He and his people were surprised at our having got across the river to-day, and pointed to where it was rushing and foaming a yard higher than its usual current. Smith lost his stick and some plants he was carrying for me, and his rifle, too, would have gone had it not been strapped to his back. No one can possibly understand the danger of these swollen torrents who has not had personal experience of them. Once off one's feet in the surging stream, running seven or eight miles an hour at the least, one's life would inevitably be dashed away on the boulders and jagged rocks which occur every few yards. Adventures of this kind look tame when calmly written down after all danger is past, and when read by a comfortable fireside, but they are really very real and exciting when one is undergoing them in person. A little later we were surprised by "Suong" and my "boy," poor little "Kimjeck," who came in looking as miserable as drowned rats. They had avoided the dangerous fords by coming along the hill-path beside the river, but my other fellows refused to come on, and took shelter from the rain in some Dusun huts midway.

"Lapayang" received us kindly, as usual, and gave us a fowl and some rice, and lent us some cooking pots. Another villager brought us eggs and a cluster of fine golden bananas—I never tasted more delicious ones—so that we dined well after all our mishaps. After dinner our host brought us in a couple of fine large tarippe fruit, just at a time when dessert was least expected; we deserved it, however, and enjoyed it accordingly. I think I never felt so fatigued before in my life, my feet and legs were sore, and the exertion of the descent yesterday, and the falls I had, made me ache all over. Added to this, my skin from head to foot was covered with irritable red eruptions, caused by a minute red parasite of acaroid nature, which my men told me came off the buffalo on which I had ridden. As we sat smoking after dinner we heard the rain falling very heavily, and it lasted most of the night. The troubles of the day are ended, and we have cause to be grateful for our preservation from its dangers.

August 20*th.*—It was at first very wet this morning, but an hour after sunrise it cleared up and the sun shone beautifully. Our laggards came in about eight o'clock, just as we finished our breakfast of fowl and rice. There are plenty of fine cocoanut trees here, and one can obtain fine fruit. "Kurow" overtook us here this morning, having, together with his little daughter and another girl, walked from Kiau since daybreak. They are going on to Kambatuan, he tells me, to trade, and the girls have baskets of tobacco on their backs. We bought some cocoanuts and paid our host "Lapayang." He particularly wanted some powder and caps for his musket, and these we gave him, together with a handkerchief or two, and looking-glasses for his sisters, two fine girls, both married to young men of the village.

We started for Kambatuan after all our men had arrived, and "Kurow" accompanied us. Altogether we had a day's rough work, two of the crossings being shoulder high and very rapid, so that only I and the buffalo could cross, and the men and Smith had to follow the windings of the river a much longer distance over rough ground, for the most part covered with coarse grasses and jungle. It rained heavily at intervals, and we did not reach the foot of Kambatuan hill much before dusk; and after half an hour's climbing up a path like a drain, sometimes stony, sometimes of slippery yellow clay, we reached the village in a regular downpour. Nowhere else in Borneo have I seen such groves of "tarippe" trees as surround this village. When we last visited "Kina Balu" in December, "langsat" fruit was in season, and met with at nearly all the Tawaran villages. Now, in August, the "tarippe," rich and luscious, is most abundant, and now and then a coarse brown fruit, something like a horse-mango, is obtained, and is agreeable for a change. The perfume of the ripe "tarippe" fruit was most cheering to ourselves and our men, and almost as soon as we had got off our wet garments, and put on dry ones, a dusky maiden appeared with four large fruit in her plump little arms. She was dressed *à la mode* Dusun, and had wire wristlets, and a heavy wire anklet an inch thick, which must have weighed two or three pounds, around her left leg. A younger child brought us some fine plump bananas, which we found to be rich and luscious as new honey, leaving an aroma in the mouth like that produced by ripe filberts and old dry port.

We had a large concourse of the villagers in to see us this evening after dinner, including "Beuhan," the head-man, who wears a head-cloth and kriss, and in general build and physiognomy resembles the Sulus much more than either Dusun or Malays. "Kurow" was the principal talker, and related all that we had done and how much he had helped us in ascending the mountain. The young girls crowded to see us, and tried hard to get speech with us. We had given the girls who brought us fruit a looking-glass each, and we could quite well understand that all were eager for a similar gift. They were very, very scantily clad; indeed the most tolerant of Lord Chamberlains might well wish to add an inch or two to their tiny petticoat, especially as 'tis the only garment of which they can boast. It answers somewhat to the American definition of a dress " which began too late and

left off too soon." Here, however, it is the customary
fashion, and as such is honoured. How graceful were
the figures of some of these young girls ! Perfect little
Amazons, lithe of limb and having regular features, eyes
full of gentle expression, and a richness of raven hair most
European ladies might envy. It is pleasant to know
that these dusky girls, lovely as some of them are, will
never be degraded to anything worse than field labour,
which is a far better lot than that of their Malayan
sisters along the coast, whose personal charms chance to
be interesting. We found out later on in the evening
that the pretty damsel who had first brought us fruit was
the headman's daughter, " Sa' Tira" by name. Most of
the evening she knelt by the fire, her dainty little fingers
busily making cigarettes for her papa's guests, many of
whom had arrived from other villages near to look at us.
Altogether we spent a very pleasant evening with these
hospitable people, and we have no doubt but that they
will long look back to our visit themselves, seeing that
whole months frequently elapse without their seeing anyone from the coast even, much less a white man or two
from far-off Labuan.

August 21*st.*—Our buffalo had wandered from her moor-
ings during the night, and so we lost some time in finding
her. She was brought in at last, however, and we prepared to start on our way. "Beuhan," the headman here,
had been very hospitable to us, first in setting aside a
good clean house for us, and he also gave our men rice
and fruit, as their supplies, like our own, were very small.
Indeed, the fellow seemed so pleased to have us at his
village, and behaved so well to us, that I felt bound to
make him a fair repayment. I found out from " Suong "
that " Lapayang " had told him of the musket which Mr.
Veitch and myself had given to him, and that " Beuhan "

wanted one too. I was glad to have the power of thus easily satisfying him. When I handed the musket to him before all his people and told him always to help the white men who came to him, he was visibly delighted, and looked at the glistening barrel and bright brass-work with rapture. I also gave him a small supply of ammunition. He had heard of my shooting down cocoanuts from the trees, both at Koung and at Kiau, and he desired me to do this at his village. Smith handed me his rifle, and luckily for my reputation, I smashed the particular nut he pointed out to atoms. Here, at this village I took leave of my old friend "Kurow," and gave his little daughter a Chinese looking-glass, which pleased her greatly. Another little girl also from Kiau was with her, and she looked so sorry that she had not one too, although pleased at her friend's good fortune, that I could not but hand her one also, and her dusky face was all sunshine in an instant. These two girls had walked all the way from Kiau yesterday perfectly barefoot over rough ground, rocks, streams, and jungle, carrying heavy loads, while "Kurow" carried only his slender-shafted spear. It is this hard work at an early age which so soon destroys the lithe figures and tiny hands and feet these Dusun children so often possess.

"Beuhan" sent two men with us as guides to Sineroup. This was a great gain to us, as they knew the road well, and conducted us by what I may call the "overland route," that is, by the hill paths, and in this way we avoided three or four of the worst crossings. We found the walking very rough and fatiguing, especially in the close gullies we had now and then to cross. About ten o'clock we reached the village of Bundoo on the opposite hill, and here, while awaiting our men, I sketched the top crags of the great mountain, of which we obtained an excellent view, and also made a sketch of some Dusun tombstones on the little village green. While waiting, a woman brought us two young cocoanuts and put them down before us, so that we might drink, which we were glad to do, as it was very hot to-day. We gave her a looking-glass, which she evidently considered a good price for her fruit. I found these Tampassuk Dusun far more inclined to be hospitable than their brethren of the Tawaran.

We passed several tiny hill villages to-day, and some of them had a neat bamboo-fence and a stile at the entrance with notched sticks for steps. Some of the houses are surrounded by luxuriant gardens, each of which contains kaladi, Indian corn, a castor-oil plant (*Ricinus*) or two, cotton bushes, and in each there is invariably a clump of cocoanut trees, and three or four slender-stemmed betel-nut palms, while here and there old stumps are verdant with the betel pepper, the leaves of which are chewed along with bits of betel-nut, and a few condiments, such as lime—made from coral reef or shells —and gambier. Here and there, too, the red-fruited rose-apple or jambosa was seen. We reached Sineroup about 3.30, and singularly enough have not had a drop of rain all day. "Gantang," the Orang Kaya, was glad to see us, and pointed with pride to the new garments he wore, made from the cloth he had earned by accompanying us to Kiau.

August 22*nd.*—We left Sineroup and its hospitable headman this morning, after having arranged with him for a guide and another buffalo as far as Ghinambaur. We descended the hill, and after crossing the river two or three times, which was easily done now, since no rain had fallen yesterday, we were surprised by meeting a young Labuan man—whom I had formerly employed. He

was a handsome young fellow named " Sallia," a relative
of poor old Musa, and from him I heard that Mr. Pretyman, accompanied by Mr. Dobree, a Ceylon coffee
planter, were following, and that their object was to proceed to " Kina Balu " in search of land suitable for coffee

KINA BALU FROM GHINAMBAUR (EVENING).

culture. A few minutes later we met them and had luncheon together on the dry stones of an old river course.
In answer to Mr. Dobree's inquiries I told him what I
had seen of the country, of the large extent either
actually under cultivation by the Dusun or lying fallow
as jungle, and that virgin soil in large tracts would only

be obtainable by felling the primæval forests on the enormous spurs of Kina Balu itself. We parted just as a
heavy shower came on, and pursued our way to Ghinambaur, which place we reached about four o'clock, drenched
to the skin and covered with mud to our waists, the roads
being in a frightful state owing to the rain. We sought
our old quarters, and soon made ourselves comfortable for
the night. We heard that a court-house was being built
here by Mr. Pretyman, but did not see it, and inquiries
as to what the " white man " was going to do were numerous, as indeed they had been all along our route.

After resting, I could not resist making the accompanying sketch of the great mountain as it loomed up through
the cloud strata just before sunset. We were four days'
journey from its base, and yet it seemed so very nigh to
us in the last hours of sunlight as to appear only a mile
or two distant through the sun-lit air of evening.

August 23rd.—We started early this morning from
Ghinambaur, having a walk of fifteen miles before us over
wretched roads ere we arrived at Mr. Pretyman's residence, " Port Alfred," on the Tampassuk. My buffalo
was nearly knocked up, and so I left her in charge of the
men, and I and Smith, trusting to our knowledge of the
way, pushed on ahead. We had a hard day's work a
greater part of the way, floundering about in the mud of
buffalo tracks, or crossing streams and creeks up to
our necks, with just such a suspicion of lurking alligators
being in them as made the thing exciting. I stayed at
one place to collect palm-seeds, and the roots of a dwarf
zingiberaceous plant, bearing pretty little white and lilac
flowers. Here and there in the jungle we also saw a
large amorphophallus, bearing erect spikes of red berries,
and a pale-leaved variety of banana had its leaves beautifully blotched with reddish purple. In one place we had

to cross a grassy plain, the mud and water being up to our waist-belts in places, and the tall coarse grasses arched over our heads so that for a mile or more one has to flounder up this grassy sewer, the effluvia from the festering mud and the heat being alike almost unbearable. We at last reached the low sandstone hills and padi fields near the Badjow village, and were glad to know that we were within a mile or two of our destination. Then came another case of floundering through a wet rice field in a drenching shower, up to the knees in unctuous black mud, remarkably warm, too, it felt to the legs and feet. After all our struggles, however, we reached the Residency about four o'clock, dirty, wet, and tired. Here we found M. Peltzer in charge, although looking very pale and ill. We found out that he was suffering from low fever and dysentery, although fortunately not in anything like its worst phases. A bath and clean dry clothes was the first thing, after which we were glad to sit and rest ourselves ere dinner time. We discovered that our friend, M. Peltzer, had formerly studied in the Horto-Agricultural College, founded by the late M. Van Houtte, at Ghent, and that he had come here to make experiments in the culture of tapioca, tobacco, and other kinds of tropical produce. He related to us an account of a journey made into the interior as far as Sineroup, in the course of which he had lost three buffaloes in the streams. Altogether we passed a very pleasant evening, glad to be so near the termination of a long, and at this time of the year, a very critical journey. The accommodation here was luxurious to what we had been accustomed to, and in spite of mosquitoes we slept the sleep of the thoroughly weary.

August 24th.—We arose soon after 5 a.m., and calling our followers, bade them prepare our boat for the home-

ward voyage. We ourselves looked after the welfare of
our plants, and packed up our roots and seeds carefully.
A party of men were sent to the sandstone hills to procure roots of the white gardenia before alluded to. At
7·50 we obtained a beautiful view of the mountain, the
top crags, ridges, and water-falls being very distinct in
the clear morning sunlight. I could not resist sitting
down on the verandah and sketching the scene. Although
my sketch was true as regards outline, nothing but colour
could represent anything of the beauty of this scene—it
is a subject worthy of Walton's skill and labour. The
tints of light are ever changing in the morning's sun, and
the cloud strata lie like downy pillows on the bosom of
a giant. No wonder the simple Dusun, gazing on this
mountain in all the radiance of its early morning glory,
has idealised it as the heaven of his race!

A small herd of water-buffaloes have come down to the
opposite side of the river to drink, and I was surprised
to see that most of them had short stumpy tails. On in-
quiry I am told that the Badjows cut the tails of their
riding buffaloes, otherwise they draggle in the mud and
dirty water so common here, and then besprinkle the
clothing of their masters. The poor beasts must feel
their loss sadly in a hot country where mosquitoes and
other blood-sucking flies are abundant, but as we cut our
sheep's tails short without so good a reason, we must not
be the first in this case to throw a stone.

We gave all our men a rest this afternoon, which they
sadly needed, for several of them were nearly exhausted.
About four o'clock we were surprised at the return of
Mr. Dobree and Mr. Pretyman, who had proceeded no
further than the hill just above Sineroup. The Chinese
cook of course received orders to augment his food supply,
and we spent a very agreeable evening. Mr. Dobree

showed us the skin of a young rhinoceros which he had shot in the mud pool near the Sagaliad river, about twenty miles from Sandakan. The lower horn was three inches in length, the upper one only just growing. Mr. Pretyman had also a small but very interesting collection of large coleoptera caught in the immediate neighbourhood.

August 25th.—We finished rigging up our boat this morning, and stowed all our plants and stores on board before breakfast. Four of my men, including " Suong," who had been very useful to me, agreed to stay at this place as policemen under Mr. Pretyman. To oblige him I allowed them to do this. About 1 p.m. we started down the river, a much easier thing than pulling the other way. We reached the mouth in about an hour, but could not get over the bar, as there was not a foot of water on the bar ; indeed we saw two native fishermen carry their little canoes over. We had to wait until 10 o'clock at night, when we got over and out to sea with a favourable breeze, but we did not reach Labuan until August 30th, since we had contrary winds, and altogether a very rough passage.

Thus ended our journey for the second time to " Kina Balu," which occupied in all thirty-one days from Labuan, of which thirteen were occupied in the sea voyage from Labuan to the Tampassuk and back ; from Tampassuk to Kiau and back thirteen ; and from Kiau to the mountain and back five days. Our last journey, viz., the Tawaran from Gaya and Menkabong, occupied in all twenty-three days, but as we happened to start just at the commencement of the dry season, we avoided the dangers and difficulties of fording rapid streams. In the dry season the Tampassuk route could be accomplished in five days, and the ground is much more level than that along the Tawaran route, which is both hilly and fatiguing, the

track being almost impassable for buffaloes. The difference in the time occupied by the two routes is in part
accounted for in this way. Thus when I and Mr. Veitch
went by the Tawaran we saved four or five days in going
by chartering a passage for ourselves by a trading steamer
which landed us at Gaya Bay the next morning after
leaving Labuan. On our reaching Labuan, poor Smith,
who had been ill in the boat for two or three days, had to
go to the hospital with a very bad attack of fever, doubtless contracted during our walk from Ghinambaur to
the Tampassuk. He fortunately recovered in a week's
time, but evidently had felt the effects of a difficult
mountain journey. All our friends in Labuan were glad
to see us back again, and the mails from home which had
arrived during my absence were of the most cheering
kind. Notwithstanding our rough passage I found my
plants and seeds in good condition, and I am glad to
know that the practical results of this journey were more
encouraging than I had expected, and many of the plants
and seeds obtained ultimately reached Chelsea alive.
Having at this time been over a year in Borneo, I had
learned a good deal of the language, and had also found
much to admire in the Malays and aboriginals, so that I
felt in a way loath to leave a land which had been fraught
with so many novelties and adventures to me.

CHAPTER XV.

THE forests and gardens of Borneo are remarkably rich in native and naturalised kinds of edible fruits, and the forests especially may be considered as the home of the mangosteen, durian, tarippe or trap-fruit, langsat, rambutan, and jintawan, all excellent, indeed unapproachable, in their way, but if one would enjoy them a journey to the East is unfortunately necessary. They are somewhat like our own luscious jargonelle pears or green gage plums, and must in a sense be " eaten off the tree." The mango, one of the finest and most variable of Eastern fruits, has been successfully cultivated in the West Indian Islands, St. Michael's, and Madeira, and has fruited out-of-doors at Lisbon, but those we have named above have hitherto resisted culture outside their own restricted habitats, if we except the solitary instance in which the mangosteen fruited in one of the hothouses at Sion House some years ago, and the trees introduced to the island of Ceylon, which have succeeded fairly well. Another extremely useful and variable fruit, the banana, is quite commonly ripened in our gardens, and with the pine-apple these may be accounted the only tropical fruits which lend themselves to anything approaching a regular system of successful culture in our hothouses at home. Our ordinary cultivated fruits are naturally found in temperate or inter-tropical countries—Europe or the cooler parts of Asia principally; and of all those cultivated in the open air of Southern Europe, such as the vine, fig, and orange, the latter is the only one which can be induced to prosper in the tropical lowlands of the far East, where its evergreen character enables it to hold its own while its deciduous neighbours seem to fail through over-excitement, the loss of their customary winter's sleep.

On the other hand the pine-apple of South America, the mango of India, and the delicious little Chinese or mandarin orange, here luxuriate in the open air, the mango yielding two crops in twelve months, while fruit of the others may be obtained all the year round. In some favoured districts in Malaya the forests almost become orchards on a large scale, so plentifully are they stocked with durian, baloona, mambangan, varieties of tampoe, luing, and other native fruits, in addition to those already named; and in many places the pine-apple is so abundantly naturalised as an escape from cultivation that one might almost be led to imagine it indigenous did we not know that, together with the white guava, the papaw, and cashew-nut—a trio forming the " weeds " among tropical fruits—it is a native of the western tropics. So abundant are the crops in some seasons that one cannot help regretting their perishable nature, by reason of which their shipment to Europe in a fresh state is prevented; and as to their preservation in the form of candied confections or "jam" no one seems to have taken up the matter. Fancy a conserve of snowy mangosteen pulp, preserved mangoes, candied rambutan, or banana marmalade. The late Dr. Lindley once said, in his usual incisive way, that "most tropical fruits were edible," but that "very few were worth eating;" but then the probability is he had never tasted a mango or a mangosteen, a tarippe fruit, or the deliciously rich apricot-like pulp which surrounds the seeds of the caoutchouc-yielding willughbeias, and certainly not a durian.

The mangoes, oranges, bananas, pomoloes, and pine-apples are all cultivated fruits in the East, just as are our best gooseberries, strawberries, apples, pears, and grapes at home; but on the other hand we have no wild fruits which can in any way be compared with the durian, jintawan, langsat, trap, tampœ, mangosteen, and rambutan, all of which are more truly wild in the Malay islands than are the so-called wild cherries, gooseberries, currants, and raspberries of our woods. It is to the tropics one must go for a drink of fresh cocoanut milk — a taste of the fascinating durian, for a luscious mango, or the delicious mangosteen; and while in the matter of flowers our cultivators at home certainly have the advantage, in the case of fruits this much can scarcely be said.

The regal durian (*Durio zibethinus*), like the finest of nectarines or melting pears, must be eaten fresh and just at one particular point of ripeness, and then it is, as many think, a fruit fit for a king. So highly is this vegetable-custard valued that as much as a dollar each is not unfrequently paid for fine specimens of the first fruits of the durian crop brought into the Eastern markets. It is a universal favourite both with Malays and Chinese, but the opinions of Europeans vary as to the merits of

this " delectable epitome of all that is perfect in fruit
food." It is a paradox, " the best of fruits with the
worst of characters," and, as the Malays say, you may
enjoy the durian, but you should never speak of it outside
your own dwelling. Its odour—one scarcely feels justified
in using the word " perfume "—is so potent, so vague,
but withal so insinuating, that it can scarcely be tolerated
inside the house. Indeed Nature here seems to have
gone a little aside to disgust us with a fruit which is
perhaps of all others the most fascinating to the palate,
when once one has " broken the ice," as represented by
the foul odour at first presented to that most critical of
all organs of sense, the nose. As a matter of course, it
is never brought to table in the usual way, and yet the
chances are that whoever is lucky enough to taste a good
fruit of it to begin with, soon developes into a surrep-
titious durian eater; just as a jungle tiger becomes a
" man-eater " after its first taste of human blood.

There is scarcely any limit to durian eating if you once
begin it; it grows on one like opium smoking, or other
acquired tastes; but on the other hand, the very suggestion of eating such an " unchaste fruit " is to many as
intolerable as the thoughts alone of supping off cheese
and spring onions, washed down with " stout and mild,"
followed by a whiff from a short " dudeen " by way of
dessert, and yet, while these incongruities are consumed
at home with enjoyment, one must not be too hard on
those abroad who relish the fragrant durian. About the
middle or end of July durian fruit are very common in
Singapore, and their spiny skins lie about the streets in
all directions. As you pass along you become aware of a
peculiar odour all around you—an odour like that of a
putrid sewer when half suppressed by holding a perfumed
handkerchief to the nose—a blending of a good deal that

is nasty with a *soupçon* of something rather sweet and nice. On opening a fruit for yourself, however, you find that the perfume, like that of the musk plant, ceases to be evident after you have once had a fair whiff at it at close quarters. The flavour of the straw-coloured, custard-like pulp which surrounds the four or five rows of large chestnut-like seeds is perfectly unique : to taste it, as Wallace tells us, is " a new sensation, worth a journey to the East to experience ; " but much depends on a good fruit being obtained when perfectly, not over ripe. You then find the pulp sweet, rich, and satisfying ; it is indeed a new sensation, but no two persons can agree as to the flavour—no two descriptions of it are alike. Its subtle action upon the palate—and perhaps this best explains the unceasing popularity it enjoys—is like the music of a well-played violin on the ear, rich, soothing, sweet, piquant. The flavour of durian is satisfying, but it never cloys ; the richness seems counteracted by a delicate acidity, the want of grape-like juiciness is supplied by the moist creamy softness of the pulp as it melts away ice-like on your tongue.

It is said that the best of whisky is that made by blending several good kinds together, and Nature seems to have blended four or five good flavours together when she made the durian. "A *macédoine* of fruits," says a modern author, "when well made and judiciously flavoured, is a delicious sweetmeat. The grape, the peach, the apricot, and the pine, meet in welcome harmony ; the pear, the apple, and the cherry, and their friendly companionship, and all these opposing elements of flavour are blended with a soft and soothing syrup." In a word, the durian is a natural *macédoine*—one of Dame Nature's "made dishes"—and if it be possible for you to imagine the flavour of a combination of corn flour and rotten cheese, nectarines, crushed filberts, a dash of pine-apple, a spoonful of old dry sherry, thick cream, apricot-pulp, and a *soupçon* of garlic, all reduced to the consistency of a rich custard, you have a glimmering idea of the durian, but, as before pointed out, the odour is almost unmentionable—perfectly indescribable, except it be as "the fruit with the fragrant stink!"

The fruit itself is in size as large as a Cadiz melon, and the leathery skin is protected by sharp broad-based spines very similar to those of a horse chestnut. The name durian, in fact, is derived from these—the word *duri* in Malay meaning a spine or thorn. There are many varieties in the Bornean woods, some but little larger than horse chestnut fruits, and having only two seeds; others larger, but with stiff orange-red pulp, not at all nice to eat, however hungry you may be; and even the large kinds, with creamy pulp and many seeds, vary very much in flavour. The trees are monarchs of the forest, as a rule varying from seventy to one hundred and fifty feet, or even more, in height, with tall straight boles and spreading tops, and the foliage is oblong acuminate, dark green above, paler and covered with rufous stellate hairs or scales below. The fruits of the finer varieties fall when ripe, and accidents sometimes happen.

I saw a native who had the flesh torn from his shoulder by a blow from one of these armed fruits, and saw several narrow escapes, but personally I gave the trees a wide berth at fruiting time. Some varieties, especially the "durianburong," or wild-bird durians, do not shed the fruits, which hang on the branches until the valves open, when the seeds fall to the ground, or are eaten by horn-bills and other large fruit-eating birds and monkeys. I saw some magnificent specimens of durian trees in the Bornean forests north of the capital, and also in other

Malayan islands, where the forests had been cleared for cultivation, and these trees left standing for the sake of their produce. Their clusters of large white flowers are produced about April, and form a great attraction to an enormous species of semi-diurnal bat, a kind which is said to be one of the greatest pests of Eastern fruit-groves. It is from cultivated trees that the finest of fruits are obtained; and, without exception, the best fruits I ever saw or tasted were from a tree in the grounds of Government House, Labuan. It does well in Sumatra, Java, Celebes, and the Spice Islands, and even as far north as Mindanao. Forests of it exist on the Malay peninsula, and very fine fruit is brought to Singapore from Siam about July or August. On the coast of the Bay of Bengal it grows as far north as Tenasserim, in lat. 14° N., but it does not succeed well in India, and cannot be grown in the West Indies. In Sumatra groves of this tree exist near the Palembang River, and in the primæval forests there are specimens fully 150 feet in height, the fruits being in perfection about September and October; but two crops are produced each year, and throughout the Archipelago one finds its seasons of ripening to be very various.

There are many different varieties, doubtless the result of promiscuous seeding, or, perchance, cross-fertilisation, and one variety actually produces flowers and fruit on its exposed roots.

Of all Eastern fruits the mangosteen is perhaps the general favourite with Europeans, and of all fruits it is one of the most delicious and refreshing. It flourishes in nearly all the islands from the south coast of Java to Mindanao, the most southern of the Philippine group, and on the mainland it flourishes as far as Bangkok, and in the interior to 16° N., but on the coast of the Bay

of Bengal only to 14° N. Attempts to cultivate it in
India have failed, and in Ceylon success is only partial.
In the West Indies all attempts to grow it have proved
abortive. In Borneo trees are not uncommon in the
forests, but the fruits generally are below the average
size, the divisions within are fewer—rarely more
than four—and each segment of pulp contains a fully
developed seed. When cultivated in richly-manured
gardens or orchards, however, as in Penang or Singapore,
not only are the fruits larger and the carpellary divisions
more numerous, but rarely more than one perfect seed is
found in each fruit, the remaining segments consisting of
edible pulp only. Similar effects may be observed in the
case of the rambi and duku, or langsat fruits, and the
best of cultivated mangoes are remarkable for their thin
and comparatively small stones, while the edible part on
the other hand is much augmented. Under cultivation
the mangosteen forms a low round or conical-headed tree,
its dark leathery evergreen foliage reminding one of that
of the Portugal laurel, only that it is of a bolder character. The waxy-petaled flowers are borne near the
extremities of the branches, and are succeeded by round
fruits, which when fully ripe are as large as a medium-
sized orange. On cutting the leathery dark purple rind
transversely about the middle of the fruit, it is found to
be of a port-wine colour in section, and encloses from
three to six segments of snow-white pulp, cool and refreshing to the taste, and with a flavour which is something like that of the finest nectarine, but with a dash of
strawberry and pine-apple added. It is one of the very
few tropical fruits of which even delicate invalids may eat
with advantage; and the dried rind, when infused in
boiling-water and drank as tea, forms an astringent which
has been proved serviceable in dysentery after all other

medicines had failed. It is the general native remedy
for this disease throughout the Malay Islands, and the
dried skins strung on strips of rattan are commonly met
with in the bazaars.

When exploring near the capital city of Brunei in
North West Borneo I frequently came across a species of
garcinia—sometimes in flower, sometimes in fruit—which
my native followers called " Prada Prada," the duplication
of particular names being usual in Borneo, for the sake
of emphasis, as also among various native tribes in South
America and elsewhere. The foliage and flowers are
somewhat like those of the mangosteen proper, the fruit,
however, is curiously shaped like a boy's " top," and of a
bright red colour, changing to purplish black when fully
ripe. The segments of edible white pulp are usually
eight in number—four containing fully developed seeds,
and four are abortive or seedless—the flavour being
similar to that of the mangosteen proper, but more
acidulous.

Of the luscious mango, Rumphius tells us that it was
introduced by the Dutch from the Moluccas to Java in
1655, but it grows in India, and as the Malay name and
that of the Javanese as applied to this fruit are evident
corruptions of that in the Sanskrit tongue, Mr. Crawfurd
thinks that it was brought to the Archipelago from the
Continent, and that it should not be considered as indigenous. Be this as it may there is no doubt that the
mango has long been introduced to the Malay Islands, in
many of which it is now perfectly naturalised, and a fruit
exactly like the mango in structure is often found in the
Bornean woods. It has the mango flavour of the most
ultra tow and turpentine type, but its juice is very grateful during hot weather, as I can testify by experience.
The cultivated mango forms a round-headed evergreen

tree, rarely over fifty feet in height, and generally not much more than half that size. The old leaves are of a deep green colour, but the young growth is often of a bright red or crimson tint. The dense clusters of pea-green flowers are followed by lax-drooping clusters of kidney-shaped fruits which, when fully developed, vary from two or three to as much as six inches in length, and nearly half that in diameter in the broadest part. These fruits consist of a tough green skin and a coat of yellow pulp surrounding an oblong fibre-coated stone, to which the flesh adheres. In the Sulu isles the mango is abundantly naturalised, some of the trees being of large size. In Indian gardens the best kinds are perpetuated and increased by grafting, and this is also the case in Manilla, where the best varieties are equal, if not superior, to those of Bombay, the excellence of which is well nigh proverbial throughout the East. This tree is of robust constitution and regularly produces two crops every year, although at times the crops are very scanty, owing to heavy rains during the flowering season.

It is one of the Eastern fruits the culture of which is moderately successful in the gardens of the West—notably in Jamaica, and very fair samples of this fruit from the West Indies now and then make their appearance in Covent Garden from the Azores. The mango, like its more fastidious neighbour the durian, is one of Nature's voluptuous productions, of which we have no representative in our gardens, although, so far as the mango is concerned, it might be cultivated successfully in our hothouses with but little more trouble and expense than that which attends the culture of pine-apples or bananas. There are varieties which fruit freely when only five or six feet high, and when only three or four years old; the greatest difficulty in the matter would be to secure the right sorts, which possibly might be had from Madeira, or even St. Michael's, where fair crops are obtained when the seasons are propitious, and even in Europe proper fruits have been produced in the open air. This was in 1874 at Necessidades, near Lisbon, the residence of the King of Portugal, the tree—a dwarf one—bearing nine fruits about the size of ducks' eggs.

Of varieties there is literally no end, a result doubtless brought about by indiscriminate propagation from seed. Some are small with tough skins, large stones, and fibrous pulp, with a strong turpentine-like flavour. Others are large, with thin stones, the skin being tender and the thick pulp quite soft, like that of a real Beurré pear, the flavour being most luscious and delicate, without a trace of the turpentine-and-tow-like combination so marked in the case of inferior kinds. The flavours of the different fine varieties are most varied, much more so than in the case of our best pears, and two or three good mangoes before breakfast form a treat sure to be appreciated by a lover of good fruit, and much as I appreciate a good durian, the mango seems to me a far more delicious and refreshing fruit for general consumption under a hot sun.

The rambutan is a common fruit in Singapore, and is the produce of a pinnate-leaved tree, thirty to fifty feet in height, the hairy fruits being borne in clusters near the extremities of the branches. On the husk being removed the edible pulp is seen surrounding the solitary seed, and is of a white jelly-like consistency, with a brisk and refreshing sub-acid flavour. There are several varieties. The common one has a red outer husk, but there are yellow and purple skinned varieties of excellent flavour. The Malay name, "boi rambutan," or hairy fruit, refers to the soft, thick hairs on the outer husk. Two other species grown in China afford fruits of

a similar character, which, dried, are sometimes met with
in this country under the name of "litchis." The fruit
is common in gardens or orchards throughout the Malay
islands, and is quite wild in Borneo.

In Batavia it ripens in February and March, and is
common in the streets of Singapore during July and
August. In the forests of North-West Borneo it ripens
in September, large basketsful of it being collected by
the natives and brought in along with tampoe fruit, and
occasionally mangosteen and fine durian. A basketful of
this fruit at first sight reminds one of strawberries, it
being singularly like them in size and colour.

The bread-fruit tree is frequently met with, but the
fruit is not so much used by the Malays as it is by the
natives of the South Sea Islands. Another member of
the same group, the "nangka," or Jack fruit, is much
more generally grown, and produces immense fruits,
varying from ten to seventy-five pounds weight. Like
the bread-fruit, it has a rough netted coating, the portion
eaten being the golden pulp which surrounds the seeds.
A smaller fruited, and altogether more delicate flavoured
species, affords the "champada," and the habit of the tree
is much like the Jack fruit, but the "champada" may be
recognised by its leaves being hairy below, those of the
Jack fruits being smooth and glossy on both surfaces.
This kind is liked both by Malays and Europeans.

The "tarippe," or "trap," is another allied fruit
borne by a round-headed tree, having entire leaves much
larger than the last, and hispid on both surfaces. They
are also of a pale, rusty-green tint, and the fruits are
borne near the extremities of the spreading branches,
as in the bread-fruit, and not produced from the main
branches or the bole of the tree, as in the case of the
Jack fruits and "champada." This is the most palat-

able of all the bread-fruits, so far as my own experience goes, the pulp which surrounds the seeds being of a milk-white colour, and very soft and juicy. The husk consists of closely packed hispid spikes, pressed closely together, and amalgamated at the base around the pulp-coated seeds. In North-West Borneo this fruit is in perfection during August and September, and it is particularly abundant around the Dusun villages near Kina Balu.

The leathery coated seeds of all these species of bread-fruits are roasted and eaten by the natives in much the same way as are chestnuts here at home. All the species have india-rubber yielding tendencies, and their inner bark is tough and useful for various purposes.

The "jintawan," or "manoongan" fruit, of which there are three kinds, is about the size of an orange, and very similar in colour, each containing from eight to twelve pulp-covered seeds.

The " tampoe," or "tampui," is another very common jungle fruit, of which but little appears to be known. There are three varieties—"tampoe shelou," "tampoe putih," and "tampoe baraja." The two first named differ in the one having yellow pulp and the other white. The last is a smaller fruit, having four internal divisions instead of six, and the pulp is of a bright chestnut colour. The part eaten is the pulp surrounding the seeds, which is agreeably sub-acid and very refreshing, the pavia-like husks, and the seed themselves, being discarded. The tree is fifty or sixty feet in height, with dark green poplar-like leaves, and the fruits hang two or three together in lax clusters, the stalks being produced from the older branches. This fruit is eaten in large quantities by the natives ; and the pulp mixed with rice and water, and afterwards fermented, affords them an intoxicating drink but little inferior to the "toddy" prepared from the cocoanut palm.

A fruit closely resembling the common "bilimbing" is found in the Lawas district, and is called "tampui bilimbing" by the natives. It is of a bright scarlet colour; and according to the native account it has large entire leaves, the fruits being borne on short few-flowered peduncles, which proceed from the main branches of the tree. The white pulp which surrounds the solitary seed is acidulous and pleasant.

Another jungle fruit, called "mandaroit" by the Kadyans, resembles a small "rambutan," but the leathery husk is quite smooth. It may possibly be produced by a species of niphelium, and is very sweet and agreeable when perfectly ripe, the fruits being kidney-shaped, and but little larger than a blackbird's egg.

"Rambeneer," a still smaller, pale yellowish-green fruit, also has sweet flesh around a stone; but in this case the husk is mango-like, having a thin and tender skin, which may be eaten with the pulp.

The fruit known to the natives as "mamhangan" is as large as an ostrich's egg, having a rough, brown skin, and when ripe the yellow flesh which surrounds a mango-like stone is rather agreeable as a juicy sub-acid accompaniment to a dish of plain boiled rice.

The "luing" is another edible fruit, but rarely seen even in its native woods. It is yellow, with brown markings, and rarely exceeds a pigeon's egg in size. After the thick, leathery husk is removed, one finds a delicate white sub-acid pulp surrounding a small stone. It is rather viscid, with a slight flavour of turpentine. The albumen of the seed is similar to that of a nutmeg.

After the durian, one of the most esteemed of native

fruits is, undoubtedly, the "langsat," which is of a pale yellow or straw-colour, borne in short clusters of four or five together, on a somewhat fastigiate pinnate-leaved tree. The individual fruits are as large as pigeon's eggs, the part eaten being the four or five segments of white gelatinous pulp within a tough, leathery husk. Of these rarely more than one contains a solitary seed, which, if tasted by accident, is found to be remarkably bitter. The seedless segments are always sweeter and more palatable than the others—indeed, this is the case generally, as exemplified in the mangosteen and rambi. In Singapore this fruit is known under the name of "duku."

The "rambi," when plucked from the stalk, is singularly like the langsat in shape, colour, and flavour. The tree, however, is more dwarf, having large entire leaves, and the fruits are borne in ropes of ten or fifteen together, on long drooping stalks. The covering of the fruit is straw-coloured, and tough like that of the langsat, but there are only three segments of pulp in each. The best I ever tasted came from the garden of the British Consulate at Brunei, but I think the "langsat" is preferable in point of flavour. The latter is very commonly seen in groves near the villages of the inland tribes; the "rambi," on the other hand, is much less abundant, and I never met with it except in European gardens.

The "mangalin" of the Kadyans is a fruit very similar in general structure to the "jintawan," and consists of ten or twelve pulp-covered seeds enclosed in an orange-like fleshy covering. The flavour is sweet, with a sub-acid after-taste.

The fruits of two kinds of jambosa, or rose-apples, are met with, but like the papaw, cashew-nut, and the apple-fruited guava, they are not esteemed of much account in a country so rich in really delicious kinds.

The sweet melons grown in Borneo are very poor indeed, but good water-melons may now and then be obtained, and are cool and refreshing in such a hot climate. All the members of the orange family do well, especially the delicious little lime, which is perfectly naturalised in many places, being with the dwarf bamboo one of the plants most commonly used for hedges. No cooling drink can possibly surpass that formed by mixing the juice of one of these deliciously perfumed limes in a tumbler of water with a little sugar, and as they keep well they are most valuable to the traveller in hot countries. Common oranges may be procured all the year round from gardens, as also may the small fruited "mandarin" variety, which is a near approach to the tangierine orange, now and then to be had in Covent Garden. It is rather a surprise to find that the oranges cultivated in the tropics have grass-green skins when perfectly ripe, the vivid "orange" fruit so familiar at home being there almost as great a rarity as a grass-green specimen to us in England.

Of all the orange tribe in the East, however, none can compare with the great-fruited pomolo, which under care-ful cultivation here attains to a state of perfection else-where unknown. The pomoloes, or shaddocks, brought to Covent Garden from the West Indian Islands and the Azores, are flavourless as a turnip when compared with the pomoloes of Bangkok or Labuan, or even with those of Northern China or Singapore. There are many varie-ties, differing much in aroma and flavour, but all are re-ferable to the lemon-fleshed or pink-fleshed types; it is extremely difficult, however, to say which type affords the best variety. A well-grown pomolo is nearly as large

as a child's head, and unless its segments be very carefully divided when serving, the copious grape-like juice
which escapes will almost swamp any ordinary dessert-
dish, and the best sorts have quite a muscatelle-like
flavour; and in addition to its other good qualities it
may, like the orange, be kept for a considerable time
without injury—so long, indeed, that pomoloes are frequently brought home to England from the Chinese ports
in excellent condition. Two sorts of custard apples are
commonly met with in Eastern gardens, but neither these
nor the apricot-like pulp of the ubiquitous papaw are
much esteemed where far better fruits are plentiful. The
same remark applies to the " santoel " fruit, which externally resembles a wizened yellow-fleshed American
peach, but it contains four stones surrounded by white
sub-acid granular pulp, which clings to the stone as in
mangosteen or rambutan. The tamarind is naturalised
near villages and houses in many of the Eastern islands,
its acid pulp being used in cookery, and by pouring boiling water over the pulp, and adding a squeeze of lime
juice and a little sugar, a most refreshing fever-drink
may be made.

Of palms the cocoanut is most plentiful, and of course
the most generally useful. Its top, or heart, may be used
as a delicious vegetable equal to asparagus, and the
scraped albumen yields the milk so essential to blend or
soften a well-made curry. The colourless water in the
fresh young nuts is peculiarly valuable and grateful as a
beverage, preferable where drinking water is in anyway
questionable ; cocoa-nut oil being, moreover, one of the
most valuable of Eastern palm products. The fruit of
the " pinang," or betel-nut palm is as essential to the
Malay races as tobacco to our own, and even the fruit of
the nipa, or "thatch " palm may be eaten. The astrin-

gent pulp which surrounds the seeds of several species of
" rattan " palms is occasionally eaten for medicinal purposes. Perhaps one of the most singular of all wild
fruits, however, is the " Bawang utan," or wild onion
fruit, which is not unlike a walnut in general appearance,

ONION FRUIT.

but which is impregnated with such a decided alliaceous
principle that a small portion of it grated forms an excellent substitute for the real esculent itself. Scientifi-
cally it is known as *Scorodoprasum borneense.* The foliage
and branches of this tree when broken or bruised give off
a strong alliaceous odour.

Last on my list, but by no means least amongst the
tropical fruits of Eastern gardens comes the " pisang," or
banana, which here, as elsewhere wherever it is cultivated,
is represented by many varieties, which differ in size of
fruit, flavour, and other particulars. One of the most
common varieties met with in the bazaars is "pisang
amas," or golden banana, the individual fruits of which
are small, but of a bright golden colour and of excellent

Y

flavour. One of the most esteemed of all is "pisang rajah," or king of bananas, a larger fruit, also of a deep golden colour, the flavour being very luscious. "Pisang hijau," the green banana, is slender and angular, but the straw-coloured pulp is of a most exquisite flavour, and it is quite a favourite in Singapore, where the "rajah" variety is comparatively scarce. "Pisang kling" is a pale yellow kind, bearing large smooth fruits, and for eating with cheese this is one of the best, being less sweet than those just named. A large horned variety of banana is common in Borneo, called of the natives "pisang tandock," the individual fruits being a foot long and two inches in diameter. The outer skin is green, changing to yellow when fully ripe, and this fruit is liked by those who do not relish the sweeter kinds.

These fruits are largely eaten by natives, and they may be cooked in a variety of ways. Banana fritters is a common Eastern dish, and stewed bananas in syrup are accounted delicious by lovers of sweet things, and pisang kling is really a nice substitute for bread when eaten with cheese.

CHAPTER XVI.

NOTES ON TROPICAL TRAVEL.

Hints on travel—Food supplies—Bathing—Medicines—Modes of travel-
    ling — Shelter — Resting-places—Barter—Articles for exchange—
    Arms in a wild land — Products of the island — Prospects of
    Borneo.

THE traveller who finds himseif for the first time in a
wild tropical country devoid of roads, railways, horses,
bridges, hotels, and Europeans, may be excused if he feels
a little anxious when called upon to make an expedition
which will require several weeks to accomplish on foot,
and during which time nearly all necessaries must be
carried by the party *en route*. A party of say twenty
natives will require a clear head to manage it rightly, and
it is only by maintaining a system that the thing can be
conveniently done. The main points to be considered
may be tabulated thus :—

Health.	Bathing.	Boating.
Food.	Packing:	Barter.
Clothing.	Foraging.	Shelter.
Cooking.	Walking.	Fire-lighting.
Medicines.	Riding.	Arms.

Health is best preserved by regular habits, taking care
to avoid chills by wearing flannel next to the skin, and

great care should be taken to put on dry clothes the first thing after a halt is made for the night. One may be drenched to the skin in the tropics without any harm ensuing if this precaution is taken. Belts of soft flannel worn around the stomach are very comfortable, and are highly recommended by many medical men. All your clothing should be light, and if of flannel so much the better. A flannel shirt and tweed trowsers secured by a belt and a light pith helmet, woollen socks, and a light pair of English walking boots cannot be improved upon as a travelling costume. A small knapsack or bag should be carried containing a clean dry jersey, shirts, socks, sarong, and light shoes ; you are then independent of your baggage-bearers, who will often linger miles behind yourself and guides. When a fire is made at night, have all your clothes dried so as to be ready for the following evening. To preserve them from wet in crossing rivers, etc., fold them into as small a compass as possible, and envelope them tightly in waterproof cloth. The old coverings as removed from bales of Manchester goods are very useful for this purpose. A couple of pairs of flannel panjamas may be taken for sleeping in. Three changes of travelling clothes will be sufficient, this gives one suit on, one being washed, and one suit dry and clean. For bedding take a waterproof sheet, a drab rug, and a red blanket. Light brushwood or palm leaves will make a good substitute for a mattress. If shelter is not obtainable and the ground is wet, a light net-hammock becomes useful, a roof to it being readily made with the waterproof sheet. Take soap and a comb.

Food is of the utmost importance. Rice, biscuits, and oatmeal may form the staple, and tinned soups, Liebig's extract of meat, and dried fish may be added. Chocolate and milk in sealed tins is convenient and refreshing. Tea, coffee, sugar, and salt must be packed in well-corked bottles to keep them dry and free from ants, etc. A bottle of Yorkshire relish or Worcester sauce, and a tin or two of bloater paste are nice relishes for soups. Fowls, eggs, fruit, and sometimes freshly-caught fish may often be purchased *en route.* A supply of fresh limes is easily carried, and no better cooling and refreshing drink can be made than that formed by squeezing a lime in a glass and adding water and sugar. Be very careful of the water drunk in travelling, and use a pocket-filter whenever it is in anyway doubtful. I always drank cocoanut water when procurable, as being pure and harmless, and with a dash of brandy it is extremely refreshing. As to the quantity of food required, two pounds of rice is ample for a man's daily supply, and less will suffice at times, as natives are generally good foragers. It is generally best, however, to pay less wages, and agree to find the men rice, otherwise they will take only a small quantity, and when that is gone much time will be lost, as they have an excuse for foraging. A few pounds of that universal vegetable, the onion or garlic, should be taken for soup. Jam in tins is also very handy, and a treat to eat with rice for a change. Each man of the party should receive his daily supply of rice every morning, and in order to facilitate progress, all cooking for the first morning's meal may be done overnight.

Cooking should be well understood by all who propose to " rough it " in a wild land, and it may be defined as the art of preparing food so that it is—1, nutritious ; 2, tasty ; 3, nice to the eye. Two cook-pots are necessary—one large enough to boil a fowl when cut up, and the other for rice. A frying-pan and a few pounds of flour render you independent of the baker, and with oat-meal oat-cakes may be indulged in. Put a few currants in your boiled rice now and then for a change. Most Madras, and some Chinese " boys" are good hands at a curry, and if you give them a share of it when made they are encouraged to excel. A favourite jungle-dish of my own was a fowl cut up and boiled with two onions, a handful of rice, salt and pepper, and thin slices of gourds, sweet potatoes or other vegetables, and three or four small chilies; when it was nearly done, a small tin of soup—julienne or ox-tail—was added. Oatmeal forms a nice change from boiled rice, and biscuits are a treat, as also are sweet potatoes nicely boiled, or corn cobs, yams, or kaladi roasted in the embers. Tinned soups are much improved by having fresh vegetables boiled in them, such as palm cabbages, sweet potatoes, or cucumbers. Eggs may be eaten boiled, poached, or beaten up in a cup of tea or coffee, in which case the yelk only should be used. A nutritious drink is made by beating up the yelk of a fresh egg with a squeeze of lime, a little sugar, whisky, or gin and water. If a dash of Angostura bitters be added, so much the better. Native cook-pots may always be borrowed, or on occasion biscuit or soup-tins form good substitutes. If pressed for supplies, corn cobs or " mealies " form a good substitute for bread, and may be varied now and then with bananas or sweet potatoes. Bananas may be eaten with cheese. The nebong (*Oncosperma*) palm, generally common beside the Malay rivers, affords a tender " cabbage," with a delicate asparagus-like flavour. Pigeons are generally plentiful, and in extreme cases even monkeys may be "potted." On boating expeditions a baited hook should always be towed astern. Most natives understand the style of fishing, and best bait to use.

Packing is important. Rice should be made up into small parcels of 10 lb. each, and wrapped in waterproof sheeting, as if it gets wet it soon turns sour, unless spread out in the sun to dry. Oatmeal should be baked in an oven, and then packed in dry bottles or tins. Biscuits should be bought in 2 lb. tins. All clothes, books, and other damageable articles should be enveloped in waterproof sheeting. In giving the stores to the carriers, put down the man's name and the stores he carries in a book, so that they may be readily found when wanted. Aneroids, thermometers, &c., should be fitted into japanned tin cases, which may be covered with leather. If tightly fitted into leather cases, they are liable to become damaged, as the leather contracts on becoming wet.

BATHING.—Always bathe in the morning. Care must be taken not to frequent alligator-infested streams. Whenever there is any doubt, never enter a stream, but bale up the water and pour it over the body. Nearly all Eastern people bath in this way, and one is not so liable to become inordinately chilled as by plunging into a large body of cold water. Never bathe at night when tired or feverish. At such times a towel-bath is sufficient if the thing is really needful. Dip a towel in water, and wring it partly dry, and then rub the body briskly and quickly all over. The dipping and wringing process may be repeated as desired, then finish with a clean dry towel. A good way of securing a refreshing bath where water is a long way off, or limited in quantity, is to send for some in a common wine or spirit bottle, in which it is handy for pouring over one's head and body, and a dry towel completes the work. When in vigorous health, a good douche-bath in a cool hill or mountain stream is a great treat in a hot land, but it must be remembered that to bathe in this way when exhausted or feverish is in the highest degree suicidal.

MEDICINES.—In nearly all towns and colonies good medical advice is obtainable, and, as a rule, preferable to self-help. On long inland journeys, however, one must frequently trust to one's own resources, and to secure a supply of medicines must be one of the traveller's first cares. The three most useful of all medicines for travellers, prospectors, hunters, or emigrants, are Cockle's pills, Collis Brown's chlorodyne, and Howard's sulphate of quinine. These and a bottle of brandy must always be taken, together with a roll of sticking-plaster, needles, silk thread, and a few long bandages. Cold compresses are easily made of towels, and a bottle of mustard may be useful for poultices on occasion. A small bottle of carbolic acid is useful for mixing with oil as a dressing for mosquito bites, scratches, or other flesh-wounds. One part of acid to fifteen or twenty parts of oil is a good proportion for ordinary use. All travellers, before leaving the beaten track of civilisation, should acquire some knowledge of bone-setting. The whole thing is easy, but nothing short of actual demonstrations can teach the elements of the art. A broken limb in the forest a month's journey from professional aid is a serious thing, and must always be regarded as a possibility. The only thing to be done is to reach some shelter where a stay can be made, and then to get the limb into position as near as possible like its uninjured fellow, and of the same length. This question of length is most important—in the leg especially—or a limping gait is sure to follow after the bones have united. Once in the right position, the thing is to secure it with a splint and bandages. A heap of sand makes a capital cushion for the limb, and also helps to hold it in position. Of course professional aid must be had if possible, and all whose business calls them far from it should be wise enough to gain the knowledge requisite to preserve life and limb as far as is possible without professional skill.

MODES OF TRAVELLING.—The only sure method of progression in a wild land is on foot; now and then ponies or buffaloes are obtainable, and along the coast, or where there are rivers, journeys may be wholly or partially made in native boats. In walking journeys, the first care is boots. These, for hot climates, should be strong, and of English make, but light. Woollen socks are softer and better suited to tender feet than cotton ones. Native guides should be obtained from some one in authority, and passports are desirable, if not actually essential. Buffaloes are often useful for riding, carrying heavy baggage and rice, and for crossing rivers. For the latter service two or three good water-buffaloes, accustomed as they are to the country and fords, are invaluable. Get a good buffalo-driver. In crossing rapid fords, keep the buffalo's head to the current, and take him well up stream, so as to allow for the force of the current, or you will find yourself below the ford, and perhaps in deep water, ere the opposite bank is reached. Ponies are best for riding (a saddle should be taken out from Europe), but are not as a rule so useful for river crossing as water-buffaloes. Nearly all coast natives are good sailors, and accustomed to make long boat journeys. Every traveller, however, should understand how to sail a boat for himself. A compass is useful for bearings either in boats or for forest travel, where it is often difficult to see the sun.

SHELTER.—A light tent of oiled calico is often useful, as timbers for it can be cut almost anywhere *en route*. A waterproof sheet will protect you from ground-damp if spread on brush-fern or palm-leaves. In the Malay islands the natives are very clever at constructing huts or tabernacles of palm-leaves, &c., but wherever there are native houses one is always welcome to the large public room, firewood, and water. Field-huts, overhanging rocks, and caves, have sometimes to be taken advantage of. I have slept very comfortably many nights in the open forest in a light net hammock swung between two trees, with a waterproof sheet put roof-fashion as a protection from the rain. It is often difficult to light a fire. I used to carry a few dry sticks, and when a fire had to be lighted, I whittled these into shavings with my knife. These light readily as a rule. A small bottle of spirits of wine may be carried, as paper soaked in it will set fire to almost anything. I have seen the Borneans wet paper with cocoanut-oil, or mix whittled shavings with melted beeswax in order to get a fire. If the matches are damp, tinder may be made by blowing a piece of rag or paper out of a gun. A small spirit-lamp cooking apparatus, if well and strongly made, is a great convenience to a traveller, enabling him to get his coffee, chocolate, or a refreshing cup of tea while the men are rigging up shelter, or lighting a camp-fire.

BARTER.—There are not many countries wherein it is now necessary to carry goods for barter. In the interior of the Malay islands, and in the far interior or mountainous districts of other countries, however, it still happens that money is useless. White or grey shirting and chopper blades are generally acceptable throughout the interior of Borneo and the Sulu islands. Black and red cloth, looking-glasses and knives, are also valued; needles and thread are currency for small trifles inland in nearly all wild lands. Muskets and ammunition are also often highly prized. The best goods for barter with natives, and all information, may generally be obtained from the bazaars in the coast towns. Whatever you take let it be good of its kind, and always remember that necessaries are more valued than beads and other ornaments. Tobacco is often highly valued, even by people who cultivate their own, as in Sulu.

The following list of articles would be useful in Borneo or Sulu Archipelago :—

40	large pocket knives.
50	packets large sewing needles.
100	reels cotton for same.
72	common Chinese-box looking-glasses.
10	pieces grey shirting.
2	,, Turkey red cloth.
10	,, black cloth.
10	cattys thick brass wire, one-eighth inch.
24	fancy battack head-cloths.
20	tins gunpowder.
10	boxes caps for Tower muskets.
12	chopper blades.

All goods for barter should be so packed that any article may be brought out for examination without exposing the remainder. The more goods the natives perceive you to have the higher will they value their own edibles or services. Beads, Birmingham jewellery, &c., may be taken for presents or for small payments.

ARMS.—The strength of right and gentleness is the best of all protections for the traveller anywhere, and in any case the moral force of firearms is generally sufficient. A good revolver is always a source of interest and amusement (perhaps sometimes of awe) to uncivilised people, and a good double breech-loading shot-gun is really useful, besides affording some amusement to the traveller who obtains food or natural history specimens thereby. Where there are wild pigs, deer, elephant, or other large game, a rifle is of service, and a Winchester repeater is both handy and effective, weighing about 10 lb. A shotgun is the most useful, however, of all weapons, and if fitted with ball or No. 1 shot cartridges is very effective at short ranges with deer, wild cattle, or pigs. It should be of what is called No. 12 bore, as cartridges of that size may be bought nearly everywhere, where ammunition is sold.

If we except the Sarawak principality and the Dutch possessions to the southward and eastward, Borneo may be called a perfectly wild country—a land where laws, jails, horses, roads, and missionaries are unknown. The future prospects of this tropical island, so rich in natural products, so fertile under rude cultivation, and withal so extensive and beautiful, are deserving of more than a passing notice. A large proportion of the country is hilly, and covered with old forest. Near the coast the land is generally well watered by shallow rivers. On the higher hill ranges which lie a few miles inland from the north-west coast, the climate, which is in the plains sultry and malarious, becomes fresh and salubrious. The natives are few in proportion to the area, and generally peaceably disposed towards strangers, but suspicious of ulterior motives, and remarkably cautious, and now then avaricious in matters of trade and barter. They invariably prefer sound useful articles, such as white or black cloth, to ornamental gewgaws.

The products of the island may be tabulated as follows :—

PRODUCTS OF BORNEO.			
ANIMAL.	VEGETABLE.		MINERAL.
Pearls. Mother - of - Pearl Shell. Trepang, Beche de Mer, or Sea Slug. Edible Swallows' nests. Tortoise Shell. Ivory. Hides. Fish in abundance. Bees' Wax. The large animals are elephant, rhinoceros, deer, pigs, wild cattle, alligators.	Sago. Camphor. Dammar. Benzoin. Gambier. Pepper. Cloves. Ginger. Cinnamon. Rattan canes. Timber. Lamba fibre. Cotton. Coffee. Tobacco. Indigo. Cocoa. Vanilla. Spices. Cocoanut oil.	Fruits [tropical of nearly all kinds, many indigenous.] Vegetables [principally Chinese varieties, edible ferns, bamboo palm cabbages, &c.] Gutta-percha. Caoutchouc, or India-rubber. Tapioca. Rice. Maize. Musa fibre or Manilla hemp (*Musa textilis*).	Coal. Iron. Tin. Copper. Cinnabar. Antimony. Gold. Diamonds. ? Plumbago.

The vegetable products are mostly indigenous, and obtainable in the primæval forests. Some few, however, such as cotton, tobacco, coffee, and cocoa have been introduced, and are only cultivated by the natives in a desultory manner. Under systematic culture, and with Chinese coolie labour, nearly all the vegetable products of tropical countries might be grown.

The mineral products are known to exist, but it is not as yet determined whether the lodes are workable, or if the metals exist in remunerative quantities. A great drawback to mining operations is the enormous rainfall. The want of British protection, and the difficulties of travel or transit inland, are against colonisation. The river Kinabatangan opens up the country from the north-east coast, and affords a good water-way by which produce could be brought down to the coast; but nearly all the other rivers to the north-west, as far as Brunei, are shallow and unnavigable, except for a mile or two near the sea; the roads inland being mere buffalo tracks, and extremely irregular on the hill slopes.

The highest land and coolest climate in the island is on Kina Balu (altitude 13,700 feet), a large mountain about five days' journey from the mouth of the Tampassuk river. The lower slopes of this range might possibly grow good coffee; cinchona would be more likely to succeed in the cool and fresh, but humid, climate of the large spurs. The land here is in places deep and rich with forest *débris*. In places good red land, with belts of luxuriant bamboo amongst the sandstone boulders, was seen. In estimating the richness of the soil, the growth of a particular species of ginger common every-where was observed, on poor soils it rarely exceeded a foot in height, but on some of the hill slopes near Kina Balu it attains a height of six or eight feet.

The bamboo is also here more luxuriant than I observed it elsewhere in the island, and the greater variety and luxuriance of undergrowth shows that the climate or soil, or both, are here better than near the coast. There are rich alluvial deposits on the plains, where wet rice, tapioca, sago, and fruits and vegetables generally, grow well. Dry or hill rice, and the cocoanut palm, succeed inland up to 3,000 feet elevation.

In Sarawak land culture has not proved to be so remunerative as the antimony and gold mines; in the north, however, this order of things might possibly be reversed. An English company has been formed for the purpose of colonising the northern part of the island,

and the cessions obtained comprise the whole northern portion from Kimanis on the north-west coast to Sabuco on the east, the total area being computed at 20,000 square miles.

It seems to me, however, that Borneo is too far from the great highway of eastern commerce to attract any but the most sanguine of planters and capitalists. I saw very good land in Jahore on Gunong Puloi, and recent explorations in Perak by Mr. Murton of Singapore (as also by practical coffee planters from Ceylon, and tobacco growers from Province Wellesley) prove that, so far as soil and climate are concerned, Perak, Quedah, and Jahore offer equal advantages for land culture, besides being much nearer to Singapore and the great sea-way between England and the East.

APPENDIX.

APPENDIX.

THE main object of my journey eastward was the collection and introduction of beautiful new plants to the Veitchian Collection at Chelsea. Botanical specimens were obtained and preserved whenever practicable, as also were birds and other objects of natural history. I was fortunate in adding about fifty new species of ferns to the lists of those already collected in Borneo, and of this number, as will be seen from the following report, about twenty were absolutely new to science. Perhaps the greatest good fortune which attended my exertions was the introduction alive of the Giant Pitcher Plant of Kina Balu (*Nepenthes Rajah*, Hook. f.). This wonderful plant and its geographical allies were discovered in 1851 by Hugh Low, Esq., C.M.G., and were figured and described by Sir Joseph D. Hooker, K.C.S.I., in Vol. xxii. of the *Transactions* of the Linnæan Society. Mr. Low made repeated journeys to Kina Balu from Labuan, but unfortunately failed in his endeavours to introduce these fine plants to European gardens in a living state. Mr. Thos. Lobb, one of the most successful of all Eastern plant hunters, attempted to reach the habitat of these plants in 1856, but was prevented by the natives. These plants are very remarkable, and, so far as is at present known, exist only on this one mountain in Borneo.

PINANGA VEITCHII.

Nepenthes bicalcarata, the "Two-spurred Pitcher Plant,"
was also for the
first time intro-
duced alive, and
is very remark-
able, its pitchers
being armed in
a really formid-
able way, and the
swollen stalks of
its urns are per-
forated by a spe-
cies of ant in a
singular manner.

Of palms a
beautiful species
of areca, having
gracefully arched
leaves and ver-
milion - coloured
sheaths, was in-
troduced alive,
as also a very
attractive dwarf
species of pin-
anga (*P. Veitchii,*
H. Wend.), the
bifurcate fans of
which are purple
below and glauc-
ous-green above,
blotched with

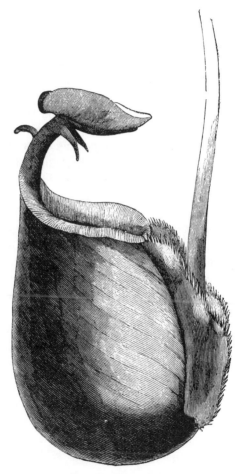

NEPENTHES BICALCARATA.

brown. Aroids are plentiful in the shady Bornean forests,
the species in some cases being extremely local in their

distribution. Of the new genera discovered two have very pretty spathes, and if they can be successfully cultivated will prove very interesting and ornamental stove plants. *Piptospatha insignis*, N. E. Br., a pretty little "rock arad," found on sandstone boulders in the beds of mountain streams, has a tuft of lance-shaped leaves and dainty white spathes tipped with pink. *Gamogyne Burbidgei*, N. E. Br., is a plant of larger growth, being a foot high but otherwise of similar habit. The spathes are of a bright rose colour. This plant grows beside mountain streams in positions where the passing water laves its roots.

Amongst new species of aroideæ may be mentioned the sub-aquatic *Cryptocoryne caudata*, N. E. Br., which has heart-shaped bullate leaves of a dark green colour, the spathe being terminated with a long tail, which reminds one of the same appendages in the arisæmas of the Himalayas. Three or four new species of alocasia were found, the remarkable being *A. scabriuscula*, *A. guttata*, and *A. pumila*. *Pothos ceratocaulis*, a fresh green climbing species, was also introduced alive, and is a plant of distinct marcgraavia-like habit. Specimens of *Schismatoglottis* and *Chamæcladon* are at present undetermined. A singular new asclepiadaceous genus (*Astrostruma spartioides*, Benth.), was discovered growing as an epiphyte on forest trees in Labuan, and in dry woods near the sea at the northern point of the last-named island, the remarkable little *Microstylis Burbidgei*, Rchb. f., was found. One of my first discoveries in Borneo itself was the new zingiberaceous genus *Burbidgea* (*B. nitida*, Hook. f.), and other novelties were *Dendrobium cerinum*, *Cypripedium Lawrencianum*, and *Bolbophyllum Leysianum*, a highly curious plant. A fine new *Bolbophyllum* was introduced alive to Chelsea from the Tampassuk river (*B. Petreianum*, Burb. MS.), which I propose shall bear the name of my whilom travelling companion, P. C. M. Veitch, Esq.

Rhododendron stenophyllum, and *Nepenthes Burbidgei,* Hook. f., were two of the more remarkable of the new plants from Kina Balu itself, where also the gigantic moss *Dawsonia superba* was collected at an altitude of 6,000 feet, these specimens being, as Mr. Mitten informs me, the first obtained northwards of New Zealand.

The three native courts of Jahore, Brunei, and Sulu were visited, and I was enabled to make extended excursions into the interior of the main island of Sulu itself. In Borneo the flora was remarkable for endemic Malasian species, intermixed more especially at high altitudes with Indian (*Rhododendra*) and Australian (*Dacrydium, Phyllocladus, Drosera,* etc.) types. In Sulu both the flora and fauna showed, as was to be expected, a marked resemblance to those of the Philippine and Celebes groups. My collections in Sulu comprised new ferns, rare mosses, and several beautiful new orchids, including *Phalænopsis Marie, Dendrobium Burbidgei* (which is mainly remarkable as being similar to the *D. d'Albertisii* discovered about the same time in New Guinea). Here also the lovely pink-blossomed *Aerides Burbidgei,* Rchb. f., was obtained, and several other species and varieties at present unnamed.

The Sulu voyage was in many ways enjoyable, but especially as being to a virgin land botanically and ornithologically, and I must here take the opportunity of acknowledging my obligations to Captain W. C. Cowie, of the steamship *Far East,* who gave me every accommodation during the voyage from Labuan, and while we lay in the little harbour at Meimbong. As will be seen, my ornithological discoveries in Sulu were a new species of jungle cock (*Gallus stramineicollis*), and a new paroquet (*Tanyg-*

nanthus Burbidgei). Sarcops Lowii was also obtained in Sulu, and the new *Buchanga stigmatops* from Kina Balu. No special endeavours were made in obtaining birds, only such species being shot as came in the way while I was searching the forest and mountain sides for plants.

The first expedition to the great mountain of Kina Balu was made in company with P. C. M. Veitch, Esq., who joined me on his return from an extended tour in Australia and the Fiji islands. The journey was a critical and tedious one, as we walked every inch of the way from Gaya Bay to the mountain, and back again to the coast, *viâ* the Koung, Kalawat and Bawang villages. We were successful in finding all the large species of nepenthes in one locality on the mountain for the first time, and in addition a distinct variety of *N. Edwardsiana* with shorter thick-winged pitchers, which it is possible may prove to be a natural hybrid between *N. Edwardsiana* and *N. villosa.*

My acknowledgments are due to Hugh Low, Esq., C.M.G., H.M. Resident in Perak, who, when he heard of my intention of ascending the mountain, very kindly sent me information as to the localities on Kina Balu where the nepenthes and other rare plants are found. To H. E. William Hood Treacher, H.M. Administrator of Labuan, and to the Hon. Dr. Leys, M.B., Colonial Surgeon of the same island, I shall always be grateful for the practical help afforded me during my expedition, and for the open-handed hospitality they extended to a wandering stranger by chance thrown in their way.

LIST OF FERNS COLLECTED IN BORNEO.

The following is an abridged account of my specimens of ferns, as written by Mr. J. G. Baker, F.R.S., and published in the *Journal of Botany*, 1879, p. 37 :—

THE following is a complete list of the species gathered, which were all obtained in the neighbourhood of Labuan and Kina Balu. To the new species I have prefixed numbers, showing the position in which they fall, according to the sequence followed in our " Synopsis Filicum ;" and I have marked with a * the names of those which, so far as I am aware, have not been gathered in the island before. I may mention that a complete catalogue of the ferns of Borneo was published in 1876 by Baron Vincent de Cesati, with a special account, with figures of some of the novelties, of those gathered by Professor Beccari.

Gleichenia circinata, Sw., var. *borneensis*, Baker.

Gleichenia dichotoma, Hook.

Gleichenia vestita, Blume, var. *palacea*, Baker.

Alsophila glabra, Hook. ?

Alsophila latebrosa, Hook.

59.* ALSOPHILA BURBIDGEI, *Baker*, n. sp. Allied to *A. latebrosa*, *Oldhami* and *Wallacei*.

Hymenophyllum Blumeanum, Spreng.

Hymenophyllum Smithii, Hook. The plant so called in Cesati's list proved to be *Trichomanes denticulatum*, Baker.

Hymenophyllum sabinæfolium, Baker.

Hymenophyllum Neesii, Hook.

Hymenophyllum formosum, Brack.

Hymenophyllum obtusum, Hook. Gathered lately in New Guinea by Beccari.

Trichomanes Filicula, Bory.

Trichomanes pallidum, Blume.

Trichomanes digitatum, Sw. Two different forms, one lengthened out, with remote branches, the other short, with close branches.

Trichomanes javanicum, Blume.

Trichomanes pyxidiferum, Linn. A handsome variety, with unusually compound rather crisped fronds.

Trichomanes rigidum, Sw.

Trichomanes maximum, Blume.

**Trichomanes apiifolium*, Presl.

Trichomanes hispidulum, Mett. This was only known before from a single sheet of specimens in the Kew herbarium, gathered by Thos. Lobb.

Trichomanes fœniculaceum, Bory.

Trichomanes Pluma, Hook. We did not know the definite station of Lobb's specimens, from which this was described and figured by Hooker. Beccari has gathered it near Sarawak.

Trichomanes trichophyllum, Moore. With the last, with which I am now inclined to think it will prove to be conspecific.

Davallia angustata, Wall.

Davallia heterophylla, Smith.

Davallia parvula, Wall.

Davallia luzonica, Hook.

**Davallia contigua*, Sw.

**Davallia Emersoni*, Hook and Grev.

Davallia pedata, Sm.

*Davallia ciliata, Hook.

Davallia elegans, Sw.

Davallia Speluncæ, Baker.

Davallia tenuifolia, Sw.

49.* Davallia (*Eudavallia*) Veitchii, *Baker*, n. sp.—A well-marked plant, reminding one in cutting and habit of the barren fronds of *Onychium japonicum* or *auratum*.

5.* Lindsaya jamesonioides, *Baker*, n. sp.—A most distinct novelty, with the habit of *Asplenium Trichomanes* or *Jamesonia imbricata*.

7.* Lindsaya crispa, *Baker*, n. sp.—Habit of the small tender forms of *Adiantum caudatum*, but the fronds neither at all hairy nor rooting at the tip.

**Lindsaya pectinata*, Blume.

Lindsaya cultrata, Sw.

Lindsaya borneensis, Hook.

Lindsaya trapeziformis, Dry.

**Lindsaya flabellulata*, Dry.

Lindsaya davallioides, Blume.

Lindsaya ensifolia, Sw.

Lindsaya divergens, Wall.

*Adiantum diaphanum, Blume.

*Cheilanthes tenuifolia, Sw.

Pteris aquilina, L.

Pteris semipinnata, L.

Pteris quadriaurita, Betz., var. *digitata,* Baker. A digitate form, like the Indian *P. Grevilleana,* Wall., but the barren and fertile fronds not dimorphic. The texture firmer than usual. The rachis with a broad wing, as in *P. biaurata,* and the veins crowded and obscure.

*Lomaria procera, Spreng.

Asplenium Nidus, L.

Asplenium tenerum, Forst.

Asplenium squamulatum, Blume.

*Asplenium caudatum, Forst.

Asplenium cuneatum, Lam.

Asplenium laserpitiifolium, Lam.

Asplenium affine, Sw.

Asplenium dichotomum, Hook. Kina Balu. The only known station. The plant has been twice gathered previously.

203.* ASPLENIUM (*Diplazium*) PORPHYRORACHIS, *Baker.*—This is the plant described by Sir W. Hooker from a single barren frond without fruit gathered by Mr. A. R. Wallace, as *Polypodium subserratum* (Hook. and Baker, Syn. Fil., p. 325). In *Asplenium* that specific name is already occupied. Of the present plant *A. zeylanicum,* Hook., is the only near ally. The same species was gathered by Beccari, near Sarawak.

*Asplenium porrectum, Wall.

*Asplenium tomentosum, Hook.

207.* ASPLENIUM (*Diplazium*) XIPHOPHYLLUM, *Baker,* n. sp.— Comes near *A. pallidum, porrectum,* and *cultratum.*

*Asplenium latifolium, Don.

Asplenium cordifolium, Mett.

*Didymochlœna lunulata, Desv.

*Aspidium aculeatum, Sw.

*Nephrodium calcaratum, Hook.

*Nephrodium pteroides, J. Sm.

*Nephrodium unitum, R. Br.

*Nephrodium cucullatum, Baker.

*Nephrodium, near *pennigerum ?* Probably new, but specimens not complete enough to characterise it.

Nephrodium molle, Desv.

Nephrodium Haenkeanum, Presl.

Nephrodium singaporianum, Baker.

Nephrodium ternatum, Baker. A fine series of specimens of this endemic species.

219.* NEPHRODIUM (*Sagenia*) NUDUM, *Baker*, n. sp.—Allied to *N. pachyphyllum*, Baker.

Nephrodium polymorphum, Baker.

Nephrolepis volubilis, J. Sm.

Polypodium Barberi, Hook.

Polypodium urophyllum, Wall. A variety with many of the sori confluent.

91.* POLYPODIUM (*Eupolypodium*) MINIMUM, *Baker*, n. sp.—Allied to the Andine *P. Sprucei*, Hook., and Mascaren *P. Gilpinæ* and *synsorum*, Baker.

131.* POLYPODIUM (*Eupolypodium*) BURBIDGEI, *Baker*, n. sp.— Habit and texture of *Davallia Emersoni*.

Polypodium alternidens, Cesati, Fil. Born., p. 25, tab. 2, fig. 4. Of this Burbidge's bundle contains a single specimen. It is a well-marked new species, discovered by Signor Beccari in the neighbourhood of Sarawak.

Polypodium cucullatum, Nees. A small slender form.

132.* POLYPODIUM (*Eupolypodium*) STREPTOPHYLLUM, *Baker*. n. sp. —Allied to *P. cucullatum*, but the pinnæ are narrower, and reach down to the main rachis, and bear the sorus at their tip.

Polypodium minutum, Blume.

Polypodium papillosum, Blume. The plant so-called by Cesati, gathered by Beccari, near Sarawak, I hold to be quite distinct from Blume's Javan type, and propose to call it *P. Cesatianum*.

Polypodium clavifer, Hook.

210.* POLYPODIUM (*Eupolypodium*) TAXODIOIDES, *Baker*, n. sp. *Polypodium soridens*, Hook.

297.* POLYPODIUM (*Phymatodes*) STENOPTERIS, *Baker*, n. sp. *Polypodium longifolium*, Mett.

Polypodium oodes, Kunze. Matches exactly Cuming's Philippine specimens, which were all that were previously known.

301.* POLYPODIUM (*Phymatodes*) HOLOPHYLLUM, *Baker*, n. sp.— Like *P. oodes* in rhizome, stipe and sori; differing by its smaller frond, crenulate border and flabellate veining.

Polypodium acrostichoides, Forst.

Polypodium angustatum, Sw.

Polypodium dipteris, Blume.

Polypodium bifurcatum, Baker.

Polypodium Phymatodes, L.
*Polypodium ebenipes, Hook.
Gymnogramma avenia, Baker.
Gymnogramma borneensis, Hook.
Gymnogramma Wallichii, Hook.
Gymnogramma Feei, Hook.
Antrophyum reticulatum, Kaulf.
Vittaria debilis, Kuhn.
Vittaria elongata, Sw.
Tænitis blechnoides, Sw. Both the type and well-marked variety,
T. interrupta, H. and G.
Acrostichum sorbifolium. L.
*Acrostichum scandens, J. Sm.
*Acrostichum subrepandum, Hook.
Acrostichum drynarioides, Hook.
*Acrostichum bicuspe, Hook. The typical form, which has only
been once gathered before by Thomas Lobb in Java.
Platycerium biforme, Blume.
*Platycerium grande, A. Cunn.
Schizæa malaccana, Baker.
Schizæa dichotoma, Sw.
Schizæa digitata, Sw.
Lygodium dichotomum, Sw.
Lygodium scandens, Sw.
*Equisetum elongatum, Willd.
Lycopodium cernuum, L.
Lycopodium casuarinoides, Spreng.
Lycopodium carinatum, Desv.
Lycopodium Phlegmaria, L.
*Lycopodium macrostachys, Hook. and Grev.
*Lycopodium volubile, Forst.
*Selaginella atroviridis, Spreng.
Selaginella caulescens, Spreng.
Selaginella inæqualifolia, Spreng.
*Selaginella Willdenovii, Baker.
*Selaginella flabellata, Spreng.
*Selaginella suberosa, Spreng.
Psilotum triquetrum, Sw.
Psilotum complanatum, Sw. = *P. Zollingeri,* Cesati.

It will be seen that altogether Mr. Burbidge has added above
fifty species to the fern-flora of the island. His exploration

quite bears out the idea that we previously entertained, that the fern-flora of the island is very rich, and that there is still a plentiful harvest to await the exploration of the interior. The added species which are not new are nearly all already known in Java and the Philippine Islands, frequently in both.

REPORT ON BURBIDGE'S FERNS OF THE SULU ARCHIPELAGO.

By J. G. Baker, F.R.S., F.L.S.

The Sulu Archipelago is a group of small islands lying between Borneo and the Philippines. They are for the most part under cultivation; but there are two mountains which attain an elevation of between two thousand and three thousand feet. So far as I am aware their botany is entirely unknown. The following is a full catalogue of the ferns which Mr. Burbidge gathered in the group :—

38.* Cyathea suluensis, *Baker*, n. sp.—Allied to *C. integra*, J. Sm., of the Philippine Islands and Amboyna.

Hymenophyllum dilatatum, Sw., var. *H. formosum*, Brack.

Trichomanes javanicum, Blume.

Trichomanes maximum, Blume.

Trichomanes rigidum, Sw.

Davallia pinnata, Cav., and its variety *luzonica*.

Pteris quadriaurita, Retz.

4.* Pteris Treacheariana, *Baker*, n. sp.—Near *P. cretica*, but much more slender and delicate in general aspect, with the lowest one to three pairs of pinnæ two to three forked. Named at the request of Mr. Burbidge in compliment to the Honourable W. H. Treacher, Acting Governor of Labuan, whose kindness and help contributed materially to the success of his expedition.

Lindsaya cultrata, Sw.

Lindsaya pectinata, Blume.

Lindsaya flabellulata, Dryand.

Lindsaya lobata, Poir.

Lindsaya davallioides, Blume.

Asplenium persicifolium, J. Sm. An endemic Philippine species.

Asplenium resectum, Smith.

Asplenium falcatum, Lam.

Asplenium hirtum, Kaulf.

Asplenium cuneatum, Lam.

Asplenium Belangeri, Kunze.

Asplenium pallidum, Blume.

Asplenium bantamense, Baker.

Asplenium cordifolium, Mett.

Nephrodium melanocaulon, Baker.

27.* POLYPODIUM (*Phegopteris*) OXYODON, *Baker,* n. sp.—A very distinct plant, allied to *P. caudatum* of Tropical America.

175.* POLYPODIUM (*Eupolypodium*) LEYSII, *Baker,* n. sp.—Allied to *P. taxifolium* and *apiculatum* of Tropical America. Named at the request of Mr. Burbidge in compliment to the Honourable Peter Leys, M.B., Colonial Surgeon, Labuan, who materially aided him during his residence there, and accompanied him on one of his expeditions into the interior.

Polypodium albo-squamatum, Blume.

Polypodium palmatum, Blume.

Vittaria elongata, Sw.

Antrophytum reticulatum, Kaulf.

Tœnitis blechnoides, Sw.

Gymnogramma Wallichii, Hook.

Osmunda javanica, Blume.

Lycopodium Phlegmaria, Linn.

Selaginella caulescens, Spreng.

Selaginella Willdenovii, Baker.

Selaginella conferta, Moore.

Selaginella caudata, Spreng.

Selaginella atroviridis, Spreng.

A CONTRIBUTION TO THE AVIFAUNA OF THE SULU ISLANDS.

By R. Bowdler Sharpe, F.L.S., F.Z.S., etc.

Senior Assistant, Department of Zoology, British Museum.

PROC. ZOOL. SOC. 1879. Part II.

[*Received March* 18, 1879.]

The present collection was formed by Mr. F. W. Burbidge during a short stay in the Sulu Islands, a most interesting locality to the ornithologist, and one of which very little is known. In my paper on Dr. Steere's collections from the Philippines, I noticed the four species of birds as yet recorded from the Sulu Islands,* and I ought to have added the common *Artamus* of the Indo-Malayan region, and a cuckoo, both recorded by Peale from Mangsi.

In addition to the birds obtained by Mr. Burbidge, I have received permission from the authorities of the Oxford Museum to describe the large Bornean collections forwarded to that institution by Mr. W. H. Treacher, Acting Governor of Labuan. Amongst them are a few birds from Sulu, but apparently not the result of a separate expedition, but presented to Mr. Treacher by Mr. Burbidge. To the latter gentleman I am indebted for the following notes :—

" Among the birds which I saw in Sulu, but could not secure, I would particularly mention—some hornbills, seemingly the common black-and-white small kind from Labūan ; a fine white harrier, with black tips to the wings (this is a distinct and handsome bird, not unfrequently seen circling over rice fields, or grassy plains) ; the ' fire-backed' pheasant ; and an owl, apparently a larger and brighter-coloured edition of our common barn-owl, or screeching species. The blue, white-ringed kingfisher (*Halcyon chloris*) of Labūan is very common here, as is also the rufous, white-headed scavenger hawk or eagle ; † and at least two other species, both larger,

* See Trans. Linn. Soc. n.s. i. p. 310.

† Doubtless *Haliastur intermedius.*

are to be found looking out for food near the wharf at Meimbong. Curlews are as plentiful here as in Sarawak and other parts of Borneo. I missed the nocturnal ' chuck-chuck ' of the goat-sucker, so common in Labūan. Water-rails and a pretty blue kingfisher are not uncommon by the margin of the Meimbong river, which is close to the harbour, and is an excellent shooting-ground. Gun-boats often come here ; and as the country is now readily accessible, much might doubtless be done in ornithology. Capital angling may be had in this little river ; and there is a good bathing place near the town, and close to the market, where one may be entirely free from the fear of an alligator lurking about in wait for a meal. Now and then the Sultan and his court, male and female, together with all the principal people in the island, meet to enjoy the fun of pig-hunting, the wild boar being very plentiful here, together with two or three species of deer. These pigs do a good deal of damage to cultivated crops ; so that now and then a regular field-day is organised, and nearly every man, pony, dog, and spear in the island are out, *versus* ' Piggy,' as many as fifty of the latter being slain in a single day. There are so many kinds of sport easily attainable here, provisions of the best are so cheap, a pony may be hired for about 1*s*. 6*d*. a day, and there is so much that is novel to be seen about the town and the court, that the wonder is that some traveller, fond of sport, and especially ornithology, does not take up his quarters here for a month or two—and particularly as the place is easily reached from Singapore, *viâ* Labūan, or from Hong-Kong, *viâ* Manila."

Mr. Burbidge left England on a botanical expedition, to collect living plants ; and his success in this department of natural history is well known. His chief attention having been devoted to plants, it only remains to thank him for the intelligent way in which he devoted his scanty leisure time to forming the present collection of birds.

The following I believe to be a correct list of Sulu birds as at present known ; and I have included the few species mentioned by Peale as procured in Mangsi by the United States

Exploring Expedition. I have also added the references to Lord Tweeddale's recent papers on the Philippine collections of Mr. Alfred Everett, and have given the ranges of the different species in the Philippine archipelago, so as to bring the subject up to the present date.

1. CACATUA HAMÆTUROPYGIA (P. L. S. Müll.).

Cacatua hamæturophygia, Wald. Tr. Z. S. ix. p. 132 ; Sharpe, Tr. Linn. Soc. n.s. i. p. 312 ; Tweedd. P. Z. S. 1877, pp. 756, 817 ; 1878, pp. 107, 281, 340, 379.

Two specimens.

[Luzon (*Meyer*) ; Guimaras (*Meyer*) ; Negros (*Meyer, Steere, Everett*) ; Zebu (*Everett*) ; Leyte (*Everett*) ; Nipar (*Everett*) ; Panaon (*Everett*) ; Butuan River, N. Mindanao (*Everett*) ; Sulu (*Burbidge*).]

2. PRIONITURUS DISCURUS (V.).

Prioniturus discurus, Wald. Tr. Z. S. ix. p. 132 ; Sharpe, Tr. Linn. Soc. n.s. i. p. 312 ; Tweedd. P. Z. S. 1877, pp. 538, 688, 756, 817; 1878, p. 379.

A single specimen, agreeing with others in the British Museum from the Philippine Islands.

[Luzon (*Meyer, Everett*); Negros (*Steere*) ; Zebu (*Everett*) ; Panaon (*Everett*) ; Mindanao (*Cuming, Everett, Murray*) ; Basilan (*Steere*) ; Sulu (*Burbidge*) ; Balabak (*Steere*).]

3. TANYGNATHUS LUCIONENSIS (L.).

Tanygnathus lucionensis, Wald. Tr. Z. S. ix. p. 133; Sharpe, Tr. Lin. Soc. n.s. i. p. 312; Tweedd. P. Z. S. 1877, pp. 538, 756, 817 ; 1878, pp. 281, 340, 612.

A single specimen, collected by Mr. Burbidge, and exactly resembling the specimens from Manilla and from Palawan in the British Museum.

[Luzon (*Meyer*) ; Guimaras (*Meyer*); Negros (*L. C. Layard, Steere, Everett*) ; Cebu (*Everett*) ; Leyte (*Everett*) ; Mindanao (*Steere, Everett*); Malanipa (*Murray*) ; Sulu (*Burbidge, Peale*) ; Palawan (*Steere, Everett*).]

4. TANYGNATHUS BURBIDGEI, sp. n.

Similis T. muelleri, *ex Celebes, sed dorso toto sordide prasino, capite flavicanti-viridi et alis omnino viridibus distinguendus.*

This fine new species of *Tanygnathus* is closely allied to *T. muelleri* of Celebes and *T. everetti* of Mindanao. It differs from *T. muelleri* in having the back green instead of yellow, while the head is yellowish green and not emerald-green ; there is also no blue on the wing-coverts, the whole wing being green.

The following is a full description of the bird.

Adult. General colour above dark grass-green, including the hind neck, entire mantle, and scapulars ; wings a little lighter green, the wing-coverts and secondaries with narrow yellow margins, the primaries blackish on the inner web, externally dark grass-green with a slight blue shade along the shaft, the first primary black shaded with blue on the outer web ; entire black and rump deep cobalt-blue; upper tail-coverts green, slightly shaded with yellow on the margins ; tail-feathers dark green, with a narrow margin of yellow at the tip, the under surface of the tail golden-yellow ; head yellowish green, the sides of the face also of this colour; the under-surface of the body bright grass-green, yellow on the throat and fore neck and passing into green on the breast and abdomen; under wing-coverts and under tail-coverts of the same green as the breast, with yellow margins ; quills ashy blackish below. Total length 15·5 inches, culmen 1·8, wing, 8·6, tail 6·4, tarsus 0·65.

On comparing *T. burbidgei* with *T. everetti,* one is struck at once by the larger size of the former and its yellowish green head, the crown being emerald-green in *T. everetti,* which also has the wing only 7·55 inches in length (Samar : *Mus. Brit.*). None of the Sulu birds, of which there are five in the collections, have the feathers of the mantle edged with blue as in the Samar individual.

5. ELANUS HYPOLEUCUS, Gould.

Elanus hypoleucus, Sharpe, Cat. B. i. p. 338 ; Wald. Tr. Z. S. ix. p. 142; Tweedd. P. Z. S. 1877, p. 757.

An adult specimen : wing 11·5 inches.

[Luzon (*Jagor*) ; Cebu (*Everett*) ; Sulu (*Burbidge*) ; N. W. Borneo (*Treacher*).]

6. SCOPS RUFESCENS (Horsf.).

Scops rufescens, Sharpe, Cat. B. iii. p. 102.

One specimen.

This bird seems to me to differ slightly from Bornean and Malaccan examples in having a much darker face, the ear-coverts shaded with black. I do not, however, propose to found a new species on a single example, and must wait for more specimens. The measurements of the Sulu bird are as follows :—Total length 7 inches, culmen 0·7, wing 4·8, tail 2·6, tarsus 0·85. It will be seen that they are a good deal inferior to those of the type of *Scops mantis,* as given by me in the " Catalogue."

7. CUCULUS FUCATUS, Peale.

Cuculus fucatus, Peale, U.S. Expl. Exp. Zool. 1848, p. 136.

C. tenuirostris, Less.; Cass. U.S. Expl. Exp. p. 244.

This cuckoo may be *Cuculus himalayanus*, which has recently been shot in Labuan by Governor Ussher; but it is difficult to decide without seeing a specimen. At present the species is only known from the plate and description given by Peale, who procured it on the island of Mangsi.

8. ARTAMUS LEUCORHYNCHUS (L.).

Artamus leucorhynchus, Walden, P. Z. S. ix. p. 174; Sharpe, Tr. Linn. Soc. n.s. i. p. 323; Tweedd. P. Z. S. 1877, pp. 544, 692, 759, 826; 1878, pp. 283, 342.

A. leucogaster (Valenc.); Sharpe in Rowley's Orn. Misc. iii. p. 170. One specimen.

[Luzon *(Meyer)*; Guimaras *(Meyer)*; Negros *(Meyer, Everett)*; Cebu *(Murray, Everett)*; Leyte *(Everett)*; Mindanao *(Everett, Steere)*; Sulu *(Burbidge)*; Mangsi *(Peale)*.]

9. ORIOLUS CHINENSIS, L.

Oriolus chinensis, Sharpe, Cat. B. iii. p. 203.

O. suluensis, Sharpe, tom. cit. p. 205.

Broderipus acrorhynchus (Vig.); Walden, Tr. Z. S. ix. p. 185; Tweedd. P. Z. S. 1877, pp. 545, 694, 760, 826; 1878, pp. 110, 285, 342, 380.

The receipt of three more specimens from Mr. Burbidge convinces me that the Sulu Islands bird, which I thought was a race of *O. frontalis*, Wall., from the Sula Islands, is not really specifically separable from the common oriole of the Philippines, called by me *Oriolus chinensis*, and by Lord Tweeddale *Broderipus acrorhynchus*. A further comparison of the series seems to show that *O. frontalis* of Wallace, from the Sula Islands, is scarcely to be distinguished from *O. chinensis*, the only difference being the slightly greater extent of yellow on the tail-feathers in the latter bird.

[Luzon *(Meyer)*; Panay *(Murray)*; Guimaras *(Meyer)*; Negros *(Meyer, Steere, Everett)*; Cebu *(Mayer, Murray, Everett)*; Leyte *(Everett)*; Panaon *(Everett)*; Dinagat *(Everett)*; Mindanao *(Steere, Murray, Everett)*; Sulu *(Burbidge)*; Si Butu *(Low)*; Balabac *(Steere)*.]

10. CORONE PHILIPPINA (Bp.).

Corone philippina, Sharpe, Cat. B. iii. p. 42; id. Tr. Linn. Soc. n.s. i. p. 343.

Corvus philippinus, Bp.; Wald. Tr. Z. S. ix. p. 201; Tweedd.
P. Z. S. 1877, pp. 548, 698, 763, 831; 1878, pp. 113, 287, 343, 381.
Three specimens.
[Luzon (*Cuming, Meyer, Everett*); Cujo (*Meyer*); Panay (*Murray*);
Negros (*Meyer, Steere, Everett*); Cebu (*Everett*); Leyte (*Everett*);
Panaon (*Everett*); Camiguin (*Murray*); Dinagat (*Everett*); Mindanao
(*Murray, Everett*); Sulu (*Burbidge*).]

11. SARCOPS LOWII.

Sarcops lowii, Sharpe, *l.c.* p. 344.
Several specimens collected by Mr. Burbidge confirm the distinctness of this species from *S. calvus.*

12. OSMOTRERON VERNANS (L.).

Osmotreron vernans, Wald. Tr. Z. S. ix. p. 210; Sharpe, Tr. Linn.
Soc. n.s. i. p. 346; Tweedd. P. Z. S. 1877, p. 764; 1878, p. 623.
A female specimen.
[Luzon (*Meyer*); Panay (*Steere*); Zebu (*Everett*); Sulu (*Burbidge*);
Palawan (*Steere*).]

13. OSMOTRERON AXILLARIS (Gray).

Osmotreron axillaris, Walden, Tr. Z. S. ix. p. 211; Sharpe, Tr. Linn.
Soc. ix. p. 346; Tweedd. P. Z. S. 1877, pp. 549, 699, 764, 832; 1878,
pp. 113, 287.
An adult specimen.
[Luzon (*Meyer, Everett*); Guimaras (*Meyer*); Panay (*Murray*);
Negros (*Meyer, Steere, Everett*); Cebu (*Everett*); Dinagat (*Everett*);
Mindanao (*Steere, Everett*); Sulu (*Burbidge*).]

14. CARPOPHAGA ÆNEA (L.).

Carpophaga ænea, Wald. Tr. Z. S. ix. p. 215; Sharpe, Tr. Linn.
Soc. n.s. i. p. 346; Tweedd. P. Z. S. 1877, pp. 764, 832; 1878,
pp. 113, 288, 344, 623.
One specimen.
[Luzon (*Meyer*); Negros (*Meyer, Steere, Everett*); Cebu (*Everett*);
Leyte (*Everett*); Dinagat (*Everett*); Mindanao (*Everett*); Sulu
(*Burbidge*); Palawan (*Steere, Everett*).]

15. CARPOPHAGA PICKERINGI.

Carpophaga pickeringi, Cass. Pr. Philad. Acad. 1854, p. 228; id.
U.S. Expl. Exp. p. 267, pl. xxvii.; Sharpe, Tr. Linn. Soc. n.s. i.
p. 353.

Procured by the United States Exploring Expedition in the island of Mangsi.

16. IANTHŒNAS GRISEIGULARIS, Wald. et Layard.

Ianthœnas griseigularis, Wald. Tr. Z. S. ix. p. 218 ; id. P. Z. S. 1878. p. 288.

One specimen.

I refer this pigeon with some hesitation to *I. griseigularis*, of which I have never seen a specimen, and only know it from Mr. Keuleman's figure in the Ibis for 1872 (pl. vi.). On the other hand, it is very closely allied to *I. albigularis* of the Moluccas, but differs in the greyish shade on the white throat, which is also more restricted, and in the forehead being grey with only a slight mark of lilac.

17. CALŒNAS NICOBARICA (L.).

Calœnas nicobarica, Cas. U.S. Expl. Exp. p. 276; Sharpe, P. Z. S 1875, p. 110.

Observed on Mangsi in some abundance by the U.S. Exploring Expedition.

18. PTILOPUS MELANOCEPHALUS.

Ptilopus melanocephalus (Gm.); Elliot, P. Z. S. 1878, p. 551. An adult specimen.

19. MACROPYGIA TENUIROSTRIS, Gray.

Macropygia tenuirostris, Walden, Tr. Z. S. ix. p. 218 ; Sharpe, Tr. Linn. Soc. n.s. i. p. 347.

Two specimens.

[Luzon (*Meyer*) ; Basilan (*Steere*) ; Sulu (*Burbidge*).]

Lord Tweeddale differs from Professor Schlegel's opinion that the same Philippine species is found in Java and Lombock, where it is *M. emiliana* of Bonaparte ; but having compared several specimens lately, I believe that the Professor's view is the right one, and that the bird is found over the Philippines, and occurs even in Borneo. Lord Tweeddale separates the Negros bird as *M. eurycerca.*

20. GALLUS STRAMINEICOLLIS, sp. n.

General colour above black, shot with green and purple ; wing-coverts like the back, the innermost and the scapulars with a slight subterminal shine of coppery brown ; primary-coverts and primaries black, the secondaries externally green ; feathers of the lower back and rump straw-yellow, with darker longitudinal centres of black or green; upper tail-coverts and tail glossy oil-green; crown of head and nape black; hind neck and neck-hackles, as well as sides of neck, straw-yellow, deeper on the hind neck, with green longitudinal centres to the feathers; remainder of under surface of body black with a green gloss; comb short and rounded; sides of face and entire throat bare. Total length 34·5 inches, culmen 1·1, wing 9·0, tail 17·5, tarsus 3·4.

Mr. Burbidge procured a single example of this jungle-fowl, which appears to be a very distinct species. He tells me that it was brought to the ship by one of the Sulu natives alive, and he cannot vouch for its having been a wild bird. I have, however, shown the bird to Mr. Gould and other ornithologists; and they agree with me that it is probably a distinct species of Jungle-fowl. Governor Ussher also has seen the bird; and he tells me that he has never seen any domesticated fowls in Borneo or the Eastern Islands which approached this species in the least.

ON COLLECTIONS OF BIRDS FROM KINA BALU MOUNTAIN IN NORTH-WESTERN BORNEO.

By R. Bowdler Sharpe, F.L.S., F.Z.S.,

Senior Assistant, Department of Zoology, British Museum.

PROC. ZOOL. SOC. 1879. Part II.

[*Received February* 14, 1879.]

The great mountain of Kina Balu has always been a locality of interest to the student of Bornean ornithology; but I am not aware that any notes on the natural history of this part of northern Borneo have ever been published. It gives me great pleasure, therefore, to give a list of the specimens obtained by Mr. Treacher's collectors,* and of a few others submitted to

* These collectors accompanied Mr. Peter Veitch and myself during the first expedition to Kina Balu, undertaken in November and December, 1877. The specimens collected by them were obtained along the route from Gaya Bay to the village of Kiau (alt. 3,000 feet). They did not ascend the mountain itself, but collected around Kiau until our return. —F. W. B.

me by Mr. Burbidge, and obtained during his recent expedition to this mountain. The latter gentleman is well known from his successful botanical researches on Kina Balu; and I shall shortly lay before the Society an account of some of his ornithological discoveries in the Sulu archipelago.

The present collection, though small, is of some importance; and the character of some of the birds seems to show that the mountains of Borneo, when thoroughly explored, will produce many species akin to those found in the mountains of Java, Sumatra, and even of the Himalayas.

1. BUTASTUR INDICUS.

Butastur indicus (Gm.), Sharpe, Cat. B. i. p. 297.
Poliornis indica (Gm.), Salvad. Ucc. Born. p. 9.

A specimen in nearly full plumage, collected by Mr. Burbidge.

2. BUBO ORIENTALIS.

Bubo orientalis (Horsf.), Sharpe, Cat. B. ii. p. 39.
B. sumatranus (Raffl.), Salvad. Ucc. Born. p. 19.

A fine adult specimen in Mr. Treacher's collection, agreeing with the diagnosis given by me (*l.c.*), and measuring 13 inches in the wing.

3. MEGALÆMA VERSICOLOR.

Megalæma versicolor (Raffl.), Marsh. Mon. Capit. pl. 22.
Chotorea versicolor, Salvad. tom. cit. p. 33.
Three adult specimens, obtained by M. Burbidge.

4. RHOPODYTES ERYTHROGNATHUS.

Rhopodytes erythrognathus (Hartl.), Sharpe, P. Z. S. 1873, p. 604.
Rhamphococcyx erythrognathus (Hartl.), Salvad. tom. cit. p. 74.

A specimen in Mr. Treacher's collection, having the two centre tail-feathers rufous at their ends.

5. HALCYON CHLORIS.

Halcyon chloris (Bodd.), Sharpe, Monogr. Alced. pl. 87.
Sauropatis chloris (Bodd.), Salvad. tom. cit. p. 103.
One specimen, sent by Mr. Treacher.

6. DENDROCHELIDON LONGIPENNIS.

Dendrochelidon longipennis (Rafin.), Savad. tom. cit. p. 122.
One specimen, collected by Mr. Burbidge.

7. CORONE TENUIROSTRIS.

Corone tenuirostris, Moore, Cat. B. Mus. E. I. Co. ii. p. 558.
Corvus tenuirostris, Tweedd. Ibis, 1877, p. 320.
One specimen, in Mr. Treacher's collection.

The constant character of the long thin bill in specimens from
N. W. Borneo impresses me with the idea that Lord Tweeddale is
right in keeping *C. tenuirostris* distinct from *C. enca*, with which I
united it in my " Catalogue of Birds " (vol. iii. p. 43).

8. DICRURUS ANNECTENS.

Dicrurus annectens, Hodgs.; Sharpe, Cat. B. iii. p. 231 ; id. Ibis,
1878, p. 414.

The first occurrence of this species in Borneo was recorded by me
in my list of Governor Ussher's Sarawak collection ; but it cannot
be uncommon in North-western Borneo, to judge from numerous
specimens which have been sent from Labuan and from the opposite
coast by Governor Ussher and Mr. Treacher. Two specimens are
contained in the collection made on Kina Balu by Mr. Burbidge.

9. CHIBIA BORNEENSIS, sp. n.

C. *similis* C. pectorali, *ex insulis Suluensibus, sed plumis lanceolatis
colli lateralis metallice chalybeo-viridibus nec purpurascentibus,
et maculis jugularibus et prœpectoralibus valde minoribus et con-
spicue metallicis chalybeo-viridibus distinguenda. Long. tot.* 10,
culm. 1·3, *alœ* 5·9, *caudœ* 4·5, *tarsi* 0·85.

An adult and young bird, in Mr. Treacher's collection.

This is an interesting addition to the avifauna of Borneo, and
seems to indicate an entirely new species. It bears considerable
resemblance to *C. bimaensis* of Timor and Lombock, but differs in
having the long silky plumes on each side of the lower back black
instead of greyish white ; while the Timor bird has not, like *C. borneensis,* any long hair-like plumes on the head. On the other hand
the latter character allies it to *C. pectoralis* of the Sulu Islands ; but
it may be recognised on comparison by the much smaller and more
metallic spots on the throat and fore neck, which are steel-green, as
also are the neck-hackles. In *C. pectoralis* the spangles are large,

dull, and incline to purplish in tint. This species appears to me to
be a thorough *Chibia,* and I do not at present see how naturalists
can avoid recognizing the existence of *Chibia* in the Malay archipelago ; nor do I understand how the Indian and Malayan species
are to be separated, when such a perfect gradation is now offered
by *C. borneensis* and *C. pectoralis.* Under these circumstances I
believe that Salvadori's genus *Dicruropsis,* which I was lately inclined to admit (Mittheil. k. zool. Mus. Dresd. iii. p. 360), cannot
be sustained ; and I therefore revert to my old opinion concerning
these birds (Cat. B. iii. p. 234). I have given this species the name
of *borneensis* to celebrate the addition of a *Chibia* to the avifauna of
Borneo. Mr. Treacher has also procured a single specimen of it on
the Lawas river.

The young bird from Kina Balu differs from the adult in being
duller black, with fewer and less metallic chest-spots and hackles.

10. BUCHANGA STIGMATOPS, sp. n.

B. *similis* B. leucophææ, *sed macula lorali alba magna distinguenda. Long. tot.* 10, *culm.* 0·9, *alæ* 5·3, *caudæ* 5·1, *tarsi* 0·7.

The presence of white on the facial region of a species of grey
Buchanga would seem to ally it at once to *B. leucogenys.* In the
Bornean bird, however, of which I have three specimens before me,
the white is confined to a large loral spot in front of the eye, whereas in *B. leucogenys* the eyebrow and ear-coverts, as well as the
feathers below the eye, are also white or whitish. The new species
is also of the same dark grey as *B. leucophœa (B. cineracea* of my
Catalogue, iii. p. 250), and not of the light pearly grey which is
another character of *B. leucogenys.* One specimen was contained in
Mr. Burbidge's collection, and two in Mr. Treacher's.

11. PERICROCOTUS IGNEUS.

Pericrocotus igneus, Blyth ; Salvad. tom. cit. p. 144 ; Sharpe, Cat.
B. iv. p. 78.

An adult male, in Mr. Burbidge's collection.

12. TRACHYCOMUS OCHROCEPHALUS.

Trachycomus ochrocephalus (Gm.), Salvad. tom. cit. p. 197.
One specimen, in Mr. Burbidge's collection.

13. RUBIGULA MONTIS, sp. n.

R. *similis* R. flaviventri, *sed multa minor et gula flava nec nigra distinguenda. Long. tota* 5·7, *culminis* 0·5, *alœ* 3·1, *caudœ* 2·8, *tarsi* 0.7.

General colour above olive-yellowish, the wing-coverts like the back ; quills and tail dull blackish brown, externally washed with olive-yellow like the back, the greater coverts also brown washed with olive-yellow ; tail-feathers paler brown at the tip of the inner web ; head crested, black, as also the sides of the face, ear-coverts, and cheeks ; entire under surface of body yellow, slightly more olive-green on the sides ; under wing-coverts yellow, the longer ones white washed with yellow ; quills sepia-brown below, white along the edge of the inner webs.

This species is almost exactly the same as *Rubigula atricapilla* of Ceylon, but has not the white tips to the tail-feathers, while its long crest distinguishes it from the Ceylonese species, which is not crested. In the form of the crest and in general appearance it is almost precisely similar to *R. flaviventris* of Pegu and Tenasserim, but is smaller, and has the throat yellow like the rest of the under surface. The single specimen obtained was in Mr. Treacher's collection.

14. CRINIGER RUFICRISSUS, sp. n.

C. *similis* C. gutturali, *sed supra ubique sordidior, supracaudalibus caudaque saturate rufescenti-brunneis ; loris et regione oculari cum genis et regione parotica sordide cinereis, gula alba, corpore reliquo subtus sordide olivascente, sub caudalibus castaneis. Long. tot.* 8, *culm.* 0·85, *alœ* 4·0, *caudœ* 4·0, *tarsi* 0·7.

This species is not very different from *C. gutturalis,* but differs in its much darker coloration, especially on its under surface, which is dull olivaceous, with a white throat and chestnut-red under tail-coverts. There is an entire absence of the pale-brown colour of the breast washed with yellow, and of the light yellow abdomen and pale fawn-coloured under tail-coverts. The crest is very long in *C. ruficrissus,* and extends nearly to the mantle.

15. IANTHOCINCLA TREACHERI, sp. n.

I. *similis* I. mitratæ (*S. Müll.*), *ex Sumatra, sed genis, mento et regione parotica sicut caput castaneis facile distinguenda. Long. tota* 10, *culminis* 0·85, *alœ* 4·15, *caudœ* 4·5, *tarsi* 1·5.

Adult. General colour above dark ashy grey, with a very slight shade of ochraceous under certain lights ; the wing-coverts slightly more bluish grey than the back : quills blackish, externally bluish grey, the primaries white along the basal part of the outer web, giving the wing a conspicuous white outer aspect ; tail-feathers dark slaty grey, shading into blackish at the end of the feathers ; entire crown and nape, as well as the sides of face, ear-coverts, and fore part of cheeks deep chestnut-red, the under cheek-feathers slightly tipped with ochraceous ; frontal plumes with lanceolate tips of light ashy grey or hoary whitish ; under surface of body dull ochraceous brown, with lighter shaft-lines of pale ochraceous, imparting a striped appearance to the throat and breast ; the sides of the body more ashy grey ; chin chestnut, like the sides of the face ; thighs dark grey, with a few chestnut feathers near the tarsal bend ; under tail-coverts chestnut ; under wing-coverts ashy grey, slightly marked with ochraceous ; quills sepia-brown below, paler along the edge of the inner web.

Four specimens are sent by Mr. Treacher, all adult, and exactly similar in plumage. On comparing them with Sumatran specimens of *I. mitrata,* a very marked difference presents itself, which shows that the Kina Balu bird belongs to a new species. Although similar to *I. mitrata* in its general coloration and white-edged quills, it is distinguished at once by its chestnut ear-coverts, while the chin and fore part of the cheeks are also chestnut.

16. TURDUS PALLENS.

Turdus pallens, Pall. ; Salvad. tom. cit. p. 256.
An adult specimen, sent by Mr. Treacher.

17. MONTICOLA SOLITARIUS.

Monticola solitarius (P. L. S. Müll.), Walden, Tr. Z. S. ix. p. 192.

A specimen sent by Mr. Treacher.

This is the second occurrence of the bird in Borneo, the first having been recorded by me under the name of *Monticola pandoo* (Ibis, 1877, p. 13), from Mr. Alfred Everett's Bintulu collection. Mr. Treacher's specimen is in full blue-and-red plumage, with the usual margins to the feathers found in the winter dress.

For permission to use the foregoing Papers, I am under obligations to James Britten, Esq., Editor of the *Journal of Botany,* and to P. L. Sclater, Esq., Secretary of the Royal Zoological Society of London.

BRADBURY, AGNEW, & CO., PRINTERS, WHITEFRIARS.